A Cookbook for People Who Hate Lawyers

(How to Become a Great Cook & Avoid Lawyers)

Stuart J. Faber

Lega-Books
3699 Wilshire Boulevard, Suite 700
Los Angeles, California 90010

Copyright© 2021 by Stuart J. Faber

All rights reserved. No part of this book may be reproduced or transmitted in any manner whatsoever without written permission from the publishers, except in the case of brief quotations embodied in critical articles or reviews.

978-0-578-31027-5

Table of Contents

Chapter 1: A Tale of Two Books	5
Chapter 2: Why People Hate Lawyers	9
Chapter 3: The Law — The Roadmap for Our Daily Lives	13
Chapter 4: A World Without Lawyers?	19
Chapter 5: The Courtroom as a Battlefield	23
Chapter 6: Reform the Laws — Remove the Lawyers	27
Chapter 7: My Kitchen to Yours	31
Chapter 8: Let's Get Started	45
Equipment For The Home Chef	46
Tips And Techniques For Becoming A Great Cook	49
A Few Words About The Use Of Ingredients	52
Chapter 9: Breakfast is Ready	55
Chapter 10: Salads, Appetizers, Soups, Stocks & Breads	61
Chapter 11: Eat Your Veggies	95
Chapter 12: Recipes from the U.S.A.	113
Chapter 13: Old World & New World Spanish Cooking	165
Chapter 14: My Favorite Italian Recipes	181
Chapter 15: Cuisine of France	209
Chapter 16: The Magic of Asian Cuisine	221
Chapter 17: Happy Holidays in the Kitchen	239
Chapter 18: Sweets and Desserts	257
Epilogue	282
A Few Additional Thoughts	284
Glossary Of Cooking Terms	287
Index	294

Acknowledgments

This book is dedicated to those folks whose devotion and skill contributed to the building of the structure and soul of my life. The influence of achievers on our growth and development cannot be overstated.

I often ignored, even squandered the positive influences that were offered to me in high school. Spike Hancock implored me to quit goofing off and savor the nectar of the French language. I was more interested in classroom frivolity. On my first trip to France, my attempts to converse in French with Parisians were met with derision and laughter. Had I taken the building blocks that high school offered, how more worldly would I be.

A.J. Cox, who taught business law (an elective), changed the course of my life. One day, he said to me: "You're a natural with the law." That's the day I took a final bow from the cut-up stage and entered the virtual courtroom. In college, I soon discovered that philosophy, history, Latin, anthropology and Shakespeare to math, chemistry, biology and physics were the building blocks that would add depth to the lawyer in me. My professional musical background provided the required cadence and dynamics for courtroom presentation. My flight instructors instilled me with discipline.

The voices of my law school professors I hear today with equal classroom clarity. I often call upon these voices. For example, Walter Cook, my contracts professor who was blind, would recite from memory a host of passages from law treatises. Years later, during a court trial, I objected to some evidence that was proffered by my adversary. When the court asked me to state the legal basis for my objection, I activated Mr. Cook's voice in my brain and quoted a passage verbatim. "I agree," responded the judge. The objection, which was sustained, brought the opposition to defeat.

Listening to Lloyd Tevis's procedure and evidence lectures was like sitting in a concert hall. When he retired from his law practice he honored me, at this point a brand-new lawyer, by turning over some of his most valued clients to me.

Role models are equally required to create an accomplished chef. My mother cooked and baked everything from scratch. I learned from her before I could ride a bicycle. Her aunts were master home chefs. I learned techniques and skills from hundreds of chefs. In Edinburgh, Scotland, the secret of how to sauté fish. In Dijon, France, the art of roasting a chicken. In China, I learned how to prepare Peking duck.

To my children, Brad and Dorothy, who are both superb cooks. We taught one another and still do. To my wife, Cheryl, who on occasion gently reminds me that the kitchen is a playground, not a temple.

To the stellar editor of this book, Victoria Bruno. We had many spirited debates on how to correctly present the prose in this book. She always won because she was always right. To Kodi Bobo, the lady who designed this book, I owe an immense debt of gratitude. Her graphic designs are testimony of her extraordinary talent.

Chapter 1
A Tale of Two Books

Hopefully, most of you will go through life without ever needing the services of a lawyer. I'm even more hopeful that most of you will travel along the highway of life without a detour through a courtroom. Unfortunately, there may be times when you might be forced to detour from a peaceful, happy litigation-free highway on to the dark, bumpy road leading to the courthouse. Generally, these will probably involve a divorce, criminal prosecution, personal injury case, landlord-tenant dispute, home/auto repair dispute, small claims, traffic or probate court.

To expand this road trip metaphor, the direction of your journey will substantially depend on the type of fuel you place into life's vehicle. If the tank is filled with hatred, poor judgment, anger, lawlessness and revenge, your destination is inevitable. If the tank is fueled with sensitivity to others, tolerance, common sense, honesty and respect for the law, your chances of crossing the threshold of a law office are diminished.

You can avoid legal pitfalls by practicing preventative law and employing logic, reason, sensitivity and a dose of reality. These measures make it more likely that you will continue along the highway of happiness and freedom from the courtroom.

I'll torture the metaphor even further. Staying in your lane of legality without drifting into the ditch of ignoring or flouting the law is the best inoculation against courtrooms and lawyers. Embracing an understanding of the law is a roadmap to freedom from stress, lawyers and the uncertainty of litigation.

I want to make clear now and throughout this book that I am not providing legal advice to anyone who reads or hears about this book. Cooking advice, yes. Legal advice, absolutely not!

If any person feels that he or she has a current, past or future legal problem, they should consult a lawyer of their choice. You should not, and cannot, rely on any of my general comments about the law to assist you in making decisions about your legal situation.

Why combine recipes with law? Because it makes sense to pair a discussion of the law with a cookbook. Here's why.

1. Both the law and food are involved in our daily lives. Therefore, a Tale of Two Books.
2. The more you keep the lawyers and the courtroom away, the more time available to cook and enjoy delicious cuisine with your family and friends.
3. Preventive law and good food both contribute to a healthy, peaceful, fulfilled and successful life.
4. A discourse on my two passions in one book saves you money.
5. Calls from clients frequently interrupt me while I'm cooking.
6. I thought it would be fun to combine two topics in one book and, in turn, be fun for you to read.

My goals with this book.

I hope to impart some tips on how to improve your culinary skills. I strive to take the mystery and fear out of cooking. I don't pretend to be a paragon of haute cuisine. I'm not a fan of gimmicky or trendy cuisine. My recipes embrace tasty, hospitable, comforting and satisfying cuisine.

I am not suggesting that my recipes will comport with everyone's standards of the healthiest foods. Some would contend that cuisine containing animal products is both unhealthy and immoral. Cardiologists might convulse at the thought of eating a hamburger, a steak or a cheese pizza. Other health care professionals shudder at the idea of consuming sugar. I have no quarrel with these ideologies. I share many of their concerns — even if I don't always follow them.

I do believe that if you love hamburgers, steak, bacon, cheese pizza, desserts, or any other category of food about which I write, you will find my recipes to be among the best. I know this to be true. Hardly a week goes by that I don't receive calls from friends and acquaintances with whom I have shared my recipes and cooking techniques. They gleefully rave about a recipe that they just tried and implore me to keep sending new ones. All have claimed that I've helped them achieve new levels of culinary skill.

The debate rages on over what foods we should consume and in what quantities. I merely suggest that if you love the variety of foods I have included in this book, you should consume (or avoid) them in accordance with your personal health concerns.

My second goal is to clarify impressions that some folks have about the law and lawyers. I consider the law as one of the most noble and essential professions in the world. If I could repeat my life, I would not hesitate to rush back to law school. Every time I achieve a result that makes life better for someone, my reward is greater than money could ever buy.

I am keenly aware that some lawyers have tarnished the reputation of the profession. I acknowledge that many folks harbor unflattering perceptions of lawyers, some of which are justified. I acknowledge that no one derives pleasure from spending hard earned money on lawyers. I hope to dispel some of this disparagement of lawyers and, if possible, create an atmosphere where there is more trust, respect and understanding of our profession.

I will sum up in three sentences my reasons for writing this book. I hope to increase a better understanding and comfort level with the law and lawyers. I hope to guide the reader through the culinary world so that he or she can experience joy and fulfillment in the kitchen. I want to share my recipes (1) for outstanding cuisine, and (2) hopefully, a lawyer-free life.

Chapter 2
Why People Hate Lawyers

Why do I love to cook? When I prepare a meal for someone, or give a cookie to a friend, the mail carrier, a client, a fellow attorney or just about anyone, I always receive an expression of thanks. But when I tell someone that I'm a lawyer, a look of fear, suspicion or contempt — even hatred, often follows. On their first visit to my office, new clients often display a palpable aura of distrust. Lawyers are frequently stereotyped as money hungry, shysters, ambulance chasers and dishonest.

Why are lawyers regarded with such derision? Over the years, I've developed a list of reasons why people hate lawyers.

1. Clients don't understand that a lawyer charges for his time.

Abraham Lincoln succinctly described what a lawyer gets paid for. "A lawyer's time and advice are his stock and trade." That has not changed over the years.

Lawyers don't sell tangible things. When a person purchases a new car, a fancy dress, takes a cruise or enjoys a sumptuous dinner, he or she receives an immediate reward in exchange for money. The transaction brings instantaneous joy and happiness.

It's not at all the same when a client hires me. Generally, I first must take his or her documents and materials for review. Then I hit the law books to assess the legal strength of the case. I may even spend several hours just thinking about the case, or I may discuss the issues with a colleague, just to get another opinion. After this, I may bill the client for 3 to 5 hours of work.

As soon as the client sees the bill, I often get a phone call. "You didn't do nuttin!"

It's true; I've yet to impart advice to the client. We haven't been to court. I haven't filed a lawsuit. As a result, I can understand that the client does not feel a sense of fulfillment and gratification. There is no "new car smell" to enjoy. As a result, most lawyers feel increasing waves of resentment as each monthly bill is mailed.

What should lawyers do? Before agreeing to represent a new client, the lawyer should make it clear that the client will be charged for the lawyer's time. The hours devoted to evaluating the case are not visible to the client. At that point, there is little noticeable progress in the case.

I explain that it's not the same as charging a customer for a cake. If a person agrees to pay the baker $300 for a wedding cake, the baker does not incrementally charge for studying the recipe, sifting the flour, measuring the amount of butter and sugar and piping a greeting on the frosting. Instead, the baker is paid for the finished cake.

2. Clients often harbor unrealistic assessments of the merits of their case.

Here is an exaggerated example. Suppose I take on a murder case. The evidence against my client consists of a video in which he is observed to sneak up behind a person, shoot him in the back of the head while saying, "I've thought about killing you for a long time." Now he claims no premeditation and wants me to plead self-defense.

When I further discover that the victim had never given my client cause to be fearful of him and that the client's motive was revenge against the victim for cheating in a poker game, I explain to the client that self-defense will not be a viable defense and that we had better negotiate a plea bargain.

The client might respond, "What did I hire you for? Whose side are you on?" Obviously, the client is not being realistic. But in his mind, he firmly believes he is correct. He will eventually conclude that I sold him down the river, that I was "in cahoots" with the prosecution or that I was incompetent.

What should lawyers do? Lawyers should make every attempt to evaluate a case as quickly as possible and then initiate a candid discussion with the client about the strengths and weaknesses of their case. The lawyer should tell the client the truth, not what the client wants to hear. The more the attorney imparts false expectations to the client, the greater the chances the lawyer will end up with a client filled with hate. Unfortunately, with some cases, it takes time to develop an accurate evaluation.

If the attorney concludes that a case has no merit, he or she should decline to represent the client. On many occasions, I've refused large fees where I knew that I could never achieve the client's expectations.

I always emphasize to the client that we are on the same side. When I point out weaknesses in the case, it does not mean that I am against the client. I'm merely doing my duty of exploring all aspects of the case.

3. Clients often have a misconception of what a lawyer can do.

It's completely understandable that clients, especially those facing litigation, are often suffering extreme distress and are searching for someone to save them.

Many clients harbor views of the lawyer as God, as their savior, or that the lawyer has some magic tricks as the client has seen on TV that will bring about a favorable result in the case. Once the client understands that the lawyer is just a person and that the outcome of the case will depend substantially on the facts and law involved in the case, a level of disappointment and resentment often displaces the hero-worship. If the client refuses to face reality, the lawyer — client relationship will erode.

There are some things a lawyer can't fix. At times, the facts in the case are beyond dispute. Of course, a good lawyer can point out inconsistencies in the facts-or discover additional helpful facts. The law may be clear or ambiguous. If possible, the lawyer can often convince a judge on how the law should be interpreted or applied. But the lawyer cannot change, deny or ignore the facts and the applicable law.

What should a lawyer do? Once the lawyer recognizes that the client views the lawyer as godlike or as a magician, the lawyer should clarify who the lawyer is and who the lawyer isn't. The lawyer should make it clear that the lawyer is friendly, but not a friend, not a God, not a magician, not a psychologist or anyone else other than someone who will exercise his or her skill, experience and dedication to the best of his or her ability. If the client cannot accept that definition of the relationship, the lawyer should withdraw from the case.

4. Does a bad result mean a bad lawyer?

In every lawsuit, there is always one winner or one loser. Perhaps the judge made the wrong decision, but nevertheless, there is still one winner and one loser. Is it the fault of the lawyer that the client lost?

Let's look at cases before the U.S. Supreme Court where, in each case, the litigants are usually represented by the best lawyers in the country. There will still be one winner and one loser. That result does not necessarily mean that the winner had a great lawyer, and the loser had a bad lawyer.

It's true that, in some cases, the reason a case is lost is that the lawyer was not a good lawyer. Of course, that lawyer should be subject to criticism. And it is likely and perhaps understandable that the client will develop negative opinions about lawyers in general. In other situations, a case may be lost because it just was not winnable. If the defendant who murdered his poker buddy insisted on a trial, it is virtually inevitable that he would be found guilty. The lawyer could be at fault for taking the case to trial.

However, there are cases where an unreasonable client insists on a trial. In criminal cases, if a client insists, a lawyer must take the case to trial. I've had a few of those cases that ended with disastrous results. In one case where a client was charged with burglary, the evidence against him was overwhelming. Nevertheless, the prosecutor made an offer: accept a charge of misdemeanor trespass with six months in the county jail. I pleaded with my client to take the deal, but he refused. The trial proceeded. The judge would not allow me to withdraw from the case and had no choice but to follow my client's demands. The evidence of guilt was indisputable. He ended up with a five-year felony prison sentence. Of course, he still blamed me.

5. There are some bad, incompetent, dishonest lawyers who deserve to be hated.

In the half-century that I have been practicing law, I've met thousands of lawyers. In my view, more than 90% of them have been honest, dedicated and competent. In the remaining group, some should be disbarred. With others, I find surprising that they were able to finish law school, let alone pass the bar.

The same can be said for many professions. Most doctors are honest and competent. Most police officers are honest and competent. However, where there are bad apples in a barrel, public perception of the good apples is often obliterated.

6. Lawyers are strictly supervised and monitored.

Every state bar has promulgated a Code of Ethics for lawyers. Strict, powerful rules exist that require lawyers to be truthful to the client, the court, other attorneys and the public. Lawyers are scrutinized to competently handle a client's case, to adequately communicate with the client and to carefully maintain money held in trust by the lawyer.

Lawyers must conduct themselves ethically in the performance of their legal duties. They are also scrutinized in other aspects of their lives. Lawyers are held to a higher standard of conduct than almost any other profession. For example, if a lawyer is dishonest in a personal business transaction not related to the practice of law, the lawyer can still be disciplined. If a lawyer commits a minor crime, especially one involving moral turpitude such as shoplifting, the lawyer can be disciplined. Most lawyers I encounter consistently think about, and discuss with other lawyers, the ethical considerations of their daily activities.

Lawyers should devote a portion of their professional time in creating good public relations. I recommend more pro bono work, more speaking tours to schools, etc. and more involvement in the community.

By the way, I'm as passionate about law as I am about cooking. Lawyer hatred does not deter me. I accept it as a challenge to convince the client that most lawyers are honest and dedicated to making his or her life better — just like the town baker.

Chapter 3
The Law — The Roadmap for Our Daily Lives

I often joke that I studied the law by watching the TV show, *Judge Judy*. In actuality, I spent four years in college and four years in law school. I studied for the bar which I passed on the first attempt. Then came hours of continuing legal education in seminars and workshops and over 50 years as a trial lawyer. I've tried hundreds of jury trials, thousands of court trials, and other courtroom procedural hearings. Even so, I'm still learning. That's because each new case usually presents a unique set of facts that may require a novel application of the law. Almost daily, a lawyer is presented with factual and legal situations never faced with previously. The law changes constantly. That is why it's called the practice of law. Clients can be harmed if I don't keep up with these changes. And these are some of the reasons why I love the law.

That being said, I still insist that lessons can be learned by watching *Judge Judy*. Of course, every litigant in her courtroom wanted to be on television, but in real life, each could have prevented their legal embroilment had they paused to exercise common sense and good judgment. The same is true with almost every person who must hire a lawyer.

Most of us rarely give this a thought: In our daily lives, we walk in the shadow of the law with almost every step we take. Consider this:

1. When you rent a place to live, you are surrounded by landlord-tenant laws.
2. When you purchase any food, be it a donut or a filet mignon, you are protected by food and drug laws.
3. When you hire a person to paint your house or fix a leaky faucet, you are subject to construction laws, contract laws and property liability laws.
4. When you embark on a date, events could occur that will trigger innumerable laws.
5. When you drive to the grocery store, you are surrounded by traffic laws and liability laws.
6. When you contemplate taking your casual date to a more romantic level, myriad laws will follow you into the bedroom.
7. Neighborhood disputes, such as loud music, barking dogs, encroaching fences and overhanging trees can bring the law to your doorstep.
8. Posting an item on social media about a friend or enemy can initiate the laws of privacy, defamation and cyber predation.
9. Cosigning for a debt of a friend or relative will assuredly end up in a lawsuit.
10. At the workplace, the law is seated right next to you.
11. Taking your dog for a walk or keeping Fido in a poorly fenced yard can impose liability laws on you.
12. Obviously, if you elect to acquire revenue or property by theft, deceit or other illegal means, the law will intervene and eventually catch up with you. If you choose to resolve a dispute or grievance by violent or deadly means, the law will certainly intervene.

Fortunately, most of us go through life without ever having to step into a courtroom as a litigant. In many instances, the path to hiring a lawyer and a trip to court depends upon you. Of course, there are occasions when the choice is made by someone else, such as a person speeding past a red light and colliding with you in the intersection. Or a vexatious litigant. Or someone who wants to get back at you for what they perceive as a wrong that you committed against them.

How to Avoid Lawyers.

CAUTION: Nothing in this book should be construed as legal advice. I am merely providing generic examples of sensible human conduct — such as "don't drive while impaired." Or "if you need money, don't commit a robbery." If any reader has a specific current or potential legal concern or problem, he or she must not use any of what is written in this book as legal guidance or advice. The reader is urged to consult a lawyer of his or her choice.

The following tips on how to avoid lawyers seem so elementary that I debated whether to include them. Following most, if not all, of these suggestions requires little more than a few moments of reflection and the exercise of common sense and good judgment.

Why do I discuss the avoidance of lawyers? The more people take steps to avoid lawyers, the less business for me and other lawyers. Nevertheless, providing tips on preventative law is the right thing to do. Just like a doctor wouldn't advise patients to not exercise and eat more fatty foods so the doctor can perform open-heart surgery on the patients.

Of course, ethical doctors will advise patients on preventative medicine. Similarly, ethical lawyers should instruct their clients about preventative law measures.

I've met many clients with superior intelligence who became entangled with the law because of a momentary act of stupidity or lapse of judgment. Common sense had abandoned these clients. They should have given my advice to themselves. They should have watched *Judge Judy*. So, I concluded that the following tips are neither obvious nor elementary. If they were, I would not have had so many clients. Perhaps schoolroom classes in common sense should be mandatory.

At the risk of appearing didactic and moralistic, here are a few of my preventative law suggestions and commonsense axioms.

1. Take a moment and think before you act.

Ask yourself, "Will my contemplated actions bring me the benefits I seek? What are the consequences if I am caught?" Here are a few examples:

One of the most common examples involves having a "few drinks" at a bar, then driving home rather than taking a taxi or Uber. The benefit is arriving home without the cost of a taxi. The consequences consist of being stopped by the police on the way home (assuming you do not have an accident and injure yourself or others). Additional consequences are thousands of dollars in fines, attorney fees, loss of driving privileges and increased insurance premiums.

The math is simple. Take a taxi and avoid a lawyer. Nevertheless, I've had numerous clients suffer multiple DUI convictions. Obviously, they didn't learn from the first encounter.

2. How important is the fulfillment of your objective when weighed against the consequences?

A few moments of unprotected sex can tether you to someone you don't like for 18 years. Although a child in your life can be a joyous and life-enhancing experience, often it is the beginning of years of heartache, custody fights, attorney's fees and child support payments. As attractive and exciting as that fleeting moment appears, do you really want to be involved with that person for the next 18 years?

Another example: If you are on a date with someone and it turns romantic and the date says "no," it's time to stop immediately. Failing to abort the pursuit of a momentary pleasurable interlude could have serious, life-long consequences.

How do we learn to control our impulses?

I'm neither a psychologist nor a behavioral therapist. The task of changing bad behavior is challenging. But it can be done. For example, to lose weight, we embark on a diet and exercise program. With sufficient discipline and dedication, we stick to the program. Folks in Alcoholics Anonymous understand that the practice of certain disciplines can lead to long lasting sobriety.

We discipline ourselves to study in school. Athletes on school and professional sports teams are disciplined by the coaches. Military boot camp is an excellent example of how to make your behavior become instinctive.

Examples of gang members, career criminals, racists and other folks who have led lives of sociopathy and have dramatically changed their behavior are not uncommon. Some people are able to transform themselves by exercising strong will. Others have accomplished success through such professional treatments as cognitive behavioral therapy or aversion therapy. Learning to change one's behavior from toxic to healthy is a teachable skill.

Learn from our mistakes.

Business executives, professionals, sports teams, political campaign managers, educators, scientists — just about everyone in the commercial world takes periodic inventory of their products and practices and then makes changes and adjustments. It's called experience, training and learning from mistakes.

A business executive might ask: Is our marketing strategy producing increased sales and revenue? If not, change it. A lawyer may review the results of previous court trials and evaluate what techniques resulted in losses. A football coach reviews videos of the last game and institutes changes. Political campaign managers consult the polls and change their message to the voters. If I create a recipe for a soup and it tastes awful, using the same ingredients and techniques for the second batch does not make sense.

Individuals should also take periodic inventory of the extent to which their conduct has added to or deterred the attainment of their goals. Repeating the same mistakes and expecting more favorable results doesn't make sense.

We must journey through life and take periodic inventory of ourselves. Ask yourself: "Are my current practices enhancing my career? Do the ways in which I conduct myself in romantic relationships contribute to the turmoil and eventual erosion of those relationships? Why are some of my friends beginning to avoid me? Why do I keep having run-ins with the law? Why don't I feel good about myself?"

Eat well and avoid lawyers.

"More than 2,500 years ago, Hippocrates said: "Let food be thy medicine and medicine be thy food." Healthy diets can optimize both short and long-term health and can help reduce risk for many health conditions. Poor nutrition is a primary contributor to morbidity globally and is associated with more than one in four U.S. deaths. About half of U.S. adults have one or more preventable chronic diseases related to poor dietary patterns or physical inactivity. Disproportionately, this affects low-income and undeserved communities. Simply put, food can help people live healthier and longer lives." *HEALTH AFFAIRS, VOL. 34, NO. 11: FOOD & HEALTH, November 2015.*

I'm neither a nutritionist nor food scientist. Any questions about the correlation between diet and mental and physical health should be directed to professionals. But there is significant research that concludes that good nutrition can reduce violence, delinquency and emotional disorders such as depression and anxiety. Good nutrition can lead to better performance by kids in school. I also contend that adults who are well nourished are better equipped to excel in their careers and their personal relationships. I've included a few academic studies to support my position.

An article in the *Indiana Journal of Psychiatry April-June 2008* concludes that current research in psychoneuroimmunology and brain biochemistry indicates the possibility of communication pathways that can provide a clearer understanding of the association between nutritional intake, central nervous system, and immune function thereby influencing an individual's psychological health status. These findings may lead to greater acceptance of the therapeutic value of dietary intervention among health practitioners and health care providers addressing depression and other psychological disorders.

Studies have been conducted in prisons to determine if proper dietary practices can reduce the amount of prison violence. *Crime and Nourishment Cause for a rethink? Lord David Ramsbotham, GCB CBE and Bernard Gesch, FRSA, March 1, 2009* is an article that describes dietary changes with inmates in California over a 24-month period resulted in a 25% reduction in assaults, a 75% reduction in the use of restraints and a 100% reduction in suicides.

Many studies indicate that school breakfast programs improve academic performance. Children who do not get sufficient meals are more likely to repeat a grade (*Alaimo et al., 2001; Kleinman et al., 1998*). It's reasonable to conclude that there might be a relationship between poor diets and juvenile delinquency.

I certainly have not provided an exhaustive list of studies that correlate good nutrition with good behavior. I should also emphasize that it is for the reader to decide the nutritional value of my recipes. However, I do suggest that we should all err on the side of health and safety. Eating well can lead to a better life. And certainly, those who enjoy good mental health are more likely to conduct themselves in a manner where they can avoid lawyers.

A waiting room full of non-learners.

You won't see many happy faces in an attorney's waiting room. The measure of gloom exceeds the level of despair in the waiting rooms of root canal specialists.

The reason for these populations of unhappy clients can often be reduced to one common denominator: An exercise of poor judgment in selecting a solution without weighing the long-term consequences.

One person may be a guy who hit his wife rather than walking away. Another might be a person who had one more drink for the road, then hopped in his car. Still another who was intimate with a person he or she did not even know. The list goes on and on.

Had each of these individuals taken a few moments to weigh the consequences of their decision against the perceived gratification they were seeking, they might be sitting at a ball game, fishing on a tranquil lake or enjoying lunch in a cozy restaurant instead of languishing in a lawyer's waiting room.

Anger is the pathway to the lawyer's office.

It's better to lose an argument than to lose your temper. Anger is a pathway to a lawyer's office and to the courtroom.

Years ago, I did the math on my anger. As I looked back at occasions where my temper displaced my reason, the dispute I was attempting to resolve did not end with good results. When I learned to interdict and convert the emerging anger into a reasoned and calm search for a solution, I invariably achieved more favorable results in my cases.

If you think that your anger is a good weapon, you are correct. It's a good weapon against yourself. One might think of it as friendly fire.

Practice makes perfect. How to reduce our anger and our urge to exercise destructive impulses.

It does not require a psychologist or behavioral therapist to tell us that, whatever your goals, practice makes perfect. When I was a student pilot, my landings were atrocious. So, I spent hours practicing landings. In so doing, I was training my brain to react instinctively to the skills that led to perfect landings.

We all have the capability of training our brains to turn bad habits or bad behavior into good habits and good behavior. We practice how to be good parents, how to engage in happy romantic relationships, how to maintain good health, how to be better in our careers. It requires discipline and the motivation to do better.

The more we train ourselves to make productive decisions and exercise good judgment, the happier, more successful and more peaceful we will travel along the highways of life, without detours to the lawyer's office.

I am convinced that most people can significantly change their behavior for the good. Of course, there are many people who cannot or will not change. Unfortunately, some people are inexorably evil, dysfunctional, self-destructive or sociopathic and unchangeable. Nevertheless, I have personally seen many clients, both in the family law and criminal law arena, make dramatic, positive changes in their lives.

Chapter 4

A World Without Lawyers?

I love to travel to places where few tourists visit. Back in the 1960s I had numerous choices but always preferred remote destinations.

One of these countries was Burma, now called Myanmar. I was intrigued by such names as Rangoon and Mandalay. I had read about WWII air corps flights over the Burma Hump. I enjoyed the song, "Road to Mandalay." Around 1963, I flew to Rangoon and was met by folks who rarely, if ever, had seen an American tourist. My first stop off the plane was the police station. It was not by choice. I was required to check in and inform the police of my daily itinerary.

Later, I inquired about taking the train to Mandalay. Once again, I was ushered to the police station where I received a permit. I boarded the rickety train and traveled through some of the most beautiful countryside I had ever seen. Although none of the passengers spoke English, we all enjoyed one another's company. I arrived in Mandalay and guess where I was escorted? To the police station to check in.

Another dream was to travel to Eastern Europe. The nations within the Balkan peninsula are extremely picturesque. The countryside is breathtaking. The cities retained much of their 18th and 19th century architecture. After WWII, Eastern Europe fell behind the Iron Curtain.

One favorite destination was Yugoslavia, the history of which I still can't figure out. In the 19th century, it was part of the Ottoman Empire. After WWI, it emerged as Yugoslavia. After WWII, Yugoslavia became part of the Soviet bloc. In 1991, Slovenia and Croatia declared their secession from the Yugoslav federation and in 1992, Serbia and Montenegro created a new federation which now covers the land that formerly was Yugoslavia.

In one respect, the Yugoslavian police state reminded me of Burma. Wherever I roamed, I had to check in. I was cognizant of being constantly under surveillance.

My traveling companion and I arrived at the Belgrade train station and started to walk to our hotel. Within moments, we were hopelessly lost. Disorientation was obvious on our faces. Several good Samaritans approached to assist us. Finally, a young man came along who spoke English.

"I'll take you to your hotel. But first, let's have breakfast," he insisted in a cordial and comforting voice. In those days, we trusted strangers, so we accompanied him to his modest home. We sat around a table and he poured huge glasses of vodka. I'm not a drinker, especially at eight o'clock in the morning. As he left the room to retrieve some pastries, I dumped the vodka into a potted plant.

We enjoyed a delightful breakfast and conversation after which he guided us to our hotel. I expressed my desire to reciprocate and invited him to meet us for dinner. We agreed to a time and place. When he arrived, he said, "Before we go to dinner, let's stop at my house for appetizers." We complied, and then headed off to a restaurant for a wonderful dinner.

After dinner, we took a stroll. He inquired about America. The conversation turned to questions about our government. "I can stand on the corner of the busiest street in the city and scream at the top of my voice, 'The President is a crook,' and no policeman can do anything to me," I bragged.

A look of shock and terror waved across his face. He nervously glanced to see if anyone heard what I had just said. His fear was that he could be arrested merely for listening to me. I immediately regretted my indiscretion. He hastily departed and we never saw him again.

Back to the U.S.A.

What does the U.S.A. have that Burma and Yugoslavia did not have? Constitutional and civil rights lawyers.

We all complain about our country. That's part of being an American. But most Americans would agree that our level of freedom is unequalled. The reason we complain is that we want to keep it free. We complain because, at times, autocrats enter government with the intent of taking away our liberties. How do we preserve these liberties?

Generally, when the government takes action to restrict our liberties, either by legislation or executive order, we turn to the courts for relief. Lawyers are called to action to enlist the courts to protect our rights.

Of the 55 Framers of the United States Constitution, 32 were lawyers. The Framers are the individuals who were appointed to be delegates to the 1787 Constitutional Convention and took part in the drafting of the Constitution.

Lawyers are the people who insure our freedom of the press.

Lawyers are the people who insure our freedom of speech.

Lawyers are the people who filed lawsuits that insured the right of women to vote.

Lawyers are the people who filed lawsuits to insure gender equality.

Lawyers are the people who bring lawsuits to protect us in the workplace.

Lawyers are the people who filed lawsuits that brought us a solidification of the right to bear arms.

Lawyers are the people who filed lawsuits that brought us women's right of pro-choice.

Lawyers are the people who filed lawsuits that brought us school integration and helped fight other forms of racial discrimination.

Lawyers are the people who filed lawsuits that assured separation of church and state.

Lawyers are the people who protect us from illegal searches and seizures by the police.

Lawyers are the people who make certain that the accused are innocent until proven guilty.

It is lawyers who make certain that we maintain our rights against self-incrimination.

It is lawyers who make certain that people who engage in violence and theft against us are brought to justice.

It is a group of lawyers who brought the right to marry same sex couples.

It is a group of lawyers who bring us and enforce our consumer protection laws.

Lawyers are the ones who make certain that we have the right to peacefully protest.

Lawyers are the ones who protect our right to vote.

Not everyone agrees that we should have all these freedoms. Some folks would like to limit gun rights. Others favor expansion. Some folks agree with a woman's pro-choice rights. Others are pro-life. Some folks would like to exclude certain religions from the right to congregate and worship. Some folks would like to bring back school segregation. Some folks would like to limit freedom of the press. No matter how repugnant the goals of some folks, lawyers will defend and fight for their rights to express them.

Let's keep the lawyers around.

Lawyers are perpetually vigilant against officials who seek to deprive us of our rights and protections. Whether you are for or against constitutional rights such as gun rights, free speech, right to life, gay rights,

rights to protest, religious rights, voting rights, plus equal rights for all races, religions, nationals and creeds, rights to protest, there will always be lawyers who will take up the cause to assure your right of expression. It doesn't matter if your views are to the far right or far left. Thanks to lawyers, each of you is protected to express beliefs and to protest the beliefs of others.

Lawyers are also there to assist you in contract disputes, compensation if you are injured, family law disputes, landlord-tenant or consumer protection. Love them or hate them; a world without lawyers would be rudderless and chaotic.

Chapter 5

The Courtroom as a Battlefield

The stereotype of courtrooms.

Courtrooms, by their very nature and history, are often perceived as battlefields. That perception has been conveyed to the American public since the early TV shows. Every show since the old black-and-white Perry Mason series glorifies a combative aura of the courtroom.

A person engaged in a dispute screams out, "You will hear from my lawyer," or "I'll see you in court." What picture is communicated by those remarks? A battlefield.

Courtrooms are bastions for the search for truth.

Although I've been hanging around courthouses for over half a century, every time I enter a courtroom, a sensation of awe, reverence and respect comes over me. I feel an ethereal warmth throughout my body whether the courtroom is in a small-town courthouse or the U.S. Supreme Court. I feel a bond with the law, a sense of duty and an awareness of my obligations — to the client, to the court and to society.

Courtrooms are not battlefields. Nor are they football fields, basketball courts or playgrounds. Courtrooms are sacrosanct halls that search for justice and the truth. Courtrooms are halls of learning on how to conduct ourselves in the future. Courtrooms are the sanctuaries of protection against unconstitutional laws. Courtrooms are where we are protected from the abuse of autocratic leaders.

We can consider our laws as the legal highways over which we take our daily journey. The laws, whether they be contract laws, criminal laws, family laws, landlord-tenant laws, civil rights laws or any other categories of human interaction, are made by our legislators and the executive branch. The courts, by interpreting and enforcing these laws, refine the highways and make them safer. They provide us with signposts with messages of legal interpretation describing where the highways will take us. They provide traffic signs, illuminated off-ramps and guardrails to protect and guide us.

Disputes should be resolved at negotiation tables or in courtrooms, not on battlefields. Rather than rush to the battlefield, let's take a thoughtful and gentle journey along the highway that leads to the courtroom — mediation, arbitration and reason.

Games Lawyers Play.

I should emphasize that this is not a lawyer-bashing book. Nevertheless, I am frequently embarrassed, and indeed often cringe, when I witness some of the "legal" antics practiced by my colleagues.

My experience has taught me that one of the most valuable services a lawyer can perform for the client is to create and implement a straightforward, yet effective solution to a complicated legal dispute. In some cases, that is virtually impossible — especially when the client insists that the lawyer "get tough" and the lawyer complies because of fear of losing the client.

But in many, many cases, especially in the field of family law, although achieving a favorable result for the client without playing games is often possible, many lawyers strive to take their cases to extra innings. They fabricate a complicated process to solve what often is a rather simple problem.

Some clients even complain when they win. I recall a criminal case where the judge interrupted the prosecutor before I ever put on my defense. "You have no case," he uttered. "I find the defendant not guilty."

The exonerated client protested. "Wait, I didn't get to tell my side of the story."

There have been many occasions where I have almost been put to sleep by the hyper-verbosity of some lawyers. Frequently I receive three-and-four-page letters from lawyers who could have expressed whatever they had to say in less than a page. These letters are often repetitious, rambling and at times, senseless.

The same is often true of many contracts, leases, court pleadings and other legal documents. Some lawyers must feel they should be paid by the word, or by the thickness of the document or the long-windedness of their oratory. To these lawyers, verbiage and bulk are financially rewarding.

These tactics remind me of the joke in which a jury trial was scheduled, and no jurors could be found. The judge ordered the bailiff to conscript people from the hallways. All the bailiff could find were twelve lawyers. "That's great," said the judge. "With their keen legal minds, they should be able to cut through the irrelevant stuff and get right to the heart of the matter."

The case was tried. The judge expected that the lawyer/jurors would return with a verdict in a matter of moments. Instead, a day passed by. Then, another day. The judge called the jurors back into the jury box. "Why haven't you reached a verdict," asked the judge?

"Well" said one of the lawyers," We are just completing our campaign speeches for whom will be elected foreman."

Let's strive to preserve and empower our courts to accomplish the goals for which they were created: The search for truth, reconciliation, guidance and stability.

Chapter 6
Reform the Laws — Remove the Lawyers

In my view, the American system of laws is the best in the world. The vast majority of our laws are fair, reasonable and make sense. They provide a workable method of how folks should interact.

Admittedly, our laws are not perfect. As human behavior evolves and times change, society should consistently strive to change and reform our laws to conform to the times.

Many of our laws are extremely complicated and serve as the basis for extended litigation. For example, in California, the laws governing family law comprised of around 7000 statutes, are contained in several 2-inch thick books. Laws involving civil and business matters are contained in books of similar bulk. Additional books contain legal rulings of appellate courts. My law library, which consisted primarily of California legal treatises, was housed in a space about the size of the average living room with floor to ceiling shelves over four walls.

I had many clients, including highly intelligent, successful and powerful folks, who were terrified of courtrooms. I recall a physician who was a witness in my case. Outside of the courthouse, he was arrogant, intimidating, self-assured and bullyish. When he took the witness stand, he clammed up. His mouth became paralyzed and he could not utter a word. Unable to testify, he retreated from the stand in disgrace. In a moment of schadenfreude, I laughed uproariously. Later, much chagrined, I lamented over his fear of a place as safe and protective as a witness stand.

Members of the general population will primarily be involved in areas of law that include divorce, paternity, consumer law, construction law, criminal law, personal injury, workplace law, landlord-tenant law and probate law. In my view, these laws should be simplified. One set of laws should be tailored for the run-of-the-mill matters in which 95% of the population might be involved. The other set should be for large businesses, industrial-commercial communities and government cases of major complexity.

Again, it's my contention that separate courts, arbitration and mediation boards should be established for the first level of cases. These forums should operate with simple and relaxed rules of evidence and procedure. Simplified forms should be created with step-by-step instructions on how to fill them out. Matters brought before these tribunals should be conducted without lawyers. Litigants who insist on the "big boy courts," should have the option to select them. No citizen should be deprived of access to these courts.

We talk about reform. How about court reform?

Most states have small claims courts which serve the public extremely well. Litigants are not permitted to be represented by lawyers. That's a good thing. Most small claims courts handle disputes where the amount of money involved does not exceed $5000. I suggest that the limit be raised to $100,000. That would provide easy access to the courts for more people who can't afford lawyers and expensive litigation. These courts could handle most routine contract disputes, accident cases, dog bite cases, neighborhood disputes, landlord-tenant disputes and other consumer-commercial transactions.

How about small claims family courts?

Family courts handle divorce cases, plus disputes involving unmarried couples where children are involved. Divorce laws, including division of marital property and spousal support, also called alimony, should be significantly simplified. As I pointed out earlier, there are almost 7000 California laws, rules and related statutes that apply to family law cases. Why should a moderate wage-earning couple who own a small house and two unpaid-for cars be required to wade through 7000 laws? I suggest that courts be established to handle divorces where the total assets are less than $100,000. These couples should also have the option of taking their marital disputes to a non-judicial board where they can quickly and inexpensively present their grievances.

Child custody disputes. Let's take them away from the courts.

One of the great mysteries to me in family law is how a couple can adore and highly regard one another to the extent that they can create a child and, within months of the child's birth, or even before, portray the other as the world's most dangerous, wicked and evil person.

Parents draw their weapons — the child — and off to battle they go. Is a courtroom the best place to resolve a child custody dispute? Should a judge decide whether it's in a child's best interest to spend Christmas with dad or mom? What is the legal principle that is employed to make that decision? Nowhere in any lawbook does it state that it's better for a child to spend Christmas with one parent or the other. What the lawbooks do assert is the general axiom that the court must award parenting time that serves the best interest, health, welfare, safety and security for the child. What that means is the child has the right to continuous, stable and meaningful time with both good parents.

The application of those principles requires the expertise of individuals trained in child psychology, child welfare, social work, marriage counseling or other disciplines of parenting and child behavior. Judges are trained in the law but aren't likely to have the training or expertise in child behavior any more than they would have to decide whether a person should have surgery, or if drugs should be used to treat a patient.

Communities should establish boards of child rights experts. The right to good parenting belongs to the child. The first task of the expert should be to encourage, or use stronger methods, to get the parents to act like adult parents and make the decisions themselves. These experts are trained to recognize and evaluate if a parent is seeking revenge against the other parent or if there is some legitimate reason why a child's welfare will be imperiled if the child spends time with a particular parent.

At times, there are no real answers to the questions of how much time a child should spend with each parent. In many cases, a coin toss might be as valid a method of resolving the dispute as the methods currently used.

Domestic Violence.

In the past few decades, there has been an alarming growth of domestic violence in this country. It occurs between married couples, unmarried parents, dating couples, neighbors and coworkers. Many cases are legitimate. An injured person is justified in seeking protection of the courts. However, domestic violence courts are often used as revenge courts. Litigants use courts to extort, bully or intimidate another person. I've seen numerous cases where one party has inflicted physical injuries on himself or herself, then calls the police and claims that the wounds were inflicted by the significant other.

One case that comes to mind involved a man who was visiting from England. He met a girl in Los Angeles, and they commenced a relationship. One night, they had a squabble over their dog. The girlfriend claimed that he grabbed the dog and she attempted to take it from him. During the encounter, she sustained a scratch on her arm. She filed for a restraining order. In court, she sobbed uncontrollably.

The judge was impressed with her histrionics and granted the order. Outside, I heard the woman laughing with a friend and saying, "I should get the academy award--that stupid judge believed me." The man was deported back to England.

These courts should be restructured to filter out the minor and baseless disputes so that they can concentrate on the serious cases. It is true that a minor act of violence can escalate into more serious, sometimes fatal encounters. Nevertheless, steps should be taken to curb the misuse of these courts. Pre-trial mediation programs should be established to focus on resolving the disputes.

Let's develop mediation and arbitration panels of experts.

America is the world's most litigious country. Instead of rushing off to file a lawsuit, I think people should be taught skills on how to settle disputes among themselves. Where a solution can't be achieved, the next step should be non-judicial halls of resolution where the rules of evidence and procedure are simplified and relaxed. Separate departments should be established where disputes can be presented before experts in each category: family law, landlord-tenant, neighborhood matters, personal injury, dog-bite cases, home construction and repairs, consumer disputes and so on.

Let's consider teaching dispute resolution in the schools.

Courses should be developed for children during early education on how to deal with life's everyday problems. I've included some suggestions for classes on teaching skills of day-to-day living that can lead to a happier and more successful life and one that hopefully can keep you from languishing in a lawyer's waiting room.

1. **Common business and consumer sense.** Classes on basic contract and commercial law, consumer law, landlord-tenant law, negotiation techniques and other subjects with which people will be involved in life could keep folks out of trouble and away from courts and lawyers.

2. **How to initiate a relationship.** Classes on how to engage in the courtship process in a lady-like and gentlemanly way. Embrace the excitement, joy and fun of falling in love without causing pain, false expectations and discomfort to one another.

3. **How to engage in a relationship.** How to resolve disputes in a relationship without ending up in court. Learn methods of de-escalation.

4. **What to look for, and not to look for, in a partner.** I've handled hundreds of divorces and partnership breakups involving folks who selected a significant other for reasons that were doomed to lead to a breakup. Classes on how to select a partner with courses on what not to look for could reduce the number of bitter breakups.

5. **Anger prevention.** When a person is convicted of an anger-related crime, judges often require anger management classes. Rather than lock the barn door after the horse gets out, we should be teaching anger prevention.

6. **Parenting classes.** No license is required to have a baby. There are no laws that require prerequisites for making a baby. No owner's manual comes with the child's birth. Although there is a modicum of sex education in the schools, youngsters are not taught the profound issues that accompany entering a relationship or the life-changing impact of parenthood.

    If boys and girls could attend classes where they discover what it's like to be a parent day in and day out, it might make them think twice about how a child can change their lives forever. Equally important, there are many existing parents who have no idea how to raise and take care of a child.

    Classes on parenting could reduce problems for the children of these parents in later life.

7. **Common sense and responsibility classes.** It's worth repeating that many folks become ensnared in the legal system because they failed to exercise common sense — or had no idea how to exercise common sense. Classes that would teach how to weigh the benefit-liability role of your decisions, plus classes on learning that we must take responsibility for our exercises in judgment would be extremely useful.

8. **General conflict resolution techniques.** When disputes arise in business, neighborhoods, on the road or elsewhere, they should be settled without violence and without a trip to the courthouse. Classes should be established to teach techniques to peacefully resolve these conflicts.

Chapter 7
My Kitchen to Yours

It took eighty years to research and write this cookbook. It's not that I'm a slow worker. I commenced the research while I was still a toddler. I began working on this book without even knowing that I would be writing a cookbook. Of course, much of the research could not have been conducted until the subjects of the research came into existence. It will all be explained in this chapter.

Ft. Atkinson Main Street. *Courtesy of the Hoard Historical Museum and the Fort Atkinson Historical Society, Fort Atkinson, WI.*

Ft. Atkinson Main Street with Bridge Over River. *Courtesy of the Hoard Historical Museum and the Fort Atkinson Historical Society, Fort Atkinson, WI.*

Our Homeland Was Our Supermarket.

I was born in 1933 and raised in Racine, Wisconsin. During WWII, our family embarked on a three-year diaspora as we traveled around the country to several military hospitals when my father was inducted as a medical officer in the U.S. Army. After the war, we returned to this agriculturally prolific region of America where I resided until I graduated from the University of Wisconsin in Madison in 1955.

In those days, cities and towns had precise, perceptible borders. Today, in my southern California community, it's difficult to tell where a city's borders begin and end. Municipalities are bunched together like sardines in a can. For example, a drive of twenty miles from Los Angeles to Disneyland will cross the elusive borders of a dozen cities. Chances are, you won't know what town you're in. One moment you may be in Norwalk. Moments later, in Downey. Cross the street and now you are in Cerritos — or, perhaps back to Norwalk. These amorphous towns, bereft of definition, have few if any detectable landmarks.

During my early Wisconsin years, cities were separated by farmland. I loved driving from Racine to the university in Madison. Sidestepping the four-lane highways and the nascent Interstates, I meandered along the old two-lane roads. My route, from home to the outskirts where I joined state Highway 12, took me through rolling acres of cornfields, soybeans, hay, dairy farms, and cultivated fields of veggies aligned in rows with military precision. I rhapsodized over the sights and fragrances of this agrarian wonderland.

Soon, I drove through Waterford, then East Troy, Whitewater, Ft. Atkinson, and Cambridge. It was clear where every town began and ended. Each had its own personality. Whitewater was home to a teacher's college. Ft. Atkinson is bisected by a majestic, covered bridge. Every town had family-operated coffee shops and dairy bars. Along the way, as I approached a small lake, a great blue heron awaited me with predictable consistency. Each time I drove by, he became airborne and faithfully soared past my windshield. I'm sure he recognized me and looked forward to greeting me.

Long before my journeys across this region, glaciers covered all of Wisconsin. The legacy of these masses of ice is the endowment of hundreds of natural lakes, streams, and rivers. These waters, brimming with native fish, were stopovers for migrating aquatic birds. I never saw an artificial lake until I moved to California. The surrounding forestland and prairies were populated with a profusion of game birds, wild turkeys, bears, deer, rabbits and other food providing animals.

In my college years, I began flying lessons. The venerable Piper Cub, a basic trainer painted in a unique yellow color, was primitive in its instrumentation. Except for a compass, the solitary navigational equipment consisted of my eyes. In winter when the entire state was blanketed in snow, navigation became even more challenging.

To fly from one city to another required the identification of landmarks such as highways, railroads, rivers and lakes. As I searched for landmarks, I flew as low as the FAA regulations allowed. If the railroad tracks intersected the outskirts of town at an exact point, as depicted on my aviation map, I knew what city I was approaching. To confirm my position, I would descend over the city's water tower — an edifice in every town, its name emblazoned in huge letters. The water tower was my GPS. As I glided to a landing, I was met with an effluence of farmland aromas, most of which were pleasing to the nose. These flights provided me with a new and expansive view of the agricultural products that were destined for our tables.

Whitewater Normal School. *Photo from the collections of the Whitewater Historical Society and used with permission.*

Whitewater Main Street. *Photo from the collections of the Whitewater Historical Society and used with permission.*

A coffee shop was the welcoming centerpiece of every airport. On Saturdays, depending on the appetites of our flying group, we selected an airport for a fly-in meal. Janesville had blueberry muffins, fresh out of the oven. Lake Lawn Lodge in Delevan continues to serve extraordinary breakfasts and lunches.

In the thirties and forties, the word, "supermarket" was not part of our lexicon. There were no such things. The first supermarkets, A&P and National Tea, did not arrive in Racine until the late 1950s. The pastures and croplands were our supermarkets. Before long, the produce and livestock in the fields that encompassed me during my journeys made its way to our tables.

We shopped at mom-and-pop corner stores. The grocer's family lived above the store. One rarely walked in and shopped. My mother phoned the grocer, placed her order, and awaited the delivery of the groceries. As soon as I acquired my driver's license, I landed a job driving the delivery truck for Sam's Quality Grocery.

Our milk, eggs, butter, and other dairy items were delivered to our home by local farmers. Bremel, an old, craggy, but pleasant German poultry farmer, delivered our chickens. In a way, he looked like a chicken.

Mr. Stauss was our butcher. In the early 1940s, we were neighbors. When he arrived home for lunch or in the evening, he dropped off our steaks, roasts, and cold cuts. Packaged meats were unheard of. Mr. Stauss butchered all meats in his store, then cut our steaks, roasts, and cold cuts to order.

Fruits and vegetables were grown within a few miles of our home by folks known as truck farmers. In winter, we were relegated to canned veggies. Fresh frozen veggies, pioneered by Birdseye, did not arrive until the early 1950s. In the summer, we picked ears of corn in the fields and ate them raw. Fresh from the stalks, the kernels were crunchy and sweet.

When fish was on the menu, my mother went to Pulda's fish market. Most of their inventory had been harvested from local waters moments before her arrival. In the summer months, we often bicycled to the Lake Michigan North Pier which was called a "jetty." We fished for smelt and perch. In an hour or two, we caught enough fish for dinner. Scores of inland glacial lakes were within a 10-mile range of our home. We often headed to these lakes, chipped in until we had two dollars to rent a leaky wooden boat, and brought home a "mess of fish."

Our City Was An International Food Court.

During the industrial revolution and up through the 1950s, Racine was a major factory town. Two international tractor manufacturers were J.I. Case and Massey-Harris. One summer, I worked on the M-H assembly line. Other heavy industry manufacturers included Modine Company, InSinkErator, Hamilton Beach, Hartman Trunk, Young Radiator, and Twin Disc. World-famous SC Johnson & Son is the centerpiece of Racine industrial history. One of the world's first automobiles was built in Racine in 1872 by J.W. Cathcart. Heavy industry plants spawned the growth of satellite companies such as foundries and manufacturers of components for the big machines. As we rode our bikes down the streets, we were serenaded by the hum and clanging of the huge tool and die machines, hydraulic presses, and blast furnaces.

In search of industrial employment that required minimal job and English-speaking skills, waves of immigrants, including Danes, Germans, Czechs, Poles, Italians, and Slovaks flooded to Racine. Thousands of Armenians escaped the Turkish genocide, many of whom flocked to Racine. Many Western European immigrants brought along their agricultural skills and made Wisconsin a garden of produce and America's Dairyland.

The throngs of immigrants brought innumerable ethnic treasures. New forms of architecture emerged. Sounds of unfamiliar music and songs permeated the neighborhoods. European fashion found its way into domestic attire. A symphony of languages, dialects, music, and dance redefined the Racine landscape.

As far back as I can remember, I yearned to travel to foreign lands. I read about distant places in our geography books and thought that visits to these lands would only be a dream. In the 1930s and 1940s, it was my perception that only the extraordinarily rich enjoyed the luxury of leisure and adventure travel. Although I knew some rather well-to-do folks who drove Cadillacs (in those times, the hallmark of wealth), and lived in big houses, I never met a person (other than military personnel returning from war), who had traveled to a foreign country. I only met folks who traveled to Racine *from* a foreign country — and those folks certainly were not rich.

It did not occur to me that exotic foreign countries existed right in my own back yard. Years later, when I finally began my world travels, I discovered that virtually every person I encountered in a foreign country added a layer of intellectual, spiritual, and social substance to my being. I was enriched by folks in these lands who entered my life — even if some contacts were ephemeral. But I had already commenced that growth back home.

Now, as I reflect on my childhood, each kid I met in school whose parents migrated to this country, each home I visited that was different from mine — Bulgarian, Italian, German, Polish, Scandinavian, Slovak or Armenian — equally clothed and enriched me with new layers of worldliness.

I've saved the best foreign treasure for last — cuisine. From the 1930s through the early 1950s, families prepared their meals in a manner markedly different from the dine-at-home practices of today. Although most of my friends were children of European-born blue-collar workers, each of these modest-income families managed to place a cooked-from-scratch dinner on the table. Today, those meals would look and taste like a banquet.

Wages were low. However, by today's standards, the cost of food products was a small fraction of wages. It has been said that in the 1940s, you carried your money to the store in a coin purse and walked home with groceries in a huge sack. Today, you take your money to the supermarket in a huge sack and bring the groceries home in a coin purse.

When I played with kids around their house, I was often invited to dinner. When we hung around my house, playmates often joined our dinner table. There were no take-out or fast-food joints. No frozen, processed dinners at the markets. Restaurant dining was reserved for special occasions — assuming that families could afford a restaurant meal. I enjoyed the experience of partaking in Armenian, Eastern European, Italian and Greek meals. I tasted foods that I had never experienced. Exotically seasoned, enormous servings of beef, pork, lamb, poultry, plus giant bowls of potatoes and veggies and always a homemade dessert were proudly placed on these modest tables.

I rarely declined an invitation for a meal at the home of families who prepared ethnic dishes handed down from their parents and grandparents. At one time, we lived next door to an Italian family. Occasionally, I'd finish dinner at home, then sprint to their house, which was always open to me as ours was to them. I'd sit down to a spread of exquisite Italian dishes for a second meal. Years later in Los Angeles, I represented a Mexican American kid who was charged with a crime he didn't commit. His parents were not wealthy. I agreed to take his case for a modest fee, but I suggested that, if I won the case, I'd be invited to their home for an authentic homemade Mexican dinner. I won the case. I arrived at their home. The dining room table, which resembled the length of a bowling alley, was covered with every Mexican delicacy I had ever seen- and then some. I gobbled up everything from one end of the table to the other. After dinner, we sang Mexican folk songs and watched 8mm home movies. I look back at this evening as one of my most memorable meals.

In countless other profound ways, the homes of Racine's European-born families were great classrooms. They broadened my knowledge, understanding and acceptance of people and cultures that were different from mine.

Except for the Scandinavian kids whose last names were universally recognizable, such as Jensen, Johnson, Peterson or Anderson, many last names included Gosieskis, Pablovich, Pavlik, Kratochvil, Itzenizer, Derderian, Kherdian, Popoff, DePasquale, Nechuta, Klabacka, Vierheilig, and Zakowski.

We never gave this diversity of names a second thought. They were as much a part of our surroundings as the variety of architecture. Ironically, architecture that we once considered obsolete, today is revered as classic. I now realize how the diversity of architecture, landscapes, and ethnicity also added layers of substance, essence, and quality to my life. Imagine a world where everyone is named Smith or Jones and every home is designed and lined up like dough on a cookie sheet.

None of these last names had anything to do with a kid's popularity or being "accepted." What did matter was if a kid was physically attractive, played on the basketball or football teams, or had an engaging personality. The Danish and Swedish kids were blonde with blue eyes. The Armenian, Italian, Greek, and Eastern European came in various hues and shades. Most of the African American children in Racine were generally younger than the kids in our group. Their parents migrated to Racine after WWII. When I was in high school, their youngsters were still infants or toddlers. I only recall two contemporaries. One, Melvin Turner, had been our junior high school student body president. The other kid, Ulysses Doss, was a first-string basketball player in high school, sang in my jazz vocal quintet, and became a prominent professor of black studies at the University of Montana.

David Kherdian, to whose Armenian home I was graciously invited for dinner where I first tasted dolma and lamb kebabs, became a renowned Armenian poet. My father was their family doctor. Norbert Goesieki, not in our class, but a fellow musician, joined several famous orchestras during the big band era. He played in one band that accompanied The Three Stooges.

Except for the owner of Lem's Chinese Restaurant, I never met an Asian person until I reached college. Hispanic families had not yet migrated to Wisconsin. I do recall one Hispanic man, Angel Callas, who ran the cafe at the Hotel Nelson where one of the best breakfasts in town was served. Angel, also a patient of my father, always greeted me affectionately. Whenever I met a person who was a patient of my dad, I was invariably received with open arms.

By the way, Norbert Goesieki's mother owned a store that sold musical instruments, sheet music, and phonograph recordings of the current hits. Small rooms were provided for listening to the records before purchase. During the holidays, I worked at the store. Positioned around a large display window were a piano and a set of drums. During the lunch hour, several of us musicians gathered in the window area and played jam sessions to entertain the window shoppers.

Teen Club Dance. (1950, August). [Advertisement for Teen Dance]. *Racine Journal Times,* 34.

While in high school, I formed a dance band known as "Stu Faber and His Students of Swing." The eight-piece band primarily consisted of older guys. I was required to join the local musician's union and hire union members. Musical talent was the only criterion by which I selected a musician. I also hosted a Saturday morning radio show on station WRAC entitled, "Stu Faber Talking," which featured jazz, bebop, and swing music.

My band played at weddings of many different ethnic families, bar mitzvahs, house parties, and Friday night dances at the YMCA. I devoured the food at the Polish wedding buffets.

A Diverse Buffet Of Cuisine And Life.

It's worth emphasizing that the variety of colors, names, and shapes of my contemporaries made no difference to us kids. It was as much a part of our life's landscape as the thousands of different trees, wildflowers, and plants that proliferated this fecund part of the country. Without this diversity, life would have been as boring as a day-after-day ham sandwich on Wonder Bread.

I'm sure that the usual amount of prejudice and bigotry loomed among some parents, but little, if any appeared to trickle down to the kids.

Although the adult members of these various ethnic groups gravitated to folks of their own ethnicity, Racine did not have defined ethnic districts such as "Little Italy" or "Little Armenia." As in all cities, there were areas with expensive homes and areas with modest homes, occupied not according to ethnicity but according to wealth.

Growing up in Wisconsin provided an omnipresent classroom of farms, cosmopolitan household dinner tables and restaurants of superb foreign and indigenous cuisine. Surfing the web or watching TV to learn about worldwide cultures were nonexistent. Roaming through the countryside, absorbing the sights, textures, and fragrances of the lakes, forests, rivers and farmland, eating food with strange names, sharing the cultures of immigrants' homes were priceless supplements to book learning.

Local Restaurant Cuisine That Formed My Culinary Ideology.

Until the late 1950s, franchised fast-food joints were virtually unheard of. Two exceptions were White Tower Hamburgers and White Castle Hamburgers. White Tower was founded in Milwaukee, Wisconsin in 1926. White Castle founded in 1921, still has some outlets. In the 1930s, the hamburgers were five cents. The Racine outlet was not our main hangout.

Racine also had an A&W Root Beer stand. On sweltering summer nights, our parents would occasionally awaken us for a midnight drive to the A&W. Food and drink were purchased by driving up to the stand where we were greeted by a waitress. After taking our order, she soon reappeared and attached the tray of goodies to the car's window frame.

Teenagers hung out at eateries referred to as "dairy bars." Harmony Dairy, The Spot, Dutch Maid Ice Cream, Homer Dary Pharmacy Soda Fountain, and Pokorny's Drug Store were places where we devoured our daily milkshake or banana split. For 25 cents, the shake was served in a conical-shaped glass with extra in a metal canister. I estimate that the volume of the thick, creamy delight approached 2 quarts. Hamburgers, hot dogs, toasted cheese or egg salad sandwiches, all made to order, were also on the menu. Cho Cho bars, an ice cream treat, now extinct, was one of my favorites.

Even to this day, my all-time favorite hamburger joint is Kewpees. It's where we held my sixth birthday party. Hamburgers were ten cents. My seventy-fifth birthday party was also celebrated at Kewpees. Prices had increased somewhat. I invited about ten guests. The bill for burgers, homemade fries, and their special root beer was around fifteen dollars.

I still visit Kewpees whenever I can. On one occasion, while my son and I were somewhere in Indiana on our annual U.S.A. exploration trip, we discussed lunch options. He suggested Kewpees. Although Racine was not part of the day's itinerary, we diverted from our intended route and drove over 250 miles for lunch at Kewpees.

Just a few years ago, he and I were in Chicago. We decided on a day trip to Racine to visit some of my childhood homes, schools and hangouts. We bypassed the interstate and cruised along the spectacular Lake Michigan shoreline. Our first stop was Kewpees. Next, we visited several Danish bakeries and sampled the world's premiere Danish pastry — the kringle. Kringles are flat, puff-pastry like sweets filled with nuts or fruit. In the 1940s, Prince's Bakery made the best kringles. Today, O&H Bakery kringles are world-famous. President Obama visited O&H during one of his campaigns. Both my son and daughter are fervent Kewpee fans to this day.

Every Wisconsin village had its cherished coffee shop or cafe. In Racine, it was the Ace Grill, which served traditional coffee shop items, such as full breakfasts, sandwiches, burgers, soups, and salads. Extremely popular were hot beef, pork, or turkey sandwiches. Freshly cooked, juicy portions of beef, pork, or turkey were heaped between two slices of plain old fashion white sandwich bread. The sandwich was covered in a rich brown or white gravy — the best part of the sandwich. Suppertime, the Ace served steaks, meatloaf and roast chicken — all made from local, fresh ingredients. Lake Superior whitefish, walleye, and other fish were consistently harvested the day they were served.

Many of the restaurants were opened over 100 years ago. My parents recounted the legend of Freddie Walters Tavern and Steakhouse. During the depression, Freddie served platters of sandwiches filled with piles of steak. How much? Free with the purchase of a 10-cent beer. Few people had money in those days. My father's medical office overflowed with patients who had no means of paying for his services. Medical insurance was virtually unheard of. Nevertheless, these patients were not turned away. By the time I visited Freddy Walters, the free sandwiches costed a dollar.

Friday night fish fry dinners, a Wisconsin tradition for over a century, still thrive today. Cliff's Boathouse in Racine, one of the most popular, closed in 2018.

The Wells Brothers Tavern, opened on Mead Street in 1920, is still going strong. The founders used recipes handed down by their Italian grandparents. The vintage mouthwatering offerings of meatballs and pasta, chicken parmigiana, veal marsala, and lasagna are still on the menu. Pizza was introduced in the 1950s by Durango's restaurant. Sadly, Brusha's Tavern, which opened in 1951, has closed.

I recall Kai-Bo Lounge, the Armenian restaurant on Main Street, which served fabulous kebabs, harissa, and lavash bread. Just up the road in Milwaukee, two superb German restaurants have served pork shanks, Wiener schnitzel, Rheinische sauerbraten, sausages, and other hearty dishes for over 100 years. Mader's Restaurant is still in business. Karl Ratzsch Restaurant, my favorite, recently closed.

Lem's Chinese restaurant served traditional Cantonese and Hong Kong cuisine, including egg foo young, chow mein and chop suey. The latter, a dish that reportedly never existed in China, is an American adaptation. Others disagree. The battle over the origins of chop suey rage on with the intensity of the current Chinese-U.S.A. trade wars.

Prior to the 1960s, unless you were Jewish, you probably never heard of a bagel — let alone lox. Isabel and Max had a small Jewish bakery and produced some great bagels.

Supper clubs, a species of restaurants that, for over a century have been a Wisconsin tradition, originated in the early 20th century as taverns, resorts, and dance halls. Fried chicken and perch, washed down with local beers, were the featured items. Eventually, these places expanded their menus. The result was the birth of cuisine we now crave — Friday fish fry, Saturday prime rib, Sunday roasted chicken and ribs. Other wholesome meat-and-potatoes entrees were dished up, such as pot roast, steaks, chops, and meatloaf. Relish trays, plus soup and salad were included with dinner.

Some supper clubs served family-style. Dining rooms consisted of large, yet clubby rooms with a welcoming atmosphere. Occasionally we would strike up a conversation with a friendly couple at an adjacent table. We'd end up sharing the same table and making new friends.

Supper clubs, which weathered the era of nouveau cuisine, are scattered throughout the state. Next door in Kenosha, the Village Supper Club is popular for crispy, flakey pan-fried fish. The Colony House on the Illinois border in the city of Trevor started off in a log cabin and still operates today. I recommend Ron Faiola's book, *Wisconsin Supper Clubs*, published in 2016 by Midway Publishers. The book narrates a comprehensive history of the clubs and where you can find them today.

Kilbourn Gardens on Highway 41 was a Sunday-drive favorite for all-you-could eat fried chicken. Danish Beer Gardens, with its farmhouse and chicken coop converted to dining rooms, was extremely popular. The fancier restaurants included The Breakers, Higgins Hob Nob, Ray Radigan's Steak House and The Corner House. Higgins and the Corner House are still in business. The cuisine was an upgraded version of the supper club offerings. However, the decor was more elegant, and the waiters were attired in tuxedos. So, the prices were higher. They also served veal Oscar, lobster thermidor, shrimp de jonghe, and oysters Rockefeller — items rarely seen on today's menus.

In the 40s and 50s, many hotel dining rooms served the best food in town. Hotel Racine is an example. The Nelson Hotel served remarkable breakfasts and lunches. Several Chicago hotel dining rooms enjoyed international fame. Examples are The Pump Room at the Ambassador East in Chicago and the Cape Cod Room at the Drake Hotel, Chicago. Both opened in the 1930s and closed around 2017.

My International Culinary Journeys.

As a food and travel journalist, I have worked with chefs all over the world. Common with many of these chefs, especially the ones I admired most, was the depth of their culinary souls which evolved in their mother's kitchen and from indigenous food cultures. Most started their careers with entry-level jobs in local restaurants. As I roamed through nearly 100 countries, chefs would invite me into their kitchens to work with them, (or I would wangle an invitation). I learned more skills than I could have acquired in the best culinary schools. I've spent hundreds of hours working in France, Germany, Spain, Denmark, Italy, Scotland, Hungary, China, Thailand, Israel, United Arab Emirates, Jordan, Morocco, Mexico, South America, Australia, New Zealand, Fiji and of course, almost every state in the U.S.A. I've done everything from peeling potatoes, cleaning fish, butchering beef, baking bread, preparing rich stocks and sauces, joining the chef for shopping at the markets and actually cooking the meal.

I've dined in foreign restaurants from sausage stands to places that charge an obscene $500 per person for dinner. When I reflect on my top twenty-five most unforgettable meals, at least half of them were experienced in rustic, down-to-earth family-owned restaurants. In my fantasy, were some benevolent person to send me to my favorite places on a private jet, I would forsake the fancy joints and return to a tapas restaurant in Alicante, Spain, a charming cafe in Edinburgh, Scotland, a cheesesteak place in Philadelphia, a BBQ joint in Houston, a fish stand in Essaouira, Morocco, a bistro in Dijon, France, a pizza place in Naples, Italy, a dim sum establishment in Hong Kong and a mansaf restaurant near Petra, Jordan. Yes, I can still taste those meals. These experiences have not displaced my Midwestern culinary soul. They have reinforced it.

Our Dinner Table.

Meals in our home resembled those served in the supper clubs. We were a typical Midwestern meat-and-potatoes family. Most dinners began with salad and homemade soup. Then a hearty meat, fish, lamb, or poultry selection along with potatoes and veggies. Dinner concluded with a homemade cake, fruit, or cream pie or an assortment of just-baked cookies.

My mother threw elaborate dinner parties, usually with two or three main dishes, an assortment of appetizers, and a fancy dessert such as a charlotte russe. Almost everything was created with local provenance and made from scratch.

Many of my mother's friends and relatives were also exceptionally accomplished cooks. My friends who resided in more modest surroundings, also served abundant, wholesome meals. It's just what folks did in those days.

The only cookbook my mother used. Notice the sexist title.   *My Mother's Roasting Pan – Over 100 years old.*

My Culinary Soul.

I am shocked when I meet people today who claim never to have enjoyed a complete, home-cooked meal. One close friend complained that his mother often roasted a chicken which invariably was brought out with a raw and bloody interior. Other friends, many from middle-class or upper-middle-class homes, were astounded when they experienced one of my dinners. They never realized that home-cooked cuisine could be better than restaurant fare. The cuisine that I now create is derived, in part, from what I learned from early 20th century Midwestern dinner tables.

My cuisine extends beyond sustenance and comfort food. It's gleeful, robust, benevolent, and inviting. Food is serene, passionate, nostalgic, stimulating, relaxing, and occasionally subtle. Cuisine is a pathway to dialogue, friendship, understanding, and acceptance. Food bonds us to the earth and implores us to safeguard, not plunder nature's bounty. Food creates, and is the repository, of wonderful memories. Years after friends have been our dinner guests, they often reminisce about how they can still taste the food I prepared.

I relish the glee on the faces of my guests as they rush past the door with outcries of being drawn by the fragrances of my offerings, as they alighted from their car.

I adore their ecstatic expressions as they scamper from the porch to the kitchen like kids who scurry downstairs on Christmas morning. Guests peek in the oven and peer into the pots as if they were shaking a wrapped Christmas package to guess its contents.

It has been said that we are what we eat. I am no exception. Our dinner table, and those of my friends, were the wellsprings of every appetite-producing cell in my body, my culinary ideology, and DNA plus my passion for hearty, identifiable substantial food. The culinary child has eternally abided within me.

It's true that I have expanded my gastronomic horizons beyond Racine. I now explore the wonders of European, Asian, Hispanic, and African cuisine. Of course, I still call upon what I learned from the groundbreaking restaurateurs of Racine. Most important, in addition to my culinary journeys I've described, in every recipe I prepare and share in this book, I include these basic secret ingredients: a combination of my mother's cooking, Bremel the egg and chicken guy, Mr. Stauss the butcher, Pulda's Fish Market, and the truck farmers.

Legal Thought and Thought for Life

Recently, a man of Indian descent came to see me.
A man of modest fiscal means, he implored me to
represent his son.
He promised to pay me a paltry sum each week.
In my experience, that promise is invariably broken.
But something about his character took my heart.
So, I relented. I agreed.
As each week came, he kept his promise.
He never failed.
During each visit, we briefly discussed his son.
And then, we launched into lengthy dialogues
about Indian life, culture, religion, geography, language and philosophy.
And how these things compare to Western life.
Bereft of money, this man was rich in worldly knowledge.
With even more wealth in morality.
I emerged with compensation
that far outweighed what money would have brought me.
The dollars he gave are gone.
The wisdom he imparted is with me forever.
Imagine my loss had I turned him down.
or dismissed him.

Chapter 8
Let's Get Started

---------- **Thought for Life** ----------

My love of travel?
Wherever I go
I'm enriched by those I meet.
Whether a person of royalty
or one whose self-perception is royalty,
or an impoverished peasant scratching sustenance from the desert.
The scenes I view,
whether a majestic hand-made edifice,
or nature's craftsmanship:
a meadow and river so stunning no artist could paint
or camera capture.
Or a desolate, shuttered town,
its only occupants
the gathering of dust.
Each contributes to my mind, heart & soul,
and eternally remains within me.
And I am nourished and grow therefrom.
At times,
the shuttered town,
or the famished peasant
are the most enriching contributors.

EQUIPMENT FOR THE HOME CHEF

Whether you are a surgeon, mechanic, artist, professional athlete or engage in any career or pastime where equipment is required, it's always advisable to purchase the best that you can afford. But keep in mind that price does not necessarily translate to the best. You should consult ratings, and friends and professionals who can make recommendations to you. I discovered long ago that a great piece of equipment results in less work and a better food product. I'll recommend some brands. I assure you, I receive no compensation from any equipment company. This list is neither exhaustive nor mandatory. When I began to take cooking seriously, I purchased every shiny culinary object that I saw. Many of these items are now in the basement. I use my favorites over and over again.

BAKING PANS	Depending on your needs, stock up on loaf pans, 8-inch and 9-inch round and square cake pans, spring form pans for cheesecakes, 8-inch and 9-inch pie pans, and 13x9-inch baking pans. You might also need a 9-inch fluted tart pan with a removable bottom. If you like Bundt cakes, a fluted pan is a must. I suggest aluminum or stainless steel. Do not use black pans — they darken the baked goods. If you make cupcakes or muffins, purchase muffin pans. They usually hold twelve muffins or cupcakes. A jelly roll pan, not only for jelly rolls, but for big batches of brownies and sheet cookies too.
BAKING SHEETS	Required for baking cookies, breads and a variety of uses. Depending on oven size, you should use what is referred to as a half hotel pan. Don't purchase black sheets. They transfer dark color to things you are baking.
BENCH SCRAPER	A wonderful tool for scraping up stuff on the cutting board. Also useful to gather chopped veggies. Purchase the metal scraper which also doubles as a dough cutter.
BLENDER	I usually employ my food processor, but a blender is also useful, especially to puree soups and sauces.
BOX GRATERS & CITRUS ZESTERS	Box graters are important for shredding veggies such as cabbage. A citrus zester is a wonderful tool for zesting lemons, grating nutmeg or shredding cheese. OXO Good Grips is my favorite.
BUTCHER'S STRING	Essential for tying up the legs of a chicken or turkey — or a rolled roast before cooking. I also use string to tie up a bunch of fresh herbs (bouquet garni). I toss the herbs in the pot and tie the other end to the pot handle.
COLANDERS	I suggest a large stainless steel colander for washing veggies. Wire mesh strainers for sifting and straining sauces, etc., are essential.
CUTTING BOARDS & WORK BOARDS	One heavy wooden carving board is suggested. Plus, several boards for cutting veggies and meat. I always use a red board for meat only and another color board for produce.
CUTTING TOOLS	You should have at least two chef knives for cutting veggies and meat. I prefer a chef's knife with a handle that's built into the blade. Chef's knife blades range in size from 8 to 12 inches. Before purchase, hold several in your hand

and see how they feel. I suggest Henckels or Wusthofs for European knives. I also have several Japanese knives which use harder steel and are excellent for precision cutting. Additionally, you will need a paring knife, serrated bread knife, boning knife, kitchen shears and poultry shears. Sharpen it regularly and you're on your way to culinary bliss. The subject of knives is quite complicated. Knives should fit your specific physical profile, such as your hand size.

DUTCH OVEN — I strongly recommend Le Creuset. I suggest the round 9-quart and the round 13¼. Not only will these last a lifetime, they will last the lifetime of your grandkids. These cast iron pots, enameled in a variety of beautiful colors, can withstand both high oven heat and stovetop burner heat.

FOOD PROCESSOR — Indispensable tool. I've owned a Cuisinart 14-cup stainless steel model for 15 years and it's still going strong. I also have a 2-cup model for grinding smaller batches, such as nuts.

IMMERSION BLENDER — I refer to mine as a hand-held motorboat. Immersion blenders are useful for any kind of pureed soup or vegetable without the burden of washing a food processor.

INSTANT-READ THERMOMETER — I could not live without my Thermopen instant thermometer. A good instant thermometer is essential to check if meat and other food items have reached desired doneness.

MEASURING CUPS & SPOONS — Pyrex and Anchor Hocking glass measuring cups are for liquids. I suggest 1, 2, 4 and 8-cup capacities.

For measuring dry ingredients, purchase a set of measuring cups and spoons, preferably stainless steel. The plastic ones seem to break and the numbers designating the capacity seem to disappear. You will enjoy a heavy metal set for life. The metal measuring cups should have a handle flush with the scoop for easy measuring. The spoons should be oval for easy dipping into spice jars — also with handles flush with the scoop.

PARCHMENT PAPER & BAKING MATS — Used to line baking sheets to keep food from sticking. A Silpat is a reusable mat, but I prefer the disposable parchment paper. Just throw the sheets away — less to clean.

PASTRY BLENDER — This handy tool is great for cutting large chunks of butter into small pieces. Also, if you love to bake by hand, it's a great tool for cutting the butter into the flour for pie crusts.

PASTRY BRUSH — For years I used brushes that were similar to paint brushes. Now, I only use the silicon brushes. They are great for basting or painting an egg wash atop a pie crust. I have separate brushes for pastry and savory use.

PASTRY WHEEL — I use the fluted wheel for cutting slices of pizza and for cutting out strips of dough for a lattice pie crust.

ROLLING PIN	Rolling pins are essential for rolling out pie crusts, pizza dough and cookie dough. I also use the rolling pin to crush crackers or nuts. I love to use the rolling pin to flatten out and shape a burger patty. I use a rolling pin that is merely a long cylinder of hard wood about 2 inches in diameter. I purchased it in Bangkok about 15 years ago and it has been my constant companion.
SAUCEPANS	A saucepan is a misnomer. It's used for everything from making sauces, roux, boiling eggs and boiling veggies. I suggest a 1-quart, 2-quart and 3-quart D3 stainless steel with covers. If you also want something just for sauces, a 1-quart saucier (a more rounded saucepan), is nice to have.
SKILLETS	I recommend a variety. Carbon steel pans, used by professional chefs, are lighter than cast iron and are great for browning meats and fish. To me, a cast iron skillet is indispensable. I have several, one of which I've had since college. Clad stainless steel skillets are also excellent. Clad means that there are three layers of bonding with a core layer of aluminum or copper. The steel is for durability and the core conducts heat quickly and evenly. Never purchase sets of cookware. The sets always include pieces you will never use. I suggest various sizes of the different materials. Recommended are 7, 9, 12 and 15-inch skillets. Non-stick skillets are very useful, but not for browning meat or fish.
SPATULAS	For scraping and stirring, I suggest silicon heat-proof spatulas. I use them for everything. I also recommend a wood spatula with a wide blade for stir-frying. I have various sizes for burgers, fish and general use. Offset spatulas are great for frosting a cake.
STAND MIXER	I could not survive without my Kitchen Aid stand mixer. Purchase the largest model you can afford. You'll use it for everything from kneading bread to whipping cream to mixing up a batch of cookie dough or a cake batter.
STOCKPOT	At times, I use my Dutch ovens for making stock. I suggest a large pot in which you can also cook pasta. I recommend Cuisinart Chef's Classic Stainless Steel 8-quart Stock Pot with Cover.
TONGS	Essential for turning meats and veggies and lifting food out of cooking vessels. Make certain that they are comfortable in your hand before you purchase.
WHISKS	I suggest several in various sizes. Great for beating eggs, custards and dry ingredients. Use silicon whisks for working with foods in nonstick pans.

TIPS AND TECHNIQUES FOR BECOMING A GREAT COOK

Over the years, I've trained several young lawyers. To this day, each of them often returns to tell me how they still employ the tips and techniques I've taught them. I've also trained several friends, (some of them not so young), on my tips and techniques for cooking. Each friend has also come back to relate how they use my suggestions to this day. One of my friends, who is a great cook, says that she keeps a special "Stuie" file of my recipes.

Of course, these validations make me happy and proud. And I don't mind bragging about it. Especially if these tips and techniques can help the reader.

I've written this book for several reasons. First, it was fun to write. Second, I want to clear the air about the law and lawyers. Third, for familial, sociological, health and other reasons, I believe that cooking in the home makes for a better life and society. If I can motivate the reader to cook at home, it will give me great joy.

Some of these techniques may seem elementary, especially to those who are already accomplished cooks. But I'm often surprised when I impart one or more of these tips, and the response is, "Gee, I never thought of that — it was a real help."

1. **Have fun.** If this is the only suggestion you take to heart, you are already on your way to being an accomplished cook. When I trained lawyers, the first thing I always said on the way to the courthouse was, "Let's have fun." At the end of the court session, I always asked (a) did they learn anything and (b) did they have fun? A day in the kitchen (or in the courtroom), should be like a day at the beach. Take it seriously, but have fun.

2. **Study your recipes and make your shopping list early.** I look at a recipe as if I were reading a favorite book. I enjoy reading recipes. I think about the project before I begin. It's like thinking about the strategy of a case before I go to court.

3. **Purchase the best available ingredients that you can afford.** Any great chef will tell you that you can't make a silk purse out of a sow's ear. A great cook can't make a great meal out of inferior ingredients. A bad cook is more likely to make a good meal out of great ingredients.

4. **Lay everything out before you start.** Every tool you will need for the project should be at your beck and call. Place them at arm's reach near the stove in the order of use. That enables you to reach for a tool almost without looking. Do the same with the ingredients. If a recipe first calls for chopped onions and celery, have these items chopped and placed at the head of the line. If the next step is to brown the meat, have that ingredient next in line and so on.

5. **Exception to rule 2 — prepare while one item is cooking.** If you determine that one item in the line will take a long time — for example if you are browning a large hunk of meat, start browning the meat and chop the onions while the meat is browning.

    A good friend of ours who came to dinner often did not believe that I could prepare an entire meal, excluding waiting time while something was cooking, in around 2 hours. I understood her disbelief.

Whenever we visited her home for a meal, she would be running around the kitchen like the Mad Hatter, looking for stuff that should have been at her fingertips hours before. The meal, such as it was, would never reach the table until over an hour after the announced time of dinner. "I've been working all day," she cried.

I invited her over to prove my point. I kept her outside the kitchen and gave her something to keep her occupied. I allowed her to inspect the kitchen to confirm that, except for purchasing the ingredients, nothing had been started prior to her arrival.

Within 2 hours of hands-on time and 4½ hours total, I served a Caesar salad, split pea soup, a roasted chicken with roast potatoes, green beans and a chocolate cake.

6. **Start first with items that take the longest.** While an item is in the oven, you could be chopping the veggies. For example, if I'm baking bread, I'll make the dough and allow it to rise while I'm doing something else. If I am baking a cake, I'll make the batter, and put the cake in the oven while attending to other things. When the cake is done, the bread is usually ready to bake, so I can use the oven without turning it on and off and wasting energy by preheating the oven twice. I don't count waiting time in my total calculation of how long it takes to make a meal. But I do try to use waiting time effectively.

7. **Season the ingredients in layers.** First, prepare and mix your seasons before starting. For example, if a recipe calls for thyme, oregano, paprika, kosher salt and black pepper, mix these items together. This results in more even seasoning. Then, as you cook each layer, such as sweating the onions, adding the bell peppers, adding the meat, etc., sprinkle some of the seasoning as you add each layer. It makes a significant difference in the ultimate flavor.

8. **Season lightly.** You can always add more seasoning later — but if you season too heavily, it can't be removed. When applying seasonings, take some between your fingers and hold your hand about 8-10 inches above the item to be seasoned. This assures even seasoning.

9. **Taste and season as you go along.** We all have different taste buds. I often add more seasoning as I go along and just before I place the final product on a serving platter.

10. **Clean up as you go along.** A messy kitchen will generally end up with a messy meal. If you clean up as you go along, it's easier to find items as you need them. Plus, it makes the after-dinner drudgery that much easier.

11. **Don't be afraid of a challenge.** A difficult or unfamiliar recipe should not frighten or intimidate you, it should inspire you. If you successfully prepare a difficult recipe, you'll not only enjoy the creation that much more, it will build your confidence.

Years ago, a judge I knew related to me that her adult daughter said to her, "Mom, you are the greatest parent in the world. But you've never made a birthday cake for me. For my gift this year, will you bake a cake?"

In her courtroom, this judge was knowledgeable, tough, composed and confident. When she asked me to be her guide in baking a cake, she was like a terrified child learning to swim. We planned a dinner together. I took her step-by-step in making my favorite chocolate cake. I required her to do everything herself while I demonstrated and watched. She made a perfect cake. Her daughter loved it and declared the cake to be one of the best birthday gifts she ever had. The judge has since baked numerous cakes. Whenever I'm before her in court, she's still tough with me.

12. **If you mess up, don't beat yourself up.** Occasionally, things just don't work out. One day, I was preparing a brunch for about ten guests. Brunch is not my favorite meal. I had my ingredients laid out and put one component in a dish that should have gone into another component — so I ended up with 2 disastrous dishes. The lesson I learned was that I should have put small labels on each component.

    We all had a big laugh. All of the other dishes came out fine. But I did not follow the advice I am now imparting to you. I was miserable. Being miserable is a waste of time.

13. **Don't let guests distract you in the kitchen.** This may not be your pet peeve, but it is one of mine. I don't like folks hanging out in the kitchen while I am putting the final touches on the meal. When they ask if they can help, I answer that the way they can help is to relax in the sun room with a drink and an appetizer. If a crowd in the kitchen does not bother you, I'm envious.

14. **Make some items the day before.** Some items made the day before will keep just fine. It saves a lot of time on dinner party day.

15. **Don't be afraid to deviate from a recipe.** Recipes are not scripture. Be creative. It's often a good idea to omit an ingredient you don't like or add a favorite ingredient. If a recipe calls for a teaspoon of a seasoning, more or less may be more to your liking.

16. **Cook foods that you enjoy.** Since cooking has to be fun, it's better to prepare things with the anticipation of enjoying them yourself. I've broken this rule a few times. For example, I hate cheesecake. I've made hundreds of them and have never tasted any that I have made. Yet, for some strange reason, folks love my cheesecakes.

17. **The more you cook, the better cook you will be.** One thing I love about cooking is that I never stop learning. It's just like the law — that's why they call it the practice of law — I'm still learning.

    Whenever I repeat an often cooked recipe, such as Bolognese sauce, it gets better each time. The reason? Experience.

18. **Have fun.** Haven't I already made this suggestion as rule 1? Yes. But it's worth repeating. HAVE FUN!

A FEW WORDS ABOUT THE USE OF INGREDIENTS

This is a brief description of some common ingredients used in cooking and baking and how to use them. This list, which is not meant to be exhaustive, is limited to items that are incorporated into other dishes. I recommend consulting specialized sources for more detailed information on these and other ingredients.

Beans. If you have the time, it's best to use dried beans. However, canned beans from a quality manufacturer are an exception to my dislike of canned products. Beans, classified as a legume, along with peas, peanuts, and lentils, are rich in fiber and a great source of protein. Black beans are a staple in many Mexican and Brazilian dishes. Cannellini, also known as white Italian kidney beans, are a popular addition to soups, salads, and many Italian dishes. Chickpeas, also known as garbanzo beans, are great for soups, salads and hummus. Great northern are another type of white bean often used in place of navy or cannellini beans. Kidney beans, with their vibrant red skin, are used in soups and chilis. Pinto beans have an orange-pink color with rust-colored specks. They are used in many Mexican and Californian dishes.

Chocolate. Hard chocolate, sold as bittersweet, semisweet, sweet and milk chocolate, contain anywhere from 10 to 85% chocolate liquor. The better quality of chocolate you purchase, the better the final product will be. Baking cocoa is dried, roasted and fermented chocolate liquor with the cocoa butter removed. Dutch process cocoa powder starts with cocoa beans that have been washed in an alkaline solution to neutralize their acidity. You can use either type in recipes that do not call for baking soda or baking powder.

Eggs. Eggs are sold in small, medium, large and extra-large. When eggs are included in this book, I refer to large eggs. Eggs are easier to separate when cold and easier to whip when at room temperature.

Fats & Oils. Butter is a fat made from cream from cows. When I refer to butter, I always mean unsalted butter. Lard is a fat rendered from pork fat. It is not in common use today, but is becoming more popular, especially as a shortening for pie crusts. Crisco®, which has been around for over 100 years, is a blend of soybean oil, fully hydrogenated palm oil, and partially hydrogenated palm and soybean oils. Smoke points, or the temperature at which oils begin to smoke and burn, is important when deciding which oil to use. The higher the smoke point, the less likely the food will burn. Avocado oil has the highest smoke point. Corn, grapeseed, peanut, safflower, light olive and sunflower oils also have high smoke points. I use olive oil to flavor foods. For stir-frying, I use canola or vegetable oil. When a recipe calls for olive oil, I always mean extra virgin olive oil. I keep two varieties. One for cooking and an even better quality for salad dressings and marinades.

Flour. Flour is a generic term for the fine grinding to a powder consistency of a variety of grains and other food items. For example, there is potato flour, almond flour or rice flour. These, and other non-gluten flours can be used in place of the wheat flour, the most common. I often use tapioca flour as a thickener. Generally, when my recipes refer to flour, I mean all-purpose flour unless another type is specified. All-purpose flour is made from a combination of high-gluten hard wheat and low-gluten soft wheat. All-purpose is sold as bleached or unbleached. They may be used interchangeably. Bread flour is an unbleached high-gluten blend of over 99% hard wheat flour. Whole wheat flour contains the wheat germ. Cake flour is a fine textured soft wheat flour. Self-rising flour is an all-purpose flour with baking powder and salt added. I rarely use this flour. Rye flour is milled from rye grain. Low in gluten, it is usually combined with all-purpose or whole wheat flour.

Leavening agents. Baking soda, known as bicarbonate of soda, is used with an acid such as lemon juice or buttermilk. Baking powder is baking soda with a moistener. Some recipes call for both. I discard and replace these agents twice a year.

Milk. Most recipes in this book use whole milk unless otherwise specified. Buttermilk is formed from skimmed milk which is cultured with lactic acid bacteria. A good substitute can be made by adding one tablespoon of lemon juice to one cup of whole milk. Evaporated milk is a canned cow's milk product with half the water removed. Sweetened condensed milk is a canned cow's milk product from which water has been removed and a sweetener added.

Potatoes. Potatoes fall into three categories, starchy, waxy and all-purpose. The most common starchy potato, the russet, is the best choice for baked, mashed or French fried potatoes. Waxy potatoes are low in starch and high in moisture. These, including red bliss, new potatoes or fingerlings, are used in casseroles, stews or just plain roasted or boiled. All-purpose potatoes include the Yukon Gold, my favorite, which I generally use in place of waxy potatoes.

Rice. There are over twenty varieties of rice. The most popular is long-grain which comes in many varieties. My favorite is jasmine rice because it is easy to whip up a batch and it always comes out fluffy and sticky. White basmati rice, grown in the Himalayan foothills, is considered to be one of the best quality white grains of rice. Widely used in Indian and Middle eastern cuisines, it has a distinctive aroma. Arborio and carnaroli rice from Italy are used for risotto and rice puddings. Bomba is another short grain rice used in paella. Avoid instant rice.

Sugar. There are around a dozen types of sugar. For this book, we use granulated sugar, confectioners sugar and brown sugar. Sugars are made from sugar cane or sugar beets. I prefer pure cane sugar. Granulated, or white sugar, is the most common. Powdered, or confectioners sugar, is white sugar that has been ground into a fine powder with some cornstarch added for stability. Brown sugar, which is granulated sugar with molasses added, is sold as light brown and dark brown. I use the light variety whenever brown sugar is called for.

Temperature of Baking Ingredients. For most baking, all ingredients should be at room temperature. For pie crust, the ingredients should be very cold. I suggest freezing the ingredients for 15 minutes before using.

Tomatoes. Although I avoid most canned foods, a quality brand of canned tomatoes is my choice for cooking. I suggest purchasing whole tomatoes. The diced tomatoes have an additive. I place the whole tomatoes in a food processor and pulse them to reach the desired consistency. I also use quality brands of tomato sauce and tomato paste. Authentic San Marzano tomatoes are one of my favorite products. Don't buy them if they say, "San Marzano Style." The legally authentic ones will have D.O.P. printed on the label.

Yeast. The two most common forms are active dry yeast and instant yeast. I prefer the instant yeast. Compressed cake yeast, which is difficult to find, is used for sophisticated or artisan breads.

Chapter 9

Breakfast is Ready

DUTCH BABY PUFFY APPLE PANCAKE

I don't often prepare breakfast for folks. I'm a very early riser and no one would show up at the hour when I have breakfast. I sometimes compromise and hold off until what some folks consider a more civilized time for breakfast. This simple creation invariably brings a standing ovation.

3 large eggs
¾ cup all purpose flour
¼ teaspoon salt
1 teaspoon sugar
¾ cup milk
¾ teaspoon vanilla
2 tablespoons packed brown sugar
¼ teaspoon cinnamon
Pinch ground nutmeg
1 medium golden delicious or Granny Smith apple
3 tablespoons butter
Lemon juice & powdered sugar

Preheat oven to 425°F. In a medium bowl, beat eggs slightly with a whisk. Add flour, salt, sugar, milk, and vanilla. Beat until combined. Do not overbeat. Set aside.

Combine brown sugar, cinnamon and nutmeg. Set aside.

Peel apple and slice thinly. Pour lemon juice over apples. Set aside.

You now have everything ready and the oven should have reached 425°F. Place butter in a deep 9-inch pie pan. Place pan in oven until butter melts. Remove pie pan, brush butter up the sides of the pan. Sprinkle brown sugar mixture evenly over the bottom of the pan. Slightly mix into the butter.

Place the apple slices in one layer over brown sugar mixture. Turn apple slices over so that both sides are coated with brown sugar.

Pour flour batter evenly over apples. Be sure that batter covers the entire pan. I transfer batter to a measuring cup before pouring. It makes it easier to pour an even layer of the batter.

Bake 30-35 minutes until puffy and deep golden brown. You can cut slices of the pancake like a pie or loosen the edges of the pancake and turn it upside down onto a heatproof plate. Either way, serve immediately. Sprinkle with lemon juice and powdered sugar.

CINNAMON STREUSEL BUTTERMILK COFFEE CAKE

This coffee cake stands out as the favorite of all my guests and friends who have tried it. It's easy to make and can be served for breakfast — or any meal for that matter.

- **1 cup brown sugar, packed**
- **½ cup granulated sugar**
- **Pinch of salt**
- **2 cups all-purpose flour**
- **⅔ cup butter, melted**
- **½ cup pecans, finely chopped**
- **1 teaspoon cinnamon**
- **1 egg, slightly beaten**
- **1 cup buttermilk**
- **1 teaspoon baking soda**
- **2 teaspoons baking powder**

Preheat oven to 350°F. Generously butter a 9-inch springform pan. In a bowl of a stand mixer, mix sugars, salt, flour, and melted butter. Transfer 1 cup of the mixture to another bowl. Add chopped pecans and cinnamon. Mix until combined.

Add the beaten egg, buttermilk, baking soda and baking powder to the mixing bowl. Mix at low speed just until combined. If you don't have buttermilk on hand, combine 1 cup of whole milk with 1 tablespoon of fresh lemon juice, mix and let stand for 5 minutes.

Pour the batter into the springform pan. Smooth and level with a spatula. Sprinkle cinnamon-pecan mixture evenly over the batter.

Bake for about 40 minutes or until a toothpick inserted in the middle of the cake comes out clean and the cake begins to slightly pull from the sides of the pan. Do not overbake.

Cool on a wire rack for 30 minutes. Then, remove the sides of the pan and cool for about 1 hour before serving.

FABE'S FRENCH TOAST

I can't escape the French culinary arts, even when it comes to breakfast. I'm not sure if the French actually invented this dish. Historians insist that, during the Roman Empire in the 5th Century A.D., the citizens employed essentially the same recipe and called it "pan dulcis." Others claim that a guy named Joseph French created the dish in 1874.

6 slices brioche or white bread (preferably 2 or 3 days old)

3 eggs

½ cup milk

2 tablespoons sugar

½ teaspoon vanilla

1 teaspoon ground cinnamon

¼ teaspoon ground nutmeg

1 tablespoon pure maple syrup

4 tablespoons butter

2 tablespoons confectioners sugar

Whisk together eggs, milk, sugar, vanilla, cinnamon, nutmeg and maple syrup in a flat-bottomed pie plate or baking dish. Place bread slices, one or two at a time, into the egg mixture and flip to make sure both sides of the bread are well-coated. Let slices sit in egg mixture for no more than a minute to soak up mixture.

Melt butter in a large skillet or on a griddle. Place the bread slices, one or two at a time, in skillet or on griddle and cook on medium heat until golden brown on each side, about 2-3 minutes. Add more butter if necessary. Sprinkle with confectioners sugar and serve with more maple syrup, if desired.

SPANISH OMELET

On the rare occasions when I make a brunch, this omelet is always a hit. This recipe calls for six eggs and could easily be doubled. If you substitute oregano and add an Italian grated cheese, it could be an Italian omelet. You could consider such things as curry, feta cheese or just about any ingredient and, presto! You have a universal omelet. I suggest a pan with low sides. If you intend to make omelets frequently, an omelet pan might be a good investment.

6 eggs

2-3 tablespoons whole milk

¼ teaspoon kosher salt

¼ teaspoon black pepper

¼ teaspoon thyme (plus more for sprinkling)

2 tablespoons butter

1 tablespoon olive oil

6-8 brown mushrooms, sliced

½ cup red onion, chopped

½ cup chopped red bell pepper

½ cup chopped green pepper

1 bunch green onions, chopped

½ celery rib, chopped

3 garlic cloves, chopped

1 cup diced tomatoes

⅛ teaspoon chili powder

½ cup grated Mexican, sharp cheddar or Monterey Jack cheese, or combination

½ cup diced tomatoes

¼ cup chopped cilantro

Place eggs and milk in a bowl. Place salt, pepper and thyme in bowl. Lightly sprinkle egg mixture with salt, pepper, and thyme. Whisk until combined. Set aside. Add butter and oil to a 12-inch non-stick skillet over medium heat. Add mushroom slices, sprinkle lightly with salt, pepper and thyme, and sauté until lightly browned. Remove from skillet, place in a bowl and set aside. Add onions, bell peppers, green onions and celery. Lightly sprinkle with salt, pepper and thyme and sauté just until soft, then add garlic and sauté for an additional 30 seconds. Do not brown. Remove from skillet and set aside in a bowl.

In a small saucepan, heat the diced tomatoes over medium low heat. Sprinkle with salt, pepper, thyme. Add chili powder. When warm, remove from heat and set aside.

Carefully pour egg mixture into the same skillet. Over medium-high heat, allow the omelet to form. Do not move the skillet or stir the egg mixture. The omelet will begin to solidify. Carefully lift an edge and allow the wet stuff on top to flow under the omelet. Continue until almost all the wet stuff is placed under the omelet. Cover the skillet, reduce heat to medium and cook just until the top of the omelet is almost set.

Add half of the chopped veggies, half the mushrooms, half the cheese and half the diced tomatoes to one side of the omelet. With a large spatula, or two spatulas, gently fold the half with no veggies over the half with veggies. Place the remaining half of the veggies, mushrooms, cheese and diced tomatoes on top of the folded omelet. Sprinkle half the cilantro over the omelet. Cover and cook just until the cheese melts.

With the spatulas, carefully slip the omelet onto a platter. It should just slide off.

Sprinkle with remaining cilantro. You can also add additional diced tomatoes and chopped green onions to the top for a little crunchiness and color. Cut into portions and serve immediately.

LET'S MAKE GRANOLA

Store-bought granola is expensive and often has stuff in it that I don't want — or lacks ingredients that I do want. This recipe is quick and easy. Plus you can add or omit items of your choice.

¼ cup plus 2 tablespoons brown sugar
½ teaspoon cinnamon
¾ teaspoon salt
3 cups rolled oats
1 cup slivered almonds
1 cup unsalted cashews
½ cup sunflower seeds
¼ cup shredded sweet coconut
¼ cup canola oil
¼ cup plus 2 tablespoons maple syrup
1 cup raisins

Preheat oven to 250°F.

Mix together brown sugar, cinnamon and salt.

Combine oats, nuts, sunflower seeds, shredded coconut and brown sugar mixture in a large bowl. In another bowl, combine canola oil and maple syrup.

Add oil-syrup mixture to dry ingredients and mix well with your hands. Spread mixture out on two sheet pans, each in one layer.

Bake for 1 hour 20 minutes. With a large spatula, mix and turn over mixtures every 20 minutes. Rotate the pans after 35 minutes.

Remove from oven and transfer to a large, heat-proof bowl. Add and mix in raisins and cool completely.

Chapter 10
Salads, Appetizers, Soups, Stocks & Breads

BARLEY SALAD WITH FRESH VEGGIES

This salad not only is beautiful to look at, it's refreshing to eat. You can add hard boiled eggs, artichoke hearts, pea pods or any number of seasonal veggies.

1½ cups pearled barley

Several broccoli crowns, green beans or cauliflower crowns

1 carrot

1 small zucchini

½ cup green olives

4 tablespoons capers

Juice of 1 lemon

3 tablespoons olive oil

1 cup cherry or grape tomatoes

1 sprig thyme leaves

Salt & pepper

1 romaine lettuce leaf

Cook barley in 6 cups water and 1 teaspoon salt. Simmer until al dente, about 45 minutes. In the meantime, bring a small pot of water to a boil. Add several broccoli crowns, green beans or cauliflower crowns. Boil until just tender. Remove and place in a bowl of ice water. Set aside.

Dice carrot and zucchini. Roughly chop olives and capers. Drain the cooked barley and rinse under cold water. Combine cooled barley with lemon juice and olive oil. Add other ingredients. Place a half cup of cooked barley on a romaine lettuce leaf and artfully place other items over and around barley. Lightly season with thyme, salt, and pepper, if desired. You may also dress the salad with a vinaigrette. To make vinaigrette, place 3 tablespoons champagne or white wine vinegar, ½ teaspoon Dijon mustard, 1 clove of minced garlic, ¾ teaspoons kosher salt and ¼ teaspoon freshly ground black pepper in a bowl. Slowly add approximately ½ cup extra virgin olive oil and whisk swiftly until emulsified. Gently drizzle over the salad.

FABE'S OUTSTANDING CAESAR DRESSING

As the story goes, this salad was invented in the 1920s by Caesar Cardini, an Italian guy who owned a restaurant in Tijuana. The original recipe included a raw egg. In the 1950s, the salad was made tableside. Today, most restaurants have eliminated the raw egg for hygienic reasons. I've sampled numerous disappointing versions in recent times. Many chefs drown the lettuce with a concoction which consists primarily of mayonnaise. I've eliminated most of the mayonnaise. I process some whole olives which add to the body of the dressing and help to hold it together. At my parties, guests always demand seconds of this version.

1 head romaine lettuce
½ garlic bulb
3 anchovy filets
5 whole green olives w/ pimento
1 tablespoon capers
Kosher salt and freshly ground black pepper
1 tablespoon grainy Dijon mustard
1 tablespoon mayonnaise
1 teaspoon Worcestershire sauce
Pinch cayenne pepper
2 tablespoons champagne vinegar
6 tablespoons extra virgin olive oil
Juice of 1 lemon
Parmesan cheese
Croutons (See recipe for Fabe's Garlic, Parmesan & Herb Croutons page 64)

Clean and dry lettuce. Place into refrigerator until ready to use. Place garlic, anchovies, capers and olives in a food processor. Carefully pulse the mixture until it forms a chunky paste. Season lightly with salt and pepper as you grind. This will assist the grinding. Add the mustard and mayonnaise and mix well. Add the Worcestershire sauce, p of cayenne, vinegar and pulse a few times more. Slowly add the olive oil, pulsing constantly until an emulsion forms. Do not add too much olive oil at one time. Add lemon juice to taste and whisk to combine. Check for seasonings. I always add more black pepper — the more I add, the better the flavor.

With your hands, tear lettuce into bite size pieces. Add to bowl and mix well with dressing. Sprinkle with Parmesan cheese and add croutons. To avoid overpowering the lettuce, I always add dressing sparingly. Or, I prepare individual bowls of lettuce for guests and let them add the dressing themselves.

Culinary Thought

The legend that Caesar Cardini invented this salad is untrue. My extensive research proves otherwise. I commissioned a group of culinary archeologists. While Marcus Brutus was plotting the assassination of Julius Caesar, he lulled him into a state of sleepiness with a huge salad.

"Et tu Brutus," uttered Caesar? "I didn't know you were a chef. How about naming this salad after me?"

FABE'S GARLIC, PARMESAN & HERB CROUTONS

2 large garlic cloves, thinly sliced lengthwise

1 teaspoon dried oregano, crumbled

1 teaspoon dried basil, crumbled

1 teaspoon dried thyme, crumbled

½ teaspoon salt plus additional to taste

½ teaspoon pepper

2 tablespoons butter

1 tablespoon Italian parsley, chopped

¼ cup olive oil

1 loaf of Italian bread, cut into ¾" cubes (about 7 cups)

¼ cup finely grated fresh Parmesan

In a small saucepan combine the garlic, oregano, basil, thyme, ½ teaspoon of the salt, pepper, butter, parsley and the oil. Simmer the mixture for 5 minutes. Discard the garlic. In a bowl toss the bread cubes with the oil mixture, then spread them in a single layer on a jelly-roll pan. Bake in a preheated 375°F oven for 8 minutes. Sprinkle the croutons with the Parmesan and bake for 7 minutes more, or until they are golden. Sprinkle the croutons with the additional salt and let them cool. The croutons may be kept in an airtight container for one week.

A Caesar salad made with grilled romaine leaves adds an additional dimension of flavor and texture. Fire up the grill. Tear off whole leaves of romaine and swish around in a bowl of ice water. Shake off excess water, lightly brush each leaf with dressing and place directly on grill, flat side down until moderately blackened. Watch closely. Turn the leaves over and grill until lightly blackened. Transfer each to a plate, add dressing and sprinkle with Parmesan cheese.

CORN AND TOMATO SALAD

An easy and refreshing salad or side dish for a summer dinner. Great during other seasons as well.

3 cups fresh corn (about 4 ears)
1 cup cherry tomatoes, halved
1 cup cucumbers, diced
½ cup red onion, chopped
3 tablespoons apple cider vinegar
3 tablespoons extra virgin olive oil
1 teaspoon each kosher salt and freshly ground black pepper
2 tablespoons Italian parsley, chopped

Bring a large pot of water to a boil. Add corn ears and boil for 5 minutes. After corn cools, place each ear, standing up, on a cutting board. Hold the ear with one hand. With a sharp knife, slice the kernels off of the ears.

Combine the corn kernels, tomatoes, cucumbers, red onion in a bowl. Mix well. In a small bowl, combine cider vinegar, olive oil, salt and pepper. Drizzle over the corn mixture. Mix well to coat all ingredients. Add more seasoning, if desired. Sprinkle parsley over corn. Serve cold or room temperature.

FABE'S SALADE NIÇOISE

This popular French salad derived its name from the City of Nice, on the Cote d'Azur in the Provence region. A very colorful and tasty salad, it lends itself to a host of variations. In my version, the three food groups are included. The classic French version does not include lettuce. But what's a salad without some lettuce? I added boiled potatoes and corn. The beauty of this recipe is that many of the cooked items can be prepared in one pot.

You could also grill the corn. You can add roasted peppers. Anchovies are a good choice. There are no limits to what you can add. I prefer the salmon to the tuna. This salad tastes best when the lettuce is cold and the other ingredients are around room temperature.

⅓ cup olive oil

Juice of 1 lemon

1 tablespoon Dijon mustard

3 anchovies, finely chopped

1 shallot, finely chopped

1 tablespoon capers

Kosher salt and freshly ground pepper

3 large eggs

½ pound haricots vert

6 baby potatoes

½ carrot, sliced along bias in ½" slices

1 ear of corn, cut in thirds

1 head red leaf lettuce

½ pint red cherry tomatoes, cut in half lengthwise

½ cucumber, sliced

3 (6-ounce) jars imported tuna in olive oil, drained (optional)

½ pound salmon filets (optional)

½ cup Niçoise olives or olive medley

In a medium bowl, whisk together olive oil, lemon juice, mustard, anchovies, shallot and capers. Season with salt and pepper. Set aside.

Place eggs in a medium saucepan. Fill with water to cover eggs. Place pan over high heat and bring to a rolling boil. Turn off heat, cover pan and let sit for 12 minutes. Eggs will be perfectly hard boiled.

Fill a large pot with water. Add haricots vert, potatoes, carrots and corn. Bring to a rolling boil over high heat, reduce heat to light boil. With tongs or a spider, remove green beans after 3 minutes. Remove corn after 5 minutes. Remove carrots and potatoes when tender, about 9 minutes total. This way, everything is cooked in one pot.

To assemble, slice eggs in half lengthwise. Slice potatoes in half lengthwise. Use a platter or a 9-inch deep dish pie plate. Place whole leafs of lettuce around the edges of the pie plate with one end on the edges and the other ends toward the middle.

Chop half of the lettuce and place in the bottom of the pie plate over the leaves. Sprinkle cherry tomatoes, cucumbers and olives over the salad. Lay out the potatoes, eggs, fish, haricots vert, carrots and corn. Whisk the dressing again. Lightly drizzle the dressing over the salad and serve.

---**Culinary Thought**---

When you serve this salad that was developed in Nice, you could call it "Nice Salad." But folks might misunderstand. All salads are nice. Tell your guests that they are about to experience a niçoise salad. I guarantee it will taste better.

I love to use an 8-ounce filet of salmon instead of the tuna. I sauté the salmon, cool it and cut it into 1" chunks. To prepare salmon, in a heavy skillet over high heat, add 2 tablespoons of olive oil. Pat salmon filet dry, then sprinkle with salt and pepper. When oil is simmering, carefully add salmon filet to skillet. Sauté for 3 minutes. Do not move it around. Check the bottom side — it should be golden brown. Flip filet and cook on the other side for 3 minutes more. Cool before cutting.

LETTUCE WEDGE WITH THOUSAND ISLAND DRESSING

These days, there are many fancy varieties of lettuce available. But there is nothing as cool and refreshing as a crisp, fresh hunk of iceberg lettuce. When served as a wedge, the iceberg salad has a delightful crunch. Beyond a dollop of dressing, that's all this salad requires. Here is my version with Cheryl's Thousand Island dressing.

- 4 tablespoons mayonnaise
- 1 ½ tablespoons ketchup
- 1 ½ tablespoons sweet pickle relish
- 6 green pimento olives, chopped
- 1 tablespoon capers
- ¼ teaspoon Worcestershire sauce
- ½ teaspoon Dijon mustard
- ¼ teaspoon sweet paprika

Cut the iceberg lettuce in half. Cut each half in half.

Mix all of the dressing ingredients together in a small bowl. Place the iceberg lettuce quarters on plates and drizzle with dressing.

SICILIAN TOMATO ONION SALAD

Several years ago, we were in Malta — a magical Mediterranean island. We were invited to lunch and met our host at an attractive outdoor café. He ordered a salad consisting of tomatoes, onions and basil. The dish was accompanied by a crusty baguette. "Is this the entire lunch," I asked myself? We dove in. To this day, we remember this as one of the tastiest lunches we've ever enjoyed. I could never duplicate the quality of that meal. The tomatoes I used are from our garden. Better than any you can get in the supermarket. My recipe comes close to the Maltese version.

3 ripe tomatoes, sliced or cut into wedges

1 brown onion, sliced (Vidalia are the best)

1 tablespoon white wine vinegar

2-3 tablespoons extra virgin olive oil

½ lemon, juiced

1 teaspoon oregano

½ teaspoon freshly ground black pepper

½ teaspoon kosher salt

6-10 fresh basil leaves

Mix tomatoes and onions in a bowl. Mix together vinegar, oil and lemon juice. Shake well to emulsify. Pour over the tomatoes and onions. Mix together oregano, salt and pepper. Sprinkle over salad and mix well. Scatter basil leaves over salad.

Legal Thought

All people, regardless of what kind of work they perform or what product they sell, want to be compensated. Lawyers are no different. Except when they cook for friends and loved ones.

FABE'S DELIGHTFUL OLIVE TAPENADE

This tapenade is great on crackers, flatbread or as a pizza topping.

1 cup Kalamata or black olives, pitted and drained

1 cup green olives with pimentos

1 cup Niçoise olives, pitted

6 garlic cloves, chopped

2 tablespoons capers

1 tablespoon Italian parsley, chopped

2 anchovy filets, rinsed

1 roasted red pepper, chopped

Extra virgin olive oil

Kosher salt and freshly ground black pepper

Pinch cayenne pepper

Combine all items except olive oil, salt, black and cayenne pepper in food processor. Pulse into rough cut. Do not puree. Slowly pulse and drizzle 1-2 tablespoons olive oil through tube — not too much or the mixture will turn to paste. Tapenade is best if there are small chunks of olives. Scrape the bowl, then add salt, black and cayenne pepper to taste.

ROASTED OLIVES

6 ounces black pitted olives, drained

6 ounces Kalamata pitted olives, drained

4.5 ounces garlic stuffed Spanish olives, drained

6 large garlic cloves, minced

5 or 6 fresh thyme sprigs

Zest of ½ lemon, finely shredded

¼ cup olive oil

Juice of ½ lemon (about 2 tablespoons)

¼ teaspoon coarse salt

Preheat oven to 425°F. In a medium bowl, combine all of the ingredients and mix well. Transfer to a 13x9-inch baking dish. Bake for 20 minutes. Cool in the baking dish.

MUSHROOMS STUFFED WITH BREADCRUMBS AND PARMESAN

Easy to make. Looks and tastes wonderful.

- 12 large brown mushrooms (cut off stems, chop and reserve)
- 3 tablespoons butter
- 4 garlic cloves, minced
- 1 ½ cups fresh breadcrumbs (use about 2 slices of stale white bread)
- ¼ cup chopped mushroom stems
- 1 ½ teaspoons oregano
- 2 tablespoons Italian parsley, chopped
- 5 tablespoons finely grated Parmesan cheese
- Kosher salt and freshly ground black pepper

Preheat oven to 350°F. With a spoon, carefully scoop out the insides of the mushrooms. Lightly coat each mushroom with olive oil.

Place a large skillet over medium heat. Melt the butter. Add garlic and sauté 1 minute. Do not allow it to brown. Add the breadcrumbs, mushroom stems, oregano, parsley, kosher salt and freshly ground black pepper to taste. Mix well until the crumbs are coated and golden brown — about 2 minutes. Mix in the cheese. Cool slightly.

Spoon the mixture into the mushrooms and pack down firmly. Place the mushrooms in a shallow baking dish. Bake for about 20 minutes.

STUFFED BABY BELL PEPPERS

These little guys are fabulous. Most markets have packages of the baby bell peppers.

12 baby bell peppers
1½ cups chopped spinach and chopped butter lettuce or arugula
½ cup Italian parsley, chopped
1 tablespoon capers
1 small can flat anchovies, oil drained
5-6 tablespoons balsamic vinegar
Kosher salt and freshly ground black pepper

Preheat oven to 325°F. Cut the tops off of the bell peppers, then scrape out the insides with a small spoon. Stand the peppers, cut side up, in a baking dish. Drizzle with olive oil. Bake for 45 minutes or until tender. Cool completely.

Add the chopped vegetables, parsley, capers and anchovies. Carefully drizzle the vinegar and mix everything well. Add just enough to moisten everything. Season with salt and pepper. Stuff each pepper and serve. You could also stuff them with chopped olive combinations.

---------- **Thought for Life** ----------

*Nature unselfishly and unceasingly
bestows us with gifts of life.
It's about time
we said, "Thank you."
And showed some gratitude.*

HONEY SOY CHICKEN WINGS

These make great appetizers or a complete meal.

2 tablespoons olive oil
¼ cup soy sauce
¼ cup Chinese rice wine
¼ cup honey
¼ cup toasted sesame oil
4 cloves garlic, chopped
1 tablespoons ground fresh ginger
1 teaspoon Chinese five-spice powder
1 teaspoon freshly ground black pepper
½ teaspoon cinnamon
3 pounds (about 14 wings) chicken wings

Preheat oven to 425°F.

In a medium bowl, combine olive oil, soy sauce, rice wine, honey, sesame oil, garlic, ginger, five-spice, pepper and cinnamon. Mix well.

Place the marinade in a large sealable plastic bag. Add the chicken and shake the bag until all of the wings are covered in marinade. Refrigerate for 4 hours or overnight.

Remove the wings from the bag and place on a baking sheet in single layers — skin side up. Pour the marinade into a saucepan. Bring the marinade to a boil, then reduce to simmer.

Place the baking sheet in the oven. Baste every ten minutes with the marinade. Cook for 25 minutes, then turn wings over and cook for another 5 minutes. Turn the wings again to skin side up, baste and cook for 5-10 minutes or until temperature of wings reaches 170°F. Garnish with thinly sliced green onions.

Serve as an appetizer or a meal with steamed or fried rice.

STU'S CHUNKY HEARTY SPLIT PEA SOUP

I'm not a big fan of thin soups. I love soups that can almost be eaten with a fork. It's important that some of the ingredients retain their identity. I want to see bits of carrots, chunks of meat or chicken and perceptible hunks of beans and pasta. In pea soup, I don't want the finished product to be pureed. Let's see some chunks of split peas. I guarantee that you will agree that this pea soup tastes and feels like no other you have ever experienced. Thickness is mandatory. But not necessarily with a thickener like flour. Take a look at my special thickening technique.

4 slices bacon

1 medium onion, chopped

2 carrots, coarsely chopped

2 celery ribs, coarsely chopped

1 medium potato, coarsely chopped

2 cloves garlic, chopped

¼ cup dry white wine

6 cups chicken stock

2 cups split peas (1 pound)

1 ham bone, or 1 cup chopped ham

¼ teaspoon cumin

¼ teaspoon ground cloves

¼ teaspoon marjoram

Pinch cayenne pepper

5 sprigs fresh thyme

Kosher salt & freshly ground black pepper

¼ cup Italian parsley, chopped

1 bunch green onions, chopped

In heavy stockpot, sauté bacon until crisp. Remove bacon, add onion and sauté until softened. Do not brown. Add carrots, celery, potato and garlic. Sauté for about 2 minutes more. Deglaze with wine. Allow wine to reduce by one-half. Add stock, split peas, bacon & ham bone. Season with spices, herbs, salt and pepper, then bring to boil. Reduce heat, partially cover and simmer for 1 to 1½ hours until peas are soft with a slight crunch. Add parsley and green onions. Reseason and simmer for about 2 minutes more. At this point, soup should be thick and chunky. If not, scoop out about ½ cup of the soup, put it in a blender and blend until it forms a heavy chunky consistency. Uncover and cook over high heat until it reduces and reaches desired consistency.

Remove ham bone, if using. With a paring knife, cut off chunks of ham and mix into the soup.

FABE'S SHRIMP WONTON SOUP
aka ONE TON SOUP

If you have read my other soup recipes, you are probably aware that I prefer hearty, chunky soups. I will abandon my preference on any occasion when I see an attractive bowl of wonton soup.

BROTH

2 quarts chicken broth

3 tablespoons soy sauce

1" fresh ginger, sliced into ¼" pieces

1 teaspoon sesame oil

WONTONS, ETC.

12-20 wonton wrappers

½ pound ground chicken

4 green onions, whites finely chopped

1 tablespoon fresh ginger, finely chopped

1 tablespoon dry sherry

2 tablespoons soy sauce

½ tablespoon sesame oil

1 teaspoon cornstarch

½ pound large raw shrimp, peeled and deveined

½ red bell pepper, julienned

1 bunch green onions, green & white, chopped ¼" (Save some green pieces)

1 romaine lettuce leaf, halved & julienned

FOR THE BROTH: Place all broth ingredients in a stockpot. Bring to a boil, then simmer for 20 minutes to allow the ginger to infuse. Turn to low.

FOR THE WONTONS, ETC.: Combine the chicken, chopped green onions, chopped ginger, sherry, soy sauce, sesame oil, cornstarch in a medium bowl. Mix well until thoroughly combined. At this point, I usually make one wonton, place it in the broth, then eat it to test for flavor.

Place a cutting board on a table. Place a cup of tap water, a salad fork, the wonton wrappers and the chicken mixture on the table. Take one wrapper and place it on the board so that one corner is pointing upward and the another corner is pointing toward you. Place 1 scant teaspoonful of the chicken directly in the center of the wrapper. If you put in too much filling, the wontons will rupture while they are cooking. Dip your index finger in the water and gently rub the wet finger along all of the edges of the wrapper. There should be just a film of water on all four edges of the wrapper. Carefully bring the top point over the filling and place it directly over the bottom point. You should now have a triangle. Carefully seal the edges of the wrapper. With the fork, press the tines around the three sealed edges. Repeat with the remaining wrappers. You should have 15-20 wontons. Cover the wontons with a clean dish towel.

With a slotted spoon or a spider, remove the ginger from the broth. Bring the broth to a gentle boil. Carefully place the wontons in the broth, one at a time. Place the shrimp and the bell pepper in the broth after you have placed all of the wontons in the broth. Cover and cook for 6-8 minutes, or until the filling is completely cooked.

Take saved green onion pieces and romaine lettuce and place in the bottom of each soup bowl. (Flat bowls are best).

CHICKEN & DUMPLINGS

Here is a dish that reminds almost everyone of their childhood. Prepare it for your kids. Create memories for them and reflect on memories of your own.

CHICKEN & SOUP

1 whole chicken
8 carrots
6 cloves garlic
2 celery ribs
2 brown onions
2 leeks
1 parsnip
Kosher salt and freshly ground black pepper
1 stick butter
½ cup flour
1 teaspoon thyme
1 teaspoon tarragon
½ teaspoon ground sage

DUMPLINGS

¾ cups milk
2 eggs
2 tablespoons butter
2 ½ cups flour
2 teaspoons salt
1 tablespoon baking powder
½ cup parsley, chopped

CHICKEN & SOUP: Cut chicken into half breasts, legs, thighs, wings. Cut carrots into 1-inch chunks.

Slice garlic. Chop celery and onions into ½-inch chunks. Slice white part of leeks. Spread layers and wash thoroughly.

In a large stockpot, fill with 4 quarts of water. Add chicken, parsnip salt and pepper. Bring to a boil, reduce to simmer, cover and cook until chicken is done. Check thick part of breast and thick part of thigh with an instant thermometer. They should read 170°F. Remove chicken from pot and cool. Cut chicken off of the bones and cut into bite-size pieces.

Meanwhile, melt stick of butter in a large skillet over medium heat. Add carrots, parsnips, celery, garlic and onion. Stir and cook until slightly soft, about 10 minutes. Add flour and mix well until you can no longer see bits of flour. Add vegetables to stockpot. Add thyme, tarragon and sage. Bring back to a boil, reduce to simmer and cook, covered for about 20 minutes or until vegetables are tender and soup has thickened slightly. Return chicken pieces to pot. Cover and simmer. Taste, then add more seasoning, if desired.

DUMPLINGS: Bring milk and eggs to room temperature. Chop butter into pieces. Mix the eggs with the milk. Mix together the flour, salt and baking powder. Add the butter and milk-egg mixture. With a pastry cutter, work the dough until it comes together. It will be moist and sticky. Add more milk, a tablespoon at a time if necessary. Do a final mix with your hands.

Moisten your hands with water. Tear off pieces of dough a little larger than golf balls. Place into the simmering soup. Cover and cook about 12 minutes. After 6 minutes, with a large spoon, turn dumplings over one at a time. Sprinkle with parsley and serve.

FABE'S OUTSTANDING BEEF & MUSHROOM BARLEY SOUP

Here is another soup that can serve as an entire meal. I love the taste and texture of barley. Nutritionists claim it is full of nutrients and very good for you. Whole grain barley is even better for you, but it's difficult to find.

¼ cup olive oil

1 pound of boneless short rib meat cut into ½" chunks (or 1 pound chuck roast cut into ½" chunks) NOTE: For extra flavor, add one soup bone. If you have bones from the short ribs, add them in.

8 cloves garlic, finely chopped

2 ribs celery, finely chopped

3 medium carrots, chopped into 1" chunks

½ each red & green bell pepper, chopped

1 large yellow onion, finely chopped

1 pound white button mushrooms, thinly sliced

2 bay leaves

¼ cup sherry

4-5 cups beef stock

1 tablespoon Worcestershire sauce

2 teaspoons soy sauce

2 fresh thyme stalks

2 teaspoons thyme leaves

1 teaspoon oregano

1 teaspoon each granulated onion & granulated garlic

Kosher salt and freshly ground black pepper, to taste

1¼ cups pearl barley

4 Yukon Gold potatoes, quartered (optional)

1 cup frozen peas

2 tablespoons fresh lemon juice

¼ cup Italian parsley, finely chopped

Heat half the oil in a 6-quart Dutch oven over medium-high heat. Brown meat on all sides. Remove and set aside. This soup can also be made with chicken. Cut the chicken (thighs and/or breasts), into 1-inch chunks. Brown chunks on all sides. Set aside. Add chicken chunks during last 20 minutes of cooking soup.

Add remaining oil, garlic, celery, carrots, bell peppers and onion, and cook until soft, about 5 minutes. Do not brown. Add sliced mushrooms, and cook, stirring, until mushrooms give off their liquid. Add bay leaves. Add sherry, and cook until evaporated, about 2 minutes. Scrape brown bits from bottom of pot to incorporate fond. Return meat to pot.

Add stock, Worcestershire sauce, soy sauce, thyme, oregano, granulated onion & garlic, salt & pepper. Reduce heat to medium-low, and cook, covered and stirring occasionally, until meat is almost tender — about 1 hour. Add barley and potatoes, if using. Stir so that liquid covers barley and potatoes. Cover and simmer until potatoes and barley are tender, about 1 more hour. Do not overcook or barley will be mushy.

Discard bones if you have used them. Discard bay leaves.

Add more beef stock or water, if necessary or desired. Mix well to incorporate meat. Reseason with thyme, salt and pepper. Add peas and cook until they are warm. Add a pinch of lemon juice. Garnish with chopped parsley.

For a thicker soup, make a roux. Place 2 tablespoons of butter and 2 tablespoons of flour in a small saucepan and place over low heat. Stir constantly until incorporated and you have a blonde substance the thickness of sour cream. Bring soup to a boil and add roux. Stir into liquid to desired thickness. The butter in the roux will add extra richness. If too thick, carefully add some water.

――――――――――――― **Culinary Thought** ―――――――――――――

Not only does food bring happiness to our tummies and nourish our muscles and bones, but food also brings us closer to our neighbors and brings new friends into our lives. So, isn't it true that food also nourishes our lives and nourishes society?

CHICKEN TORTILLA SOUP

It took several attempts to develop a recipe that made me happy. This version has made everyone who tried it extremely happy.

1½ pounds boneless chicken

8 corn tortillas

2-3 tablespoons olive oil

1 (14.5 ounce) can whole tomatoes

1 (6 ounce) can tomato paste

1 teaspoon kosher salt

1 teaspoon black pepper

1 teaspoon smoked paprika

1-2 tablespoons chopped jalapeño

1 cup onion, chopped

1 red bell pepper, chopped

2 cloves garlic, chopped

1 bay leaf

2 teaspoons cumin

1½ teaspoons ground coriander

1½ teaspoons oregano

1½ teaspoons chili powder

⅛ to ¼ teaspoon cayenne

1 (15 ounce) can black beans

1 (15 ounce) can corn

5 cups chicken stock

1 lime, juiced

¾ cup cilantro leaves, chopped

1 bunch green onions, chopped

Cut chicken into ¼-inch thick strips. Cut tortillas into 2-inch wide strips. Heat 1 tablespoon oil in a large Dutch oven. Place tortilla chips in oil, cook for 1 minute or until golden. Remove with a slotted spoon and place on a paper towel.

Add tomatoes and tomato paste to a food processor. Pulse until the mixture reaches the consistency of oatmeal.

Add one more tablespoon of oil to the pot. Add chicken and season with salt, pepper and paprika. Cook until pink disappears — about 2 minutes. Remove and place on cutting board. Cut into shreds.

Before chopping jalapeño, remove membranes and seeds and discard. Add onions, jalapeño and bell pepper to the pot. Sauté for 1 minute, then add garlic and sauté for 30 seconds. Add the bay leaf, cumin, coriander, oregano, chili powder, paprika and cayenne and mix well. Add the tomato mixture and chicken stock and mix well. Add shredded chicken, black beans and corn (drained). Bring to a boil, cover and simmer for 15 minutes. Add juice from the lime in 1 teaspoon increments. Check seasoning.

Add cilantro and green onions, stir and cook for 1 minute. Add tortilla strips and cook for one minute. Remove bay leaf.

Serve topped with shredded Monterey Jack cheese, tortilla chips, avocado, etc.

BUTTERNUT SQUASH SOUP

Butternut squash arrives with autumn. This soup is tasty and as colorful as the deciduous leaves.

1 large butternut squash (about 3 pounds), halved vertically and seeded

1 tablespoon olive oil, plus more for drizzling

1 teaspoon kosher salt

Freshly ground black pepper, to taste

1 celery rib, chopped

1 carrot, chopped

2 small white potatoes, chopped

2 large shallots or 1 small onion, chopped

4 garlic cloves, pressed or minced

Up to 4 cups chicken stock

1 teaspoon maple syrup

⅛ teaspoon ground nutmeg

⅛ teaspoon cinnamon

½ teaspoon allspice

2 tablespoons brown sugar

1 teaspoon thyme

¼ cup Italian parsley, chopped

1 to 2 tablespoons butter

1 bunch green onions, chopped

Preheat oven to 425°F and line a rimmed baking sheet with parchment paper. Place the butternut squash on the pan and drizzle each half with just enough olive oil to lightly coat the squash on the inside (about 1 teaspoon each). Coat the inside of the squash with oil. Sprinkle it with salt and pepper.

Turn the squash face down and roast until it is tender and completely cooked through, about 45 to 50 minutes. When the squash is cool enough to handle, scoop the flesh and place in a bowl. Set aside.

In a medium Dutch oven, warm 1 tablespoon olive oil over medium heat until shimmering. Add the chopped celery, carrot, potatoes, shallot or onion and 1 teaspoon kosher salt. Cook, stirring often, until the veggies have softened, about 3 to 4 minutes. Add the garlic and cook until fragrant, about 1 minute, stirring frequently. Do not burn.

Add the roasted squash to the pot, then add the stock, maple syrup, nutmeg, cinnamon, allspice, brown sugar, kosher salt, thyme and black pepper. Bring the mixture to a simmer and cook, stirring occasionally, for 15 to 20 minutes until the potatoes are soft. Remove about 2 cups of soup and the large chunks. Blend with an immersion blender. Return to the soup pot and mix well. If you want a creamier texture, blend all of the soup with the immersion blender. Add chopped parsley. Add 1 to 2 tablespoons butter or olive oil, plus spices to taste. Serve and top with chopped green onions or pumpkin seeds.

STU'S PASTA E FAGIOLI

This soup, nicknamed "pasta fazool," is very hearty and makes a complete meal. The beans are high in protein. If you desire vegan "pasta fazool," you can omit the ham, bacon and anchovies, use vegetable stock and a no-egg pasta.

1 branch rosemary, about 6 inches

1 bay leaf

3 medium onions, chopped (3 to 4 cups)

2 slices bacon, chopped

1 celery rib, chopped

Olive oil

4 cloves garlic, chopped

⅓ pound diced ham or ham bone or 2 ounce can flat anchovies, drained & chopped

4 cups chicken stock, preferably homemade

Kosher salt & freshly ground black pepper

¼ to ½ teaspoon dried oregano

½ teaspoon dried thyme

1 pound chopped tomatoes, or 1 (14 ounce) can diced tomatoes

2 (15-ounce) cans cannellini beans

6 ounces short tube pasta, such as penne, ditalini or mostaccioli

1 tablespoon butter

Italian parsley, chopped

Parmesan cheese to taste (about ¼ cup)

Tie rosemary branch and bay leaf together with butcher's string to make a bouquet garni. Sauté onions, bacon and celery in olive oil for about 15 minutes until soft, but not brown. Add garlic and ham or anchovies and sauté additional 5 minutes. Add stock, bouquet garni, salt, pepper, oregano, thyme, and ham bone if using. Immerse bouquet garni into liquid and tie other end to handle of pot. Add tomatoes and beans and simmer additional 40 minutes. During last 10 minutes, add pasta and cook until al dente.

If desired, remove 1 cup of beans and liquid and process or blend until chunky. Return processed beans to pot. Remove bouquet garni. Add butter, parsley and Parmesan.

This can also be made with Italian sausage. Cook sausage, then slice and place in soup.

FABE'S SOUTHERN LENTIL & HAM HOCK SOUP

Folks who have sampled this soup claim, not only that it's the best lentil soup, it's the best soup of their dining life. I don't agree. I prefer my French version with lentils du puy, but this is a close second. And it's easy to make. The secret to this soup, as with any, is the quality of the chicken stock.

2 tablespoons olive oil

2 medium onions, diced

2 celery ribs, diced

½ red & ½ green bell pepper, chopped

2 large carrots, diced small

Freshly ground black pepper

4 cloves garlic, chopped

1 (6 ounce) can tomato paste

2 bay leaves

1 teaspoon dried sage

½ tablespoons oregano

¼ teaspoon dried red pepper flakes

1 tablespoon fresh thyme

½ cup dry white wine

2 ham hocks

8 cups homemade chicken stock

2 tablespoons Worcestershire sauce

2 tablespoons soy sauce

1 pound green or red lentils

Kosher salt

Handful Italian parsley, chopped

Heat oil in large Dutch oven. Add onions, celery, bell peppers and carrots. Season with pepper only. The ham hocks could make this soup very salty, so wait until later to add salt if necessary.

Sauté the onions, celery, bell peppers and carrots until the onions become translucent. Don't allow them to brown. Add garlic and sauté for an additional minute. Add tomato paste and spread over bottom of Dutch oven. Add bay leaves, sage, oregano, pepper flakes and thyme and sauté for 30 seconds. Add white wine. Increase the heat to high and cook just until wine almost disappears. Add ham hocks and stock, bring to a boil and simmer. Add Worcestershire sauce and soy sauce.

Add the lentils and bring to a boil again and cook until the lentils are slightly al dente. This takes about 30 minutes. Do not cook to the mushy stage. At this point, reseason and use salt, if necessary. Remove the ham hocks and cut off the lean meat into very small morsels and add to the soup.

At this point, I remove about a cup or two of soup and place it in a blender — or, if you have an immersion blender, better yet. Blend until it is the consistency of thick, smooth gravy. Return blended stuff to soup. It will create a great consistency. Reseason if necessary. Add chopped parsley and serve.

This soup could also be made with a ham bone or ¾ cup cooked ham or bacon.

CHICKEN NOODLE SOUP

If you look at my Chicken in the Pot recipe, you will notice the similarity between that chicken dish and this soup. In essence, the soup is a watered down version of chicken in the pot. Chicken soup is claimed by many nationalities and religions as their comfort and/or healing soup. Chicken soup is often referred to as "Jewish Penicillin." I'm not a doctor and don't give medical advice, but when the kids come down with a cold or the flu, or when they need something light on their sore tummies, this soup might be the remedy. By the way, I am a strong believer in homemade chicken stock. Whenever I need stock, I make this soup. We eat the chicken and veggies, and a cup or so of soup. The balance of the liquid, I strain and place in freezer-proof containers, usually 1-cup sizes, and freeze for future use.

- 1 whole chicken, about 4-5 pounds, cut up (or your favorite pieces)
- Olive oil for rub, plus 2 tablespoons
- 1-2 teaspoons kosher salt
- 1 teaspoon freshly ground black pepper
- 1 ½ teaspoons fresh thyme leaves or 1 teaspoon dried thyme
- 4 cloves garlic, chopped
- 8-12 cups water
- 3 large carrots, cut in 1" chunks
- 1 medium parsnip
- 3 medium onions, peeled and quartered
- 2 celery ribs, chopped into 1" chunks
- 1 leek (white part only), halved and rinsed
- ½ pound mushrooms, sliced
- 1 bay leaf
- 1 teaspoon ground sage
- 1 teaspoon tarragon
- Potatoes (optional)
- 2 tablespoons butter, softened
- 2 tablespoons flour
- 1 cup dry rice or ½ pound noodles
- ½ cup Italian parsley, chopped
- Peas
- Grated zest and juice of ½ lemon

Preheat oven to 375°F. Pat chicken parts dry. Lightly rub with olive oil. Sprinkle with salt, pepper, thyme leaves. Place 2 tablespoons of olive oil in a large Dutch oven over medium heat. In batches, place chicken parts in Dutch oven and lightly brown on each side. This should take about 10 minutes. In traditional chicken soup, the chicken is not browned — most French chicken recipes call for browning. Remove chicken parts and set aside. Add chopped garlic and sauté for 30 seconds. Do not burn. Remove garlic and set aside. Wipe the Dutch oven clean, then add water. Add cooked garlic, carrots, parsnip, onions, celery and leek. Return chicken to Dutch oven. Over medium heat, bring chicken stock to a boil. Then, reduce to simmer. Add mushrooms, salt, pepper, thyme, bay leaf, sage and tarragon. Add potatoes if using. Cover the Dutch oven and place in the preheated oven. You could cook the recipe on the stove top, but the oven will produce a heartier dish.

Cook for approximately 45 minutes. Remove from oven and test veggies for tenderness. With an instant-read thermometer, check the largest pieces of chicken. They should register 170°F.

Place the Dutch oven on a burner and, over medium heat, bring to a simmer. (It should already be simmering).

While the chicken is in the oven, make the roux by adding 2 tablespoons of soft butter, plus 2 tablespoons of flour to a small saucepan. Over medium-low heat, stir the butter and flour constantly until they are combined and the mixture turns a light beige color, about 2 minutes. Also, cook noodles or rice in another pot of boiling water according to package instructions. For more flavor, when the chicken and veggies are done, and before you introduce the roux, remove from the pot and cook the rice or noodles in the chicken stock, then remove rice or noodles with a mesh spoon and return other ingredients to the Dutch oven.

Add the roux to the Dutch oven and stir to combine. The mixture should thicken to the consistency of gravy. If too thin, make and add more roux. If too thick, add some water to desired thickness. Add chopped parsley, peas, lemon juice and zest. Cook 2 minutes to warm peas. Taste and reseason. Don't forget to eat the veggies, especially the onion quarters. Some insist they are the best part.

---————————————————— **Legal Thought** —————————————————---

A person who commits perjury
contaminates justice
And himself
Just like throwing a virus in a clear mountain spring
And drinking the water.

FABULOUS CHICKEN OR TURKEY STOCK

One secret to the wonderful flavor of many of my recipes is no secret at all. If you take a little extra time to make your own stock, you gain at least two benefits. The first is that you can eat the chicken used to make the stock — add some of the stock and some noodles or rice and you have a complete dinner. The second benefit is to freeze the stock for later use. Throughout this book are many recipes that call for chicken, vegetable or beef stock. To prove the value of homemade stock, I have made several of the same dishes, one with homemade stock and the other with store-bought stock. Every ingredient other than the stock was identical. I conducted several taste tests and, without exception, everyone chose the dish made with homemade stock.

I usually make a pot of stock and save a little for a chicken soup dinner. The rest, I strain into 1-cup containers and put them in the freezer. This recipe will yield about eight cups of stock.

1 whole chicken (4-5 pounds)

4 carrots, cut into 1" pieces

2 onions, halved

2 celery ribs, cut into 1" pieces

1 parsnip, cut into 1" pieces

1 piece fresh ginger-about 1" (optional)

4 cloves

1 bay leaf & 4 sprigs fresh thyme or 2 teaspoons dried thyme

6 whole cloves of garlic, smashed

½ cup Italian parsley, chopped (stems are fine)

Kosher salt, freshly ground pepper, poultry seasoning & more dried thyme to taste

Cut up carrots, onions, celery & parsnip into large chunks. Wrap and tie ginger, cloves, thyme sprigs & bay leaf in cheesecloth. It's best to butterfly the chicken, however it's fine to use it whole. Wash chicken thoroughly. Use everything except for the liver. Place chicken, garlic and vegetables in large stock pot, preferably stainless steel or enameled cast iron. Fill pot with water just enough to cover chicken & vegetables.

Add parsley and seasonings. Bring to a boil, uncovered. Then, cover, reduce heat and simmer for about 45 minutes to 1 hour or until chicken and vegetables are tender. If you prefer a broth that is more clear, cook over a lower flame and do not cover. If water reduces and no longer covers chicken completely, turn the chicken over halfway through cooking. But don't add more water.

Occasionally, remove scum from top of liquid with a ladle or large spoon. About 10 minutes before chicken is done, taste and reseason with salt, pepper, poultry seasoning & dried thyme. For more intense flavor, remove the chicken and vegetables, increase heat and reduce liquid by approximately 20 percent. Remove and discard cheesecloth and stuff contained therein.

Save the chicken, carrots, parsnip and onions. Use some of the stock and enjoy chicken soup with noodles or rice. Strain the balance of the liquid through a fine mesh strainer. If the strainer is not fine mesh, place a piece of cheesecloth in the strainer. Place stock in large bowl or 8-cup measuring cup. Refrigerate for two hours. The fat will rise to the top. Remove fat, then pour stock into 1-cup plastic containers with covers and freeze.

TURKEY STOCK VARIATION: You can use the turkey neck, wings, heart and gizzard. Some poultry shops sell turkey necks and turkey backs. You will need about 3 pounds of bones and giblets. Prepare the same as the chicken stock. You will probably end up with about 5 cups of stock. That should be enough for a holiday dinner. You can always combine it with some chicken stock.

WHITE SANDWICH BREAD

1 tablespoon instant or dry active yeast

1 tablespoon sugar

2 cups warm water (110-120°F)

3 tablespoons melted butter, slightly cooled

5 ¼ cups bread flour or unbleached all-purpose flour

2 teaspoons kosher salt

In the bowl of a stand mixer, with a paddle attachment, combine the yeast, sugar and two cups warm water (110-120°F.). Test temperature with an instant thermometer. Stir to dissolve. Wait 3-5 minutes until it foams. The sugar promotes the blossoming of the yeast.

Add the melted butter and 2 cups of flour. Mix until well combined and smooth. Add the salt. (Adding the salt earlier can impede the blossoming of the yeast).

Add the remaining flour, one cup at a time. Mix until the dough pulls away from the sides of the bowl. The dough should be sticky. With the dough hook, knead the dough for 10 minutes. The dough must remain sticky.

Dust some flour on your hands. Remove the dough from the bowl and place on floured board. Punch dough down to remove all air bubbles. Place dough in a bowl greased with canola oil or melted butter. Cover bowl with a clean kitchen towel and put in a warm place until it doubles, about 1 hour. Gently press two fingers into the dough about ¼-inch deep. If the indentations remain, the dough has properly risen.

Grease or butter two 5x9-inch loaf pans. Punch dough down, cut into two equal portions. Roll each portion into a rectangle, 9-inches wide, then roll each rectangle like a jelly roll. Taper and pinch each end. Place each roll into a loaf pan. Cover and let rise for 45 minutes or until the loaves rise about 1-inch above each pan.

Preheat oven to 400°F. With a razor blade or serrated bread knife, slice three diagonal ½-inch slits in each loaf. Bake the loaves until golden brown on top for 30-35 minutes. Each loaf should register 210°F. on an instant thermometer. Remove loaves from pans and brush tops with more melted butter. Cool completely.

FRENCH BREAD & ROLLS

Bread baking is comforting and rewarding. I love to watch the dough as it rises and observe the loaves as they brown in the oven. The fragrances permeate the house. There are few culinary pleasures greater than tearing off a piece of bread, still warm from the oven.

2 ¼ cups warm water (110-115°F)
2 tablespoons sugar
1 tablespoon instant yeast
5 to 5½ cups bread flour or unbleached all-purpose flour
¾ teaspoon salt
2 tablespoons olive oil

In the bowl of a stand mixer, with a paddle attachment, combine the warm water, sugar and yeast. Allow the mixture to sit for about 5 minutes until it begins to foam and bubble. Add about 3 cups of flour and mix until combined. Add salt and olive oil. (Adding salt too early can inhibit growth of yeast). Add more flour in ¼ cup intervals. When the dough begins to pull away from the sides of the bowl, it is almost ready. Carefully add more flour, 1 tablespoon at a time and mix until the sides of the bowl are clean. The dough is now ready. The dough will be sticky, but that's the way you want it. Attach the dough hook and knead for about 5 minutes.

Dust some flour on your hands. Remove the dough from the bowl and place on a floured board. Gently press the dough down and knead for another 2-3 minutes. Roll the dough into a ball and place in a lightly oiled bowl. I use the mixing bowl. Roll the dough around to lightly coat it with oil.

Cover the bowl with a clean kitchen towel and set in a warm place until the dough doubles in size — about 1 hour. I place a small desk lamp next to the bowl for just the right amount of heat. To test for proper proofing, gently press two fingers into the dough about ½-inch deep. After 30 seconds, the holes should substantially remain at the same depth.

Remove the dough from the bowl and place on a lightly floured surface. Divide the dough in half. If you are making hoagie rolls, divide one of the halves into four equal parts. Pat the large half (or both halves for 2 loaves), into a thick rectangle about 9x12-inches. With the heal of your palm, press all bubbles out of the dough. With the 12-inches part facing you, roll the dough, like a jelly roll, into a cylindrical roll. With the heel of your palms, gently roll the cylinder back and forth from the center of the cylinder to the edges. Pinch the edges to seal. Repeat with second half.

If you are making dinner rolls, pat each piece of dough into a rectangle, around 6x6-inches. Roll and pinch in the same manner as you did the loaves. Place each roll, seam side down, on a baking sheet that has been dusted with cornmeal. You can also use two baking sheets and bake in two batches. Cover with a kitchen towel, put in a warm place and proof until loaves are puffy and doubled in size, about one hour.

After 30 minutes, preheat oven to 375°F. Place an oven rack at the center level. When the loaves have risen, gently cut several slashes in each loaf and/or roll about ¼-inch deep. Use a serrated bread knife. Place the pan of rolls and/or loaves in oven. For a crunchier crust, spray the rolls/loaves with water. I use a water spray bottle.

Bake for 25-30 minutes, or until the loaves are golden. Half-way through, rotate the baking pan for even baking. Tap the bottom of a loaf. It should sound hollow. If you have an instant thermometer, each loaf should register 210°F. The rolls may be done before the loaves. If so, remove them and place on a wire rack. Brush loaves and rolls with soft butter. Cool completely.

dough will be slightly sticky, but that's the way you want it. Cover the bowl with a kitchen towel. Let it rest for 15 minutes. Place the dough hook on the mixture and knead for about 5 minutes. The interior of the bowl should remain clean. If the dough partially adheres to the bottom of the bowl, add some flour, 1 tablespoon at a time.

Dust some flour on your hands. Remove the dough from the bowl and place it on the floured board. Using the heal of your hand, knead the dough, turning it 90°F after each knead, for about 2-3 more minutes.

Lightly grease a large bowl with olive oil. Place the dough in the bowl, turning it over so that the entire ball of dough is lightly coated with oil. Cover the bowl with a kitchen towel and let it rise in a warm place (I put the bowl under a lamp), for about 45 minutes or until doubled in size. If an indentation remains in the dough after you have gently punched two fingers into it, the dough has risen enough.

Punch dough down and let rest for 5 minutes. Divide in half. Cover one half and, with the other half, roll the dough into a 12-inch rope, slightly tapered at the ends. Repeat with the second half. Place the ropes on a large baking sheet (or a baking stone), sprinkled with cornmeal. Let rise for 25 minutes or until doubled in size. Preheat oven to 450°F. Uncover the dough. With a razor blade or a serrated bread knife, carefully cut three diagonal slits across the top of each loaf.

Bake for 20 minutes or until browned. Tap the bottom of a loaf. It should sound hollow. If you have an instant thermometer, the loaves should register 210°F.

CRUNCHY HARD ROLLS

These rolls are great for sandwiches or as buns for burgers. I usually make a batch, then freeze the buns individually so that I can grab one when needed.

1 ½ cups warm water (110°F/45°C)

1 tablespoon active dry yeast

2 tablespoons granulated sugar

2 tablespoons vegetable oil

4 cups bread flour

1 teaspoon salt

In a mixing bowl, stir together warm water, yeast, and sugar. Let stand until foamy, about 10 minutes.

To the yeast mixture, add the oil and 2 cups flour. Using a paddle attachment, stir in the remaining flour, ½ cup at a time, plus the salt, until the dough has pulled away from the sides of the bowl. With a dough hook, knead for 5 minutes. Turn out onto a lightly floured surface, and knead until smooth and elastic, about 2 minutes more. Lightly oil a large bowl, place the dough in the bowl, and turn to coat. Cover with a kitchen towel, and let rise in a warm place until doubled in size, about 1 hour.

Turn the dough out onto a lightly floured surface and punch it down to deflate air bubbles. Divide the dough into 16 equal pieces, and form into round balls. Lightly dust two baking sheets with cornmeal. Place the rolls on the baking sheets at least 2-inches apart. Cover the rolls with a kitchen towel, and let rise until doubled in volume, about 40 minutes.

Preheat oven to 400°F. Bake for 18 to 20 minutes or until golden brown on top. Tap the bottom of one roll with your fingers. A hollow sound means that the rolls are done. Rolls should register 210°F with an instant thermometer. Cool completely on a wire rack.

BANANA CHOCOLATE CHIP BREAD

This is a quick bread that requires no kneading or rising. Soft and delicious, its texture is almost like a cake. At times, I can't decide whether to serve it with the meal or for dessert.

8 tablespoons butter, room temperature

3 or 4 medium bananas, very ripe (1 ½ cups)

1 ¼ cups sugar

2 large eggs

¼ cup buttermilk*

1 teaspoon vanilla extract

2 ½ cups all-purpose flour

1 teaspoon baking soda

1 teaspoon salt

1 cup semi-sweet chocolate chips or mini-chips

Preheat the oven to 350°F. Butter bottoms only of 2 (8x4-inch) pans or 1 (9x5-inch) pan.

Place bananas in a bowl and mash until consistency of mashed potatoes.

Combine the butter and sugar in mixing bowl. Using a stand mixer, cream the butter and sugar until light and fluffy.

Add the eggs, one at a time. Mix after adding each egg.

Add the buttermilk, bananas and vanilla. Mix until combined.

In a separate bowl, whisk together the flour, baking soda, and salt. Add the flour mixture to the batter in the stand mixer in three stages. Mix just until combined.

Scatter the chocolate chips over the batter and gently fold them in.

Pour the batter into the prepared loaf pan(s). Smooth the top of the batter.

Bake the 8x4 loaves for 1 hour, or bake the 9x5 loaf for 1 hour fifteen minutes, or until a toothpick inserted in the center comes out clean.

Remove pan(s) from oven and place on cooling rack. Cool for 10 minutes, then cut around edge of pan(s) with a sharp knife to loosen. Invert pan(s) and gently remove bread. Cool completely before cutting.

*Substitute for buttermilk: Add ½ tablespoon of fresh lemon juice to ½ cup of milk. Let sit for 5 minutes.

WHOLE WHEAT SANDWICH BREAD

Easy to make, this is a soft, hearty sandwich bread.

¾ cup (6 oz, 180ml) warm water

1 packet (2 ¼ teaspoons) dry yeast

¼ teaspoon granulated sugar

2 cups (10 oz, 280g) bread flour, divided

1 cup (8 oz, 240ml) milk

1½ tablespoons honey

1½ teaspoons salt

1½ cups (7.5 oz, 210g) whole wheat flour

Preheat the oven to 350°F. Lightly grease a 9x5-inch loaf pan with vegetable oil or baking spray. In the bowl of a stand mixer, combine the water, yeast, sugar and ½ cup of the bread flour. With a paddle attachment, mix on low speed to combine. Cover the bowl for a half hour. The mixture should then be foamy.

In a small saucepan over low heat, warm the milk to about 100° F. Add the milk, honey and salt to the yeast mixture. Mix on low speed to combine.

Add the whole wheat flour and ½ cup of the bread flour. Mix until the batter comes together.

With the mixer running, slowly add the bread flour in ½ cup increments. Continue adding bread flour until the dough forms a ball on the paddle and pulls away from the sides of the bowl. You may need less or more of the bread flour. Change to a dough hook and knead the dough for 5 minutes.

Transfer the dough onto a lightly floured surface. The dough should be soft and slightly sticky. Knead to form a smooth ball.

Place the dough in a lightly oiled bowl, turning once to coat the entire ball of dough. Cover the bowl with a clean towel and let stand in a warm spot until the dough doubles in size — about 1 to 1½ hours.

Turn the dough out onto a lightly floured surface. Form the dough into a 9-inch rectangle. Beginning at the long end at the top, roll the dough into a log. As you roll, pinch the ends of the dough to form a tight roll.

Place the dough into the pan and cover with a towel. Set in a warm place and let rise until the dough almost doubles in size, about 1 hour.

With a serrated knife or razor, cut a ½-inch deep slash down the center of the length of the loaf. For a darker, shiny surface, brush an egg wash over the top of the loaf.

Bake about 30-35 minutes until golden brown, With an instant thermometer, the loaf should be about 190-210° F.

Cool in the pan about 5 minutes. Transfer the bread to a cooling rack. Cool one hour before slicing.

Chapter 11

Eat Your Veggies

(and your carbs, legumes, & sides)

SAUTÉED BRUSSELS SPROUTS WITH GREMOLATA

I am shocked at the number of folks I meet who don't like Brussels sprouts. These bright green, mini cabbage jewels are near the top of the list of my favorite veggies. Here are two recipes that might change the minds of the anti-Brussels sprouts coalition.

BRUSSELS SPROUTS

1 pound Brussels sprouts (you can also use asparagus or green beans)

2 shallots

2 cloves garlic, crushed

2 tablespoons butter

2 tablespoons olive oil

½ cup chicken stock

GREMOLATA

2 tablespoons butter

½ cup breadcrumbs

1 teaspoon lemon zest

1 clove garlic, chopped

¼ cup Italian parsley, chopped

Pinch red pepper flakes

BRUSSELS SPROUTS: Cut each sprout in half. Finely chop the shallots. In a large, non-stick skillet over medium heat, heat the butter and oil. Place the sprouts in one layer, cut side down. Scatter the shallots and garlic over the Brussels sprouts.

When the sprouts begin to caramelize, turn them over and cook for another 5 minutes. Add just enough stock to cover the base of the skillet. Cover and allow the sprouts to steam until the liquid has almost evaporated and the sprouts are tender.

GREMOLATA: Melt the butter in a small skillet. Add breadcrumbs and sauté until they are toasty brown. Add lemon zest, garlic, parsley and pepper flakes. Sauté for 1 additional minute. Remove from heat. When the sprouts are done, sprinkle the gremolata over the sprouts and serve immediately. Sprinkle with grated Parmesan if desired.

WINNER'S CIRCLE BRAISED BRUSSELS SPROUTS

¼ pound pancetta or bacon, diced (½ cup)

1 tablespoon olive oil

½ cup diced carrot

⅓ cup minced shallot (2 or 3 medium)

⅛ teaspoon red pepper flakes

2 pounds Brussels sprouts, cut lengthwise, about ¼"

1 ½ cups chicken stock

1 sprig fresh thyme

1 tablespoon butter

1 teaspoon lemon zest

In 12-inch skillet, over medium heat cook bacon or pancetta in olive oil until lightly browned. Increase heat to medium high, stir in carrot, shallot, pepper flakes and cook for 2 minutes.

Add sprouts, season lightly with salt and pepper, stir to coat with fat and cook until a few sprouts are lightly browned, about 2 minutes.

Add stock and thyme, cover with lid slightly ajar and cook until sprouts are barely tender, about 5 minutes. Remove lid, increase heat and stir until all liquid is gone, about 3 minutes. Remove from heat and stir in butter and zest.

VEGETABLE AND BREADCRUMB MEDLEY

Eat your vegetables! It may take less persuasion with the kids with these veggies. This recipe will serve ten people. For a small family dinner, you can cut recipe in half.

4 cups breadcrumbs
5 slices bacon
1 cauliflower, cut into florets
1 pound Brussels sprouts, halved
2 crowns broccoli, cut into florets
3 carrots, sliced thin on bias
1 red bell pepper, cut into 1" squares
1 pound green beans
4 shallots, chopped
½ cup chicken stock

Homemade bread crumbs Homemade breadcrumbs are the best. Two slices of white bread pulsed in a food processor until the consistency of dry oatmeal will do the trick. You may want more or less breadcrumbs in this dish. You can also use store bought breadcrumbs. Sauté breadcrumbs in butter and olive oil until golden brown. Remove breadcrumbs from skillet. In the same skillet, fry the bacon until crisp. Chop into small pieces and set aside. Blanche cauliflower, Brussels sprouts, broccoli, carrots, bell pepper and green beans for about 5 minutes until crisp-tender. To blanche, place in a pot of boiling water, remove and immediately place in a bowl of ice water. Drain and set aside.

Sauté shallot in bacon drippings, then add vegetables and sauté until just tender. Add bacon pieces. Add just enough chicken stock to moisten the veggie medley. Mix in breadcrumbs and serve immediately.

BOSTON-CALIFORNIA BAKED BEANS

When time permits, I love to bake the long-term version of baked beans. During my lazy moments, I opt for the quick version. The photo on the next page is the quick version. My guests rave about both versions.

1 pound great northern beans
1 pound bacon, chopped
1 onion, chopped
1 jalapeño, chopped
1 (6 ounce) can tomato paste
¼ cup brown sugar
¼ cup molasses
1 tablespoon honey
Vegetable or chicken stock
Pinch cayenne pepper
1 teaspoon granulated garlic
1 teaspoon freshly ground black pepper
2 teaspoons kosher salt
2 teaspoons mustard powder
2 tablespoons Worcestershire sauce
¼ cup BBQ sauce (see recipe on page 114)
2 tablespoons ketchup
2 teaspoons Dijon mustard

Soak beans overnight for up to 12 hours. If pressed for time, you can use the quick soak option. For quick soak, cover beans with water in a stockpot. Bring to a boil, cover, then reduce heat and simmer 2 minutes. Turn off heat and leave covered for 1 hour. Heat oven to 250° F.

Place Dutch oven over medium heat and stir in the bacon, onion and jalapeños until some fat has rendered from the bacon and the onions are softened, but not brown — about 5 minutes. Stir in the tomato paste, brown sugar, molasses and honey.

Drain beans and reserve soaking liquid. Add drained beans to Dutch oven. I prefer cast iron. Place soaking liquid in measuring cup and add enough stock until liquid raises to level of 4 cups. Add liquid to pot and bring to boil over high heat. Add cayenne pepper, granulated garlic, black pepper & salt. Add remaining ingredients. Give a good stir, cover and place pot in oven.

Cook beans for 6-8 hours, or until tender. Most of the liquid should be absorbed. Check seasoning.

─────────────── **Thought for Life** ───────────────

Jealousy and distrust of your mate's fidelity
is often without reason.
But jealousy and distrust
demand no reason
to ignite.
But know this:
often folks are guilty
of what they distrust in others.
These irrational emotions
could be a pathway to the courthouse.

BAKED BEANS — QUICK VERSION

1 pound bacon, chopped
1 yellow onion, diced
1 green bell pepper, diced
1 red bell pepper, diced
4 cans pork & beans
1 cup ketchup
2 tablespoons dry mustard
1 tablespoon black pepper
½ tablespoon kosher salt
½ tablespoon garlic powder

Cook bacon in a 12-inch skillet over medium heat until bacon is crispy and fat is rendered. Strain fat from bacon, reserving 2 tablespoon of bacon fat, and set bacon aside. Place reserved fat back into the sauté pan and add onion and bell peppers.

Sauté for 5-10 minutes until onions are translucent and bell peppers are tender. Remove from heat and set aside.

Preheat oven to 350° F.

In a 9x13-inch casserole dish combine all remaining ingredients. Stir well to combine. Cover the pan with foil. Bake for 45-60 minutes or until sauce has thickened. Stir occasionally. Let cool for 15 minutes before serving.

---------- **Culinary Thought** ----------

*When you teach your children how to cook,
your kitchen becomes more than a culinary classroom.
It's a classroom of language, geography, love
and people working together.*

GREEN BEANS & BACON

These green beans are full of flavor. It's very likely that they will convert folks who hate their vegetables.

½ cup chopped toasted pecans

Kosher salt

2½ pounds green beans, trimmed

½ pound bacon, roughly chopped

1 small yellow onion, finely chopped

3 cloves garlic, minced

1 teaspoon red pepper flakes

Juice of ½ lemon

Freshly ground pepper

To toast the pecans, place them in the sauté pan you are about to use for the bacon and green beans. Over medium high heat, let them sit in a single layer for 1 minute, then turn them with a spatula. After 3 or 4 minutes, turn them again and continue until they are fragrant. Wipe the skillet with a clean towel.

Bring a large pot of water to boiling, add kosher salt and green beans and cook until the green beans are bright green in color and crisp-tender, about 5 minutes. Drain the green beans and shock in a large bowl of ice water to stop the cooking. Drain the green beans again and pat dry.

Cook the bacon in a large, heavy sauté pan until crisp, about 5 minutes. Remove the bacon to a paper towel-lined plate. Remove all but 2 tablespoons of the bacon grease from the pan. Add the onion to the pan and sauté until soft and very tender, 4 to 5 minutes. Sprinkle in the garlic and red pepper flakes and sauté until just fragrant, about 1 more minute. Do not allow garlic to brown. Add the green beans and the pecans and cook until heated through, 5 to 6 minutes more. Return the bacon to the pan and drizzle with lemon juice. Season with salt and pepper.

BABY BOK CHOY WITH GARLIC, GINGER & SPINACH

Bok choy, a member of the cabbage family, contains folate, vitamin C, vitamin E, and beta-carotene. These nutrients have powerful antioxidant properties. Plus, cooked or raw, bok choy tastes great.

- 1 ½ pounds baby bok choy
- 2 tablespoons oyster sauce
- 2 tablespoons chicken stock
- 1 teaspoon cornstarch
- ¼ teaspoon sesame oil
- 2 bunches green onions, chopped (optional)
- 1 bunch spinach
- 2 large cloves garlic, chopped
- 4 slices ginger, chopped

Place oyster sauce, chicken stock, cornstarch and sesame oil in a bowl. Mix with a whisk until cornstarch is dissolved. Trim bok choy by removing a few loose leaves from each. If you can't find baby bok choy, purchase regular bok choy and cut each in half lengthwise.

Heat oil in wok, add bok choy and season with kosher salt. Toss frequently until slightly browned. Add green onions (if using), spinach, garlic and ginger. Stir-fry until tender, about 2 minutes. Cook until bok choy and spinach are tender, then add sauce and mix well. Stir until sauce thickens, then serve.

FABE'S ANTI-MAO POTATO SALAD

Years ago, the first time I visited China, Chairman Mao Tse-tung was in charge. He was a hard-line commie — even more of a Marxist than Groucho. Well, I was attending a state dinner with some Chinese dignitaries. It was a potluck affair — in honor of Pol Pot of Cambodia. You know, the Khmer Rouge guy who killed millions of his own people.

I wanted my culinary contribution to be classical American, so I decided to make my mother's recipe for potato salad. At the time, I was watching my weight, so I wanted to make the dish without mayo. I appeared at the banquet and presented my creation and made the following proclamation:

"Ladies and gentlemen, I present to you a traditional American culinary delight--what makes it great is that I've eliminated the mayo." An unfortunate choice of words.

Instantaneously, a thunder of boos and shouting filled the chamber. I was immediately shackled and rushed off to prison. They didn't even allow me to stay for dessert or open my fortune cookie. Imagine what it would have said. A few hours later, I was released from custody. Mao himself appeared with the key.

"Mister Faber," he said with a smile. "That was the best potato salad I've ever eaten."

¾ cup extra virgin olive oil
¼ cup champagne vinegar
½ teaspoon fresh lemon juice
2 tablespoons onions, finely chopped
1 teaspoon sugar
1 teaspoon Dijon mustard
½ teaspoon dried basil
¾ teaspoon dried oregano

¾ teaspoon dried thyme
¾ teaspoon kosher salt
½ teaspoon freshly ground black pepper
2 cloves garlic, minced
2-3 pounds Yukon Gold potatoes
1 tablespoon dried dill
1 bunch green onions, chopped

¼ cup red onion, chopped
1 tablespoon capers
¼ cup green olives, chopped
4 slices bacon, cooked and chopped
3 eggs, hard boiled and chopped
¼ cup Italian parsley, chopped

Mix together olive oil, vinegar, lemon juice, finely chopped onion, sugar, mustard, basil, oregano, thyme, salt, pepper and minced garlic. Place in a jar and shake well until emulsified. Set aside.

Place the potatoes, with skin on, in a large pot. Fill with water until level is 2-inches over tops of potatoes. Bring to a boil and cook until potatoes are tender when a fork is inserted. Do not overcook.

Add dill to dressing. Shake well again. When potatoes are cool enough to work with, (you can place them in a colander and run cold water over them), cut into 1-inch squares. Place potatoes, chopped green onions, chopped red onion, chopped celery, capers and olives and in a large bowl. Add dressing and mix well. Add chopped bacon and chopped eggs and remix gently. Reseason if desired. For extra flavor, you can add a few tablespoons of bacon drippings and pickle juice. Refrigerate for at least 2 hours before serving. Add chopped parsley and remix just before serving.

Anti-Mao Potato Salad

French Potato Salad

FRENCH POTATO SALAD

3 pounds Yukon Gold potatoes
3 hard boiled eggs
5 slices bacon
¾ cup mayonnaise
2 tablespoons Dijon mustard
2 teaspoons sugar
1 teaspoon kosher salt

1 teaspoon black pepper
½ teaspoon paprika
½ teaspoon granulated garlic
2 tablespoons pickle relish
2 tablespoons capers
8 gherkins, chopped
1 celery rib, chopped

1 small red onion, chopped
1 bunch green onions, chopped
½ each red & green pepper, chopped
3 tablespoons Italian parsley, chopped

With the skin on, boil the potatoes until fork tender. Remove, drain and cool slightly. Cut into 1½-inch squares. Most of the skin will fall off. Place squares into a large bowl. Cut up the hard boiled eggs and add to the potatoes.

In a large skillet, fry the bacon until crisp. Cool on paper towels. Cut into ½-inch pieces. Reserve the bacon drippings.

Mix the mayonnaise, mustard, sugar, salt, pepper, paprika, granulated garlic, pickle relish, and capers. When the bacon drippings cool, add about 3 tablespoons to the mayo mixture and mix well.

Place the gherkins, celery, onion, bacon pieces, green onions and bell peppers in a bowl. Mix well and add to the potatoes. Add the mayo mixture in three batches and mix after each batch. Place in refrigerator for about 3 hours. Sprinkle parsley flakes on salad before serving. Serve cold or room temperature. It's also great to serve it warm just after you make it.

QUICK, CRISPY ROAST POTATOES

These potatoes, which require only 10 minutes of hands-on preparation, are superb accompaniments to any meat, poultry, or fish entrée.

- **2 pounds Yukon Gold potatoes, quartered**
- **4 tablespoons olive oil**
- **1 tablespoon fresh rosemary, chopped**
- **1 tablespoon thyme**
- **1 tablespoon paprika**
- **2 teaspoons granulated garlic**
- **½ teaspoon black pepper**
- **2 teaspoons kosher salt**

Preheat oven to 450°F. Place olive oil in a large bowl. Place potato quarters in olive oil immediately after cutting them. Do not remove skins. Mix the potatoes with the olive oil to coat completely. Combine rosemary, thyme, paprika, garlic, pepper and salt. Sprinkle spice mixture generously on all sides of the potatoes.

Place potatoes in a single layer in an oven-proof baking pan, cut side down. Bake for approximately 1 hour 15 minutes or until potatoes are golden brown and tender. Halfway through roasting, turn each potato quarter to the cut side that was not facing down. Baste every 15 minutes.

GREEN BEAN AND TOMATO CASSEROLE

This is a colorful, tasty version of green beans. Even the kids will love them.

6 slices bacon
1 ½ pounds green beans
1 (28 ounce) can whole tomatoes with juice
1 large onion, chopped
Kosher salt and black pepper
½ teaspoon dried thyme
Pinch cayenne pepper

Cut the bacon strips into 1-inch pieces. Cut the tips from the green beans. Crush the tomatoes with your hands or in a food processor until chunky. Set aside. In a large skillet, cook bacon over medium heat. Cook until lightly golden. Add the onions and cook until soft and translucent, and the bacon is golden brown. Do not allow onions to brown.

Add the green beans and tomatoes, and season to taste with salt, pepper, thyme and cayenne. Stir to combine. Bring the mixture just to a boil, then reduce heat and simmer until the beans are tender.

FABE'S O'BRIEN POTATOES

I've been to Ireland many times. I met a number of men and women whose last name was O'Brien. But I never met the person who invented these potatoes. I searched for the inventor because I wanted to meet the person and shake his or her hand. Perhaps the inventor was not even Irish. My research tells me that these spuds were claimed to be invented in Boston at Jerome's restaurant. Jack's restaurant in Manhattan disputes that claim and insists that the recipe was created by their restaurant in the early 1900s. Perhaps we should not assume that this is an Irish dish. Corned beef and cabbage, which we love to eat on St. Patrick's day, would be difficult to find in Ireland. One would also be hard put to find Potatoes O'Brien in Ireland. But who cares? These spuds are a wonderful accompaniment to steak, lamb and pork dishes. They also can star as breakfast potatoes.

2 pounds Yukon Gold potatoes
4 tablespoons unsalted butter
4 tablespoons canola oil
1 medium brown onion, chopped
½ green bell pepper, chopped
½ red bell pepper, chopped
3 cloves garlic, chopped
Kosher salt and freshly ground black pepper
1 tablespoon fresh thyme leaves or ½ tablespoon dry thyme leaves
½ teaspoon paprika
¼ cup Italian parsley, chopped
1 bunch green onions, chopped

Place the potatoes in a large pot and cover with cold water by 2-inches. Add 2 tablespoons salt and bring to a boil. Cook until a fork inserted into the center of each potato meets with no resistance, about 20 minutes.

While the potatoes are boiling, heat 2 tablespoons each of butter and oil in a large skillet. Over medium-high heat, add the onions, bell peppers and garlic. Season with salt, pepper and thyme. Sauté until soft. Do not brown. Remove from skillet and set aside.

When the potatoes are done, place in a colander and run cold water over them. When cool enough to handle, cut into ½-inch cubes. Do not remove the skin. Heat 2 more tablespoons each of butter and oil in the same skillet. Add the potatoes and spread into one layer. Season with salt, pepper, paprika and thyme. Press potatoes down with a spatula and cook until crisp and golden brown on the bottom. Turn potatoes over, press down and season the other side. Stir in the onion-garlic-bell pepper mixture. Add the parsley and chopped green onions. Taste for seasoning and serve.

MASHED POTATO CASSEROLE

Over the years, I've made tons of mashed potatoes. I have always enjoyed them, but I'm never quite satisfied. After intense research and a considerable amount of tinkering, I came up with this version. Even before they went into the oven, I took a bite. WOW! These are the crown jewels of mashed potatoes. For holiday dinners, or any dinner for that matter, these can be made a day ahead of the festivities.

4 pounds russet potatoes, peeled and cut into 1" squares

½ cup heavy cream

½ cup chicken stock

12 tablespoons unsalted butter (1 ½ sticks), cut into pieces

2 garlic cloves, minced

1-2 tablespoons Dijon mustard

½ cup grated Parmesan, plus more for topping

2 teaspoons salt

¼ teaspoon black pepper

¼ teaspoon paprika

4 large eggs

¼ cup Italian parsley, finely chopped, plus more for topping

1 bunch green onions, chopped, plus more for topping

Preheat oven to 375°F. Place potato pieces in a pot of water that covers potatoes. Bring to a boil. Cover and boil until fork tender, about 20 minutes.

Place cream, chicken stock, butter, garlic, mustard, Parmesan, salt, pepper, and paprika in a medium saucepan. Simmer over medium-low heat until everything is mixed, and the butter has melted. Stir and set aside.

Drain potatoes and place in the bowl of a a stand mixer with the paddle attachment. At low speed, beat the potatoes while slowly adding the cream-butter mixture until potatoes reach desired consistency. Add eggs, one at a time and mix on low speed until incorporated. Do not overmix. With rubber spatula, fold in the chopped parsley and green onions.

Butter a 13x9-inch glass baking dish. Transfer the potatoes to the baking dish and smooth the top until level.

Cover the dish with aluminum foil and bake for 30 minutes. Remove cover and sprinkle more chopped parsley, green onions and Parmesan. Bake for an additional 5-10 minutes until Parmesan melts. Remove from oven and cool for 10 minutes. Serve. This recipe can be partially made the day before. Fill the baking dish with the potato mixture. Cover with plastic wrap and refrigerate overnight. Remove the baking dish from the refrigerator 1 hour before baking.

Legal Thought

Love is a human treasure.
But don't fall in love with your lawsuit.
It will consume you.
Keep it at bay,
and go about your life.
Better yet,
fall in love with your kitchen.

PAN FRIED POTATOES

Not only do these potatoes look beautiful, the taste is divine. They can accompany almost any meat or poultry dinner. When I need a carb overload, I'd consider these as a complete meal.

5-6 Yukon Gold potatoes
1 large onion
2 tablespoons bacon fat
1-2 tablespoons paprika
Kosher salt & freshly ground black pepper

Slice potatoes very thin. Leave skin on. Slice onion. Melt bacon fat in skillet. Add onions and sauté for 2-3 minutes. Add potatoes, salt, pepper and paprika. Add bacon, if used to render fat. There should be enough to make potatoes almost orange.

Cover and fry over medium heat, until soft and tender, about 30 minutes. Potatoes will not be crispy. If potatoes start to stick, add a little water.

---- **Legal Thought** ----

The strength of a lawyer's argument in court is measured not by the volume of his presentation, but by its content.

WILD RICE WITH PECANS, MUSHROOMS & SHALLOTS

I'm surprised at the number of folks I meet who have never tried wild rice. This product has a unique, nutty flavor and earthy texture. Actually, wild rice is not rice. Northern wild rice is an annual wild plant native to the Great Lakes region of North America. For decades, Native Americans have harvested this product in the aquatic areas of Northern Ontario, Alberta, Saskatchewan and Manitoba in Canada and Minnesota, Wisconsin, Michigan and Idaho in the United States. The wild version can still be purchased in these regions. In recent years, farmers have learned how to plant and cultivate the product — I suppose that cultivated wild rice is an oxymoron. I have purchased cultivated wild rice in local markets and on the internet and the difference is barely perceptible.

1 to 1 ½ cups wild rice

4 cups chicken stock

1 cup pecans, chopped

1 celery rib, diced

3 shallots, diced

½ - 1 pound shitake mushrooms

3 cloves garlic, minced

1 tablespoon fresh thyme, chopped

½ cup Italian parsley, chopped

Butter, salt, pepper

Wash rice three times. Place rice and stock in pot. Add salt. Bring to boil. Cover and simmer for about 1 hour until barely tender. The rice will blossom slightly with small white blossoms atop the black rice. Drain rice and reserve stock. Set aside rice and reserved stock. Should yield about 3-4 cups of rice.

Sauté pecans and celery in butter in a large skillet for about 5 minutes. Add shallots, mushrooms and garlic. Sauté for about 3 minutes more. Add cooked rice, thyme and parsley. Add about ½ cup of reserved stock. Cook an additional 3-5 minutes or until tender and slightly chewy. Season with kosher salt and pepper and a few pats of butter for extra richness. Stir and fluff with a fork. Serve immediately.

This rice dish is a wonderful accompaniment to lamb chops, a roasted chicken or roasted duck. If you really want to splurge, purchase a crown lamb roast from the butcher. See recipe for Crown Roast of Lamb With Mustard Crust on page 117. After the roast is cooked, stuff the center with Wild Rice Pecans, Mushrooms & Shallots and return to oven. Reduce heat to 375°F and cook for 10 more minutes.

SAUTÉED BROCCOLI, CAULIFLOWER & CARROTS

Folks seem to have a problem imparting flavor and texture to veggies. The secret is butter and chicken stock. Whenever I want a side dish of veggies, be it broccoli, Brussels sprouts, asparagus, zucchini, bok choy or green beans, this is my go-to recipe. A drizzle of lemon juice at the end brightens the flavor.

3 tablespoons unsalted butter

2 tablespoons olive oil

3 cups broccoli florets

3 cups 1″ cauliflower florets

1 cup carrots, sliced or chopped into 1″ pieces

½ teaspoon kosher salt

¼ teaspoon freshly ground black pepper

½ cup chicken stock

1 teaspoon fresh lemon juice

Heat the butter and 2 tablespoons of the oil in a large skillet over medium-high heat.

Add broccoli, cauliflower and carrots in a single layer, sprinkle with ½ teaspoon salt and ¼ teaspoon of pepper. Add chicken stock and cover the skillet and cook until the veggies are tender, about 3-5 minutes.

Drizzle with lemon juice. With a slotted spoon, remove veggies from skillet and serve.

FRENCH GLAZED CARROTS

One of the beauties of French cooking is that they are able to take a few simple ingredients and make the final creation to taste more than the sum of its parts. This French classic, aka carrots Vichy, is an example. Just four simple ingredients. Sauté the carrots with sugar, water, lemon juice and butter until they are tender and glazed with the melted sugar. Care must be taken to avoid overcooking and burning the sugar mixture.

1 pound carrots, peeled (about 4-5 medium carrots)

Kosher salt and freshly ground pepper to taste

½ teaspoon sugar

¼ cup water

1 tablespoon fresh lemon juice

2 tablespoons butter

Italian parsley, chopped

Cut the carrots into ½-inch slices. Place carrots in a skillet. Add salt, pepper, sugar, water, lemon juice and butter.

Cover tightly and sauté over medium high heat. Shake the skillet occasionally. Cook until carrots are tender, about 7 minutes. Watch carefully until the liquid has just evaporated and the carrots are lightly glazed. Remove carrots immediately. Overcooking can cause the sugar to burn the carrots. Sprinkle with chopped Italian parsley.

BEETS WITH ORANGE JUICE & BROWN SUGAR

Beets are infrequently served in restaurants. I love to cook beets at home. Even roasted without the sauce, these are delicious.

3 fresh beets
2 tablespoons butter
1 tablespoon brown sugar
1 teaspoon cornstarch
Zest from 1 orange
½ cup fresh orange juice

Preheat oven to 350° F. Remove stems from beets, then wash but do not peel. Drizzle beets with olive oil. Mix with your hands to coat entire surfaces. Wrap beets in foil and place in a baking pan. Roast until tender, about 45-60 minutes. To test for tenderness, pierce with a paring knife. It should go through without resistance.

In the meantime, in a medium skillet, melt butter over low heat. Stir in brown sugar and cornstarch, then orange zest and juice. Increase heat to medium, cook and stir until mixture thickens and becomes bubbly. Remove from heat.

When beets are done, cool slightly, then peel skin which now will come off easily. Cut beets into quarters. Over low heat, warm sauce, then add beets and coat well with the sauce.

ASPARAGUS PARMESAN

Asparagus is a veggie that lends itself to roasting. Parmesan adds an extra level of flavor.

1 pound asparagus (thick spears are best)
½ teaspoon kosher salt
¼ teaspoon black pepper
¼ teaspoon granulated garlic
¼ teaspoon thyme
2 tablespoons extra virgin olive oil
½ cup shredded or grated Parmesan cheese (Romano cheese can also be used)

Preheat oven to 400°F. Cut off the woody ends of the asparagus spears. Combine salt, pepper, granulated garlic and thyme. Set aside.

Place the spears in one layer in a 13x9-inch glass baking dish. Lightly sprinkle the spears with olive oil. Mix with your hands to coat each spear. Lightly sprinkle with spice mixture. Spread cheese evenly over asparagus. Bake just until the cheese begins to brown and a fork easily punctures the thickest part, and the spear is tender, about 8-12 minutes.

Chapter 12

Recipes from the U.S.A.

(Plus, Americanized Recipes and Other Favorites)

FABE'S BBQ RIBS

BBQ ribs are one of the few items that can never be duplicated at home. Famous BBQ joints smoke their ribs for up to 16 hours. However, this recipe comes very close. I suggest using of St. Louis ribs. They have more meat than the baby back ribs and less waste than spare ribs. The other secret to great ribs is to use a great rub and sauce. I think that you will find my sauce recipe to be superior to the store-bought bottled stuff.

BBQ RUB
2 tablespoons paprika
1½ teaspoons chili powder
1½ teaspoons cumin
1½ teaspoons brown sugar
1½ teaspoons kosher salt
¾ teaspoons oregano
1 teaspoon thyme
¼ teaspoon celery salt
½ teaspoon granulated onion
½ teaspoon granulated garlic

¾ teaspoons black pepper
¼ teaspoon cayenne pepper

BBQ SAUCE
1 cup ketchup
1 cup tomato sauce
½ cup brown sugar
½ cup red wine vinegar
¼ cup unsulfured molasses
2 teaspoons hickory-flavored liquid smoke
1 tablespoons butter

¼ teaspoon garlic powder
¼ teaspoon onion powder
¼ teaspoon chili powder
½ teaspoon paprika
¼ teaspoon celery seed
⅛ teaspoon ground cinnamon
¼ teaspoon cayenne pepper
1 teaspoon salt
1 teaspoon freshly ground black pepper

BBQ RIBS
1 rack pork back ribs or St. Louis ribs
½ cup Fabe's BBQ rub
1 cup Fabe's BBQ sauce
1 cup chicken stock
2 tablespoons apple cider

FOR THE RUB: Mix all of the ingredients together in a plastic food container with a cover. Cover and shake well. This will stay fresh for up to one month.

FOR THE SAUCE: Place all of the ingredients in a medium saucepan. Bring to a boil over medium heat. Reduce heat to low and simmer for about 20 minutes or until the mixture reaches the consistency of BBQ sauce. With a rubber heat-proof spatula, stir occasionally and scrape the sides of the saucepan. This can be refrigerated for up to one month.

Preheat oven to 250°F. Dry ribs with a towel and remove the silver skin (membrane). Generously rub all sides of ribs with Fabe's BBQ rub. Wrap the ribs in a kitchen towel and place in refrigerator for 1 hour or overnight.

In a large baking pan, mix chicken stock and vinegar. Place ribs in pan. Liquid should come up to about ¼-inch of ribs.

Wrap top of pan tightly with foil. Place in oven for 2½ to 3 hours. Do not peek.

In the meantime, heat grill to high. Place a cast iron griddle over flame for at least 15 minutes. After 2½ hours, you can peek. Remove foil and gently insert the blade of a sharp knife into the meat. The blade should enter without resistance. When ribs are done, remove from pan. Pour liquid into a saucepan and bring to a boil over high heat on top of stove until reduced by half. Remove from heat. Add about 1 cup of

Fabe's BBQ sauce and mix well.

In the meantime, lightly coat both sides of rack with Fabe's BBQ sauce and place rib rack on griddle and grill for 3-5 minutes on each side or until nicely charred. Watch carefully.

Remove ribs from grill. Cut into individual ribs and place in saucepan and coat each side. Place ribs on serving plates and add more of the BBQ sauce that has not been mixed with stock.

---— **Legal Thought** ---—

I'm not ribbing when I advise you:

A one-night stand
Can take command
Of your whole life
And cause you strife.

STU'S CHILI FOR EIGHT PEOPLE

I make chili for almost every one of my big parties. There are never any leftovers. Folks beg to take some home. If you do have any leftovers, this dish freezes well for a month or so.

- 1 tablespoon kosher salt
- 1½ teaspoons freshly ground black pepper
- 1½ teaspoons chili powder
- ¾ teaspoon cumin
- ¾ teaspoon thyme
- ¾ teaspoon oregano
- ½ teaspoon granulated garlic
- ½ teaspoon granulated onion
- 2 teaspoons sugar
- Pinch red pepper flakes
- 1 tablespoon olive oil
- 2 pounds ground chuck
- ½ pound mild Italian sausage
- 2 medium onions, chopped
- 5 cloves garlic, chopped
- 1 green bell pepper, chopped
- 1 red bell pepper, chopped
- 1 red chili pepper or 1 serrano chili pepper, seeds removed & chopped
- ½ pound mushrooms, sliced
- 2 carrots, chopped
- 2 celery ribs, chopped
- 1 (28 ounce) can diced tomatoes
- 1 (15 ounce) can tomato sauce
- 1 (6 ounce) can tomato paste
- 1 can corn, drained
- 3 cans beans, 1 great northern, 1 red kidney & 1 black, drained
- ¼ cup cilantro, chopped
- 1 bunch green onions, chopped

Mix together salt, pepper, chili powder, cumin, thyme, oregano granulated garlic, granulated onion, sugar and red paper flakes. Place 1 tablespoon of olive oil in Dutch oven or large heavy pot. Over medium high heat, add chuck and sausage. Lightly season with a pinch of the seasonings just mixed. When the meat is browned, remove from pot, place in a bowl and drain and discard meat juices. Add 2 more tablespoons olive oil and sweat onions, garlic, bell peppers, chili peppers, mushrooms, carrots & celery. Lightly dust with seasoning mixture and stir into vegetable mixture. Add diced tomatoes, tomato sauce and tomato paste. Bring to a boil, add all the remaining seasonings, cover and simmer for 1½ hours. Add corn, beans, cilantro and green onions. Stir into pot, heat for 5 minutes and reseason.

You can substitute ground chicken, ground turkey or a combination of several ground meats. If you are a vegetarian, or even a vegan, this chili is fantastic with no meat whatsoever. You can top your bowl of chili with raw onions, shredded cheddar cheese, tortilla chips or more cilantro. Or, boil up some macaroni and have chili mac.

STU'S CROWN ROAST OF LAMB WITH MUSTARD CRUST & WINE PAN SAUCE

If you want to be the talk of the town for years to come, I suggest that you throw a dinner party and serve a crown roast of lamb. The completed edifice looks like it was prepared by a master chef. The truth is that, after making the crust in a food processor, the roast is placed in the oven and your work is practically finished. Most good butchers will assemble the racks together for you. They will also French the bones which means that they will strip the meat from between the top portions of the ribs. For extra flavor, I prefer to leave this fatty meat on the ribs. If the butcher won't tie the racks together, it's quite easy to do on your own.

CROWN ROAST

1 roast, 2 or 3 racks

HERB CRUST

½ cup breadcrumbs

2 teaspoons garlic, minced

2 tablespoons chopped herbs

1 teaspoon salt

¼ teaspoon black pepper

2 tablespoons olive oil

2 tablespoons Dijon mustard

PAN SAUCE

1 teaspoon garlic, minced

½ cup red wine

½ cup lamb stock

1 teaspoon fresh thyme

1 teaspoon Dijon mustard

2 tablespoons butter

Salt & pepper

FOR THE ROAST: Preheat oven to 475° F. French the bones if desired, by cutting off the fat between each rib. With butcher's string, tie 2 or 3 lamb rib racks together (about 1-inch from the meaty base of the racks), to form a circle. Meaty side should be inside. The roast will look like a crown. Three 8-rib racks will feed six people. In a very hot cast iron skillet, sear all sides of the crown. Cover outside with crust as described below. Place roast in skillet and roast for approximately 20 minutes. Reduce oven temperature to 375° F. Add filling (such as wild rice). Place in oven and roast about 10 minutes more. Remove, let rest for 10 minutes. Test for desired doneness with an instant thermometer. It should read 135° F for medium.

FOR THE CRUST: Combine all ingredients except mustard and oil in a small bowl or blend in a food processor. For herbs, I suggest chopped fresh rosemary. Sprinkle in olive oil. Spread the crumbs in a flat pan. After the rack is seared, brush it with the mustard. Roll rack in breadcrumbs until it is well coated. Place in oven as described above.

FOR THE PAN SAUCE: Pour off excess fat from skillet. Leave juices behind. Place pan over medium heat and add garlic. Cook for 15 seconds, add wine, increase heat to high and deglaze pan. Reduce wine by one-half. Add stock and thyme and boil until mixture turns syrupy. Whisk in the mustard until the sauce is smooth. Whisk in butter, season with salt and pepper.

Filling Roast with Wild Rice. A wild rice accompaniment is a wild addition. The recipe for wild rice with pecans, mushrooms and shallots is on p. 109.

Legal Thought

There is a timeless axiom among lawyers: "A bad settlement is always better than a good lawsuit." A lawyer does a greater service to a client by promoting peace and conciliation between opposing parties. The lawyer exerts a disservice to a client by escalating derision between opposing parties.

STU'S GREATEST MEAT LOAF WITH POTATOES & GREEN BEANS

I've met some folks who don't like meat loaf. After sampling some versions in restaurants, I can understand why. I've asked these folks, "Do you like meatballs?" Most answer in the affirmative. Well, a meat loaf is just a big meatball. I've converted many anti-meat loaf people with this recipe.

- 1 large onion, chopped
- 2 tablespoons butter
- 3 cloves garlic, minced
- ¼ pound mushrooms, finely chopped
- ¾ cup matzo meal, breadcrumbs or cracker crumbs
- ½ cup milk
- 2 large eggs, lightly beaten
- 2 pounds ground beef
- 1 pound ground pork or ground sausage
- 2 tablespoons ketchup mixed in ½ cup beef stock
- 2 tablespoons horseradish
- 1 tablespoon capers
- 1 tablespoon Worcestershire sauce
- ½ cup Italian parsley, chopped
- 1½ tablespoons kosher salt
- 1 teaspoon pepper
- Pinch cayenne pepper
- 1 teaspoon dried thyme
- 1 teaspoon dried oregano
- 1 teaspoon dried mustard
- 6 strips green or red bell pepper, or combination
- 2 teaspoons olive oil
- 3 strips bacon
- Ketchup
- 4-5 Yukon Gold or medium white potatoes
- 1 tablespoon rosemary, chopped
- 2 teaspoons paprika
- Green beans

Preheat oven to 375°F. Sauté onion in butter until caramelized, about 10 minutes. Add garlic and mushrooms after 5 minutes. Remove from pan and cool. Mix breadcrumbs or matzo meal with milk and beaten eggs. Meanwhile, combine beef, pork, breadcrumbs mixture, ketchup & stock, horseradish, capers, Worchestershire sauce and parsley. Combine salt, pepper, cayenne, thyme, oregano and dried mustard, then add to the mixture. Add onions, garlic & mushrooms. Combine thoroughly. Take a small portion of the meat loaf mixture, place in skillet and cook for tasting sample. Adjust seasonings.

Form into loaf or two loaves. Add handfuls of mixture at a time to build the loaf. Do not pat down too tightly. Place loaf or loaves in large baking sheet pan or baking pan. I prefer a baking sheet lined with parchment paper. Drizzle bell pepper strips with olive oil. Drape bacon strips and bell peppers across top of loaf. Brush top of everything with ketchup.

Cut 4-5 medium white or Yukon gold potatoes into ½-inch slices. Drizzle with olive oil and some butter. Season with salt, pepper, rosemary and paprika (paprika makes them brown beautifully). Scatter around meat loaf in a single layer and bake along with meatloaf. Turn potatoes occasionally.

Bake for 1 to 1 ½ hours, or until a thermometer registers 155°F. Allow loaf or loaves to rest 10 minutes before serving.

For the green beans, parboil in a saucepan for 2 minutes. During the last 15 minutes while meat loaf is cooking, drain green beans and place in the meat loaf pan.

You can substitute some ground turkey and/or mild Italian sausage for some of the beef. For example, try ½ pound beef, ½ pound pork, ½ pound ground turkey, ½ pound sausage.

---------------------------------- **Legal Thought** ----------------------------------

*If you steal a TV,
Every time you turn it on,
No matter what channel,
It will remind you
That you are a thief.*

CHERYL'S STUFFED BELL PEPPERS

Cheryl and I are together all the time. Our life together is a joy. There are few activities in life in which we don't jointly participate. One is fishing. Another is aviation. The third involves the kitchen. She insists that I'm too fussy when I cook. I agree. I'm passionate, dedicated and rejoiceful when I cook. I prefer to work alone. There are several dishes which Cheryl makes which are outstanding. When she cooks, which is infrequently, I stay out of the kitchen. Here is a recipe that was handed down from her mother. It's one of my favorites.

PEPPERS & STUFFING

6-8 bell peppers, red and green

1 ½ to 2 pounds ground chuck

1 egg, lightly beaten

¼ cup milk

1 cup cooked white rice

1 teaspoon kosher salt

1 teaspoon freshly ground black pepper

½ onion, finely chopped

2 cloves garlic, chopped

1 ¼ tablespoons Worcestershire sauce

SAUCE

3 (8 ounce) cans tomato sauce

1 (15 ounce) can diced tomatoes

1 bay leaf

2 cloves garlic, chopped

1 teaspoon sugar

¼ cup Italian parsley, chopped

PEPPERS & STUFFING: Select wide peppers that will accommodate filling. Wash and dry peppers, then cut off the tops from about ½-inch from the stemmed top. Chop up the tops and set aside. With a spoon, clean out the seeds and the white veins.

Place the ground beef in a large mixing bowl. Beat the egg and milk together, then add to the meat. Add the rice, salt, pepper, chopped onion, chopped garlic, chopped pepper tops and Worcestershire sauce. Mix well with your hands. Do not overmix.

Pack each pepper with enough of the beef mixture so that the mixture is about ½-inch over the top. Do not pack tightly. The amount of mixture will depend on the size of each pepper.

SAUCE: Mix all of the sauce ingredients together.

Preheat oven to 350°F. In a 13x9-inch baking dish, place each pepper, beef side up. Pour the sauce evenly around the peppers. Cover with foil and bake for about 1½ hours. We prefer the peppers to be very soft and starting to wrinkle. Baste every 15 minutes. Remove the foil for the last 15 minutes of baking.

FABE'S BBQ BUTTERFLIED CHICKEN

Butterflying a chicken or turkey is a method that offers faster, more even cooking. The technique is also referred to as "spatchcocking" a chicken. Unless I want the drama of presenting a whole roasted chicken, when I prepare a chicken on the grill, (or even in the oven), I generally use the butterfly method. Some recipes call for the removal of the backbone entirely. It's your choice.

1 chicken, about 4 pounds

⅓ cup canola oil

1 teaspoon Dijon mustard

1 tablespoon ketchup

1 teaspoon Worcestershire sauce

1 teaspoon soy sauce

1 teaspoon Fabe's BBQ sauce (See BBQ ribs recipe, p. 114)

2 tablespoons Fabe's BBQ rub (See BBQ ribs recipe, p. 114)

Kosher salt and freshly ground black pepper

Preheat grill or oven to 400°F. Best to use a flat, nonstick griddle placed on top of the grill. Heat griddle.

Butterfly chicken by cutting along each side of the back bone from the tail to the neck cavity. Use a sharp chef's knife or poultry shears. Turn chicken over and, with the heel of your palm, smack the center of the breast until the chicken is flattened.

Combine oil, mustard, ketchup, Worcestershire sauce, soy sauce, BBQ sauce. With your hands, rub sauce on chicken until it is entirely covered with a coat of sauce. Then sprinkle the entire chicken with BBQ rub. Drizzle with salt and pepper.

Place chicken, breast side down, on griddle. Close cover of grill and cook for 15 minutes. Turn chicken breast side up and baste with oil mixture. Baste every 15 minutes. The skin will start to turn black-don't worry — that's where the flavor is. Don't add more BBQ sauce until just before chicken is done, or it will burn. If the chicken is becoming too burned, reduce temperature to 375°F.

For a complete meal, cook the chicken with potatoes, onions and peppers. For the potatoes, slice about four white or red potatoes ¼-inch thin. Julienne some onion rings and red and green bell pepper and mix in with the potatoes. Coat in olive oil, then sprinkle with rub. Spread the potatoes and peppers in one layer around the chicken. Baste potatoes occasionally. If they become too brown, remove before chicken is done.

Continue to grill until breast and thigh reach 170°F with an instant thermometer — about 45 minutes to 1 hour 15 minutes. During the last 10 minutes, brush with Fabe's BBQ sauce and sprinkle with Fabe's BBQ rub, salt and pepper. Serve with more BBQ sauce.

If you are not in the mood for BBQ chicken, omit the sauce and rub. Add some dried thyme leaves.

FABE'S ROASTED DUCK WITH ORANGE/RASPBERRY SAUCE

For reasons I don't quite understand, duck has diminished in popularity. I've met folks who have never tried duck, either at home or in a restaurant. Fresh ducks are available in quality butcher or poultry shops. I purchase fresh ducks at the Asian markets in Los Angeles. In a pinch, a frozen duck will work just fine. Don't hesitate to try this recipe. It's no more difficult than roasting a chicken. This duck recipe is the centerpiece of our annual Valentine's Day dinner.

1 (4-6 pound) duck
1 cup freshly squeezed orange juice
Zest from 2 oranges
1 tablespoon fresh lemon juice
¼ cup chicken stock
3 tablespoons apricot jam
⅛ teaspoon ground mustard
⅛ teaspoons kosher salt
4 tablespoons sugar
1 teaspoon freshly ground ginger
2 tablespoons butter
1 tablespoon cornstarch dissolved in 2 tablespoons cold water
½ teaspoon orange liqueur
¼ teaspoon cognac
¼ cup fresh raspberries

Preheat oven to 425°F. Clean duck and dry completely. If you purchase a fresh duck, ask the butcher to cut off the legs and webbed feet.

Sprinkle salt and pepper on surface of duck and in cavity. Stuff cavity with reserved orange peels. Fold wings back under the duck. With kitchen string, tie the legs together with the tail. Place the duck on a rack and place duck and rack in a heavy roasting pan. With a serving fork, pierce the skin all over. Insert the fork at an angle and pierce about ¼-inch deep. Pour about ½-inch of water into the bottom of the pan.

Roast uncovered for one hour. In the meantime, make the sauce. Mix orange juice, orange zest, lemon juice, chicken stock, apricot jam, ground mustard, salt, sugar, ginger, and butter in a medium saucepan. Bring to a boil over medium heat, then add cornstarch mixture. Continue to boil until the mixture thickens to about gravy consistency. Add liqueur and cognac and simmer for an additional minute more. Add raspberries and simmer for about 2 more minutes, until soften. Set aside.

Rotate pan and continue to roast the duck for another 30 minutes. Reduce temperature to 375°F. Baste duck every 15 minutes with sauce. Roast until the breast registers 165°F when an instant thermometer is inserted into the thigh and/or breast — about 2 hours depending on the size of the duck. If the skin is beginning to get too dark, cover the duck loosely with aluminum foil.

Remove duck from oven and place on a cutting board. Cover with foil and allow to rest for 15 minutes before carving. Serve with sauce.

--- **Legal Thought** ---

Want to save your marriage — or drop your divorce case? Pack up your nasty divorce papers, flee from the courthouse and head to the kitchen. If you and your spouse cook together and each develops a special culinary skill, you become indispensable and will live happily ever after.

For accompaniments to this masterpiece, I suggest Asparagus Parmesan (p. 112) along with wild rice and mushrooms (p. 109) or Pommes de Terre Boulangères (p. 214).

―――――――――――――――――――――― **Legal Thought** ――――――――――――――――――――――

Thus, we can go through life with the secure feeling that the law will protect us against those who break their promises in our daily business lives. What would life be without that predictability and security?

MOLLEE & ED'S ROAST CHICKEN

One evening about 10 o'clock, my phone rang. The screen revealed the caller to be my doctor.

"That's strange," I thought. "Why is he calling me?"

First of all, doctors rarely call patients anymore. Second, and most important, most doctors hate lawyers. They perceive lawyers as ganging up and suing them for medical malpractice.

Whenever I'm introduced to a doctor, I open with, "Hi, I'm Stuart the lawyer. I don't do medical malpractice cases."

Well, this particular doctor and his wife are dear friends of Cheryl and me. Mollee and I often cook together. But Mollee is usually the one who calls. Perhaps Ed was calling to tell me he was reviewing my chart and wanted to tell me that he discovered a medical problem that meant I had only months to live.

With heightened trepidation, I answered the phone. "Stuie," the doc cried out. "Mollee just made your roast chicken recipe. She's been roasting chicken for 30 years and they've never tasted this good. It was so juicy — the skin was crispy and a gorgeous color."

He continued. "Oh, the potatoes — crispy on the outside and creamy on the inside."

"And the gravy. I drank it like it was soup," he rhapsodized.

Now, when I visit his office, I get special treatment. He even puts on a pair of brand new gloves before he examines me. Unlike the staffs in many medical offices these days, Ed's staff is not mean and condescending to me. Most important, Ed now loves lawyers!

The story does not end there. A few years ago, during a stay at a central California resort, we met a lovely couple, also from Los Angeles. They had been married for about 15 years and had two beautiful kids. We were enjoying breakfast around the pool at the hotel and struck up a pleasant conversation. The subject turned to cooking and I mentioned this roast chicken story.

"I've never roasted a chicken," she admitted with obvious embarrassment. "Do you have to clean out the cavity?"

I was shocked. Married 15 years and she never roasted a chicken. What's happening to family values in this country? I gently reviewed the recipe with her. I hope to change that pattern for her and also do my part for the preservation of American family values — so this recipe is also dedicated to her as well as Mollee and Ed.

Warning: This recipe looks lengthy, difficult and complicated. As an honest lawyer, let me assure you that it is simple, quick and most important, extremely rewarding. I have droned on because (1) the recipe has been fun to write and (2) lawyers tend to be quite long winded.

1 (3 to 5 pound) whole chicken

4 tablespoons olive oil, divided

2 tablespoons butter, softened (optional)

Kosher salt and freshly ground black pepper

1 sprig fresh thyme-or 2 teaspoons dried thyme, divided

2 teaspoons paprika, divided

½ medium brown or yellow onion, peeled

3 cloves garlic, peeled and smashed

4-6 medium Yukon gold potatoes, sliced ¼" thick

1 green or red bell pepper, cut into 1" slices (or half red, half green)

½ cup dry white wine

2 cups chicken stock

FOR THE MIREPOIX: In uniform sizes, chop about ½ cup each of onions, celery and carrots. Mix together.

FOR THE ROUX: Place 4 tablespoons of butter in a small, heavy saucepan. Melt slowly, then add 4 tablespoons of flour. Over a low flame, mix ingredients together until no bits of flour are visible. Stir constantly with a wooden spoon. Continue to stir until the roux becomes medium blonde in color, about 3-5 minutes. Remove from heat. Never leave the roux until you remove it from the heat!

Preparation of the chicken and accompaniments should take no longer than 20 minutes. You can prepare the roux while the chicken is in the oven.

FOR THE CHICKEN: This recipe requires a heavy roasting pan or a large heavy skillet either of which will withstand a hot oven and the finishing of the gravy over a hot burner.

Place the mirepoix in the center of the pan or skillet. It should be gathered to the approximate dimensions of the chicken. The mirepoix will serve not only to enhance the flavor of the chicken and the gravy, but also doubles as a rack. Preheat oven to 450°F.

Remove all giblets from the cavity. Place opening of the cavity under faucet and run cold water into cavity for about 30 seconds. Turn cavity upside-down and let water drain out. With paper towels, wipe dry both the cavity and the exterior of the chicken. Place the chicken, breast side up, on top of the mirepoix. Drizzle 1 tablespoon of olive oil on the chicken, then rub the oil around the entire exterior of the chicken. If using the soft butter, take small portions with your hand, lift the skin around the breast and distribute the butter evenly between the skin and the breast meat.

Rub approximately 1 teaspoon each salt, pepper and thyme into the cavity of the chicken. Stuff the onion, garlic and thyme sprig, if using, into the cavity. Mix approximately 1 teaspoon each of salt, pepper, thyme and paprika together. You can add ½ teaspoon of garlic powder if you like. Rub the mixture evenly over the entire exterior of the chicken. If the chicken is large, you may need another batch of the rub.

Place the sliced potatoes and bell pepper slices in a medium bowl. Drizzle with 1 tablespoon olive oil. Mix together 1 teaspoon each salt, pepper, paprika and sprinkle over the potatoes and vegetables. Use more if necessary. You could also add a teaspoon of dried rosemary. With your hands, mix everything together so that the potatoes and peppers are evenly coated with the oil and spices. Place the pepper and potato slices around the chicken — in as much of a single layer as possible.

Place the pan and its contents in the oven. After 30 minutes, baste the chicken with the juices that have gathered on the bottom of the pan. A silicon basting brush is the best choice.

Baste every 15 minutes thereafter. Turn the potato and pepper slices every 30 minutes. Roast for a total of 1½ hours or until the breast reaches an internal temperature of 170°F.

Remove the pan from the oven and place on the counter. Remove the chicken, place on a cutting board and tent with foil. Remove the potato and pepper slices and place in a covered serving dish. Remove all but 1 tablespoon of the drippings from the pan. Remove the mirepoix and discard.

FOR THE GRAVY: Place the roasting pan on the stovetop over high heat. Carefully pour the wine into the pan and, with a wooden spatula, simultaneously scrape the browned bits from the bottom. Do not remove the browned bits. These are called the fond (another fancy French word). They will enhance the flavor beyond belief. Continue to scrape until all but 1 tablespoon of the wine remains. Then, add the chicken stock and bring to a boil. As the liquid starts to boil, add the roux and mix well until the gravy thickens to your desired consistency — perhaps the thickness of a hearty soup. The gravy will not thicken until the liquid boils. Reduce heat to a point where the liquid barely simmers. Check for taste and add some salt, pepper and thyme if necessary. For extra flavor and richness, add 2 tablespoons of butter and ¼ cup milk or cream and stir until incorporated. Remove from heat otherwise the gravy will thicken too much or reduce to nothing. Strain the gravy into a gravy boat.

Culinary Thought

The quintessential food processing plant of the universe? Nature.

FABULOUS MOIST SAUTÉED CHICKEN BREASTS

Rarely will I eat chicken breasts. To my taste, they are dry and tasteless. This recipe is a game changer. The breasts are moist and full of flavor. If you prefer, you can use boneless thighs. Cheryl and I have been together for 45 years. One of the secrets to our happy, blissful relationship is that Cheryl hates the dark meat of the chicken and I hate the white meat. Since I developed this recipe, all that has changed. For the sake of the marriage — and for the preservation of family values — I double the recipe.

4 boneless chicken breasts or boneless thighs

½ cup flour

Kosher salt & freshly ground black pepper

5 tablespoons butter

1 large shallot, minced

¾ cup chicken stock

½ cup dry white wine

2 tablespoons dill, chopped

1 tablespoon tarragon

1 tablespoon whole grain mustard

1 tablespoon capers

1 tablespoon green olives, chopped

Flatten breasts or thighs so that they are the same thickness throughout. Place breasts or thighs between two sheets of plastic wrap and roll with a rolling pin until around ¼-inch thick.

If chicken breasts are really thick, you will need to use the butterfly method. To butterfly a chicken breast means splitting the chicken breast horizontally and opening it like a book. The French call these paillards. Place a chicken breast on a cutting board lengthwise. Place your palm on the chicken. With a very sharp boning knife, beginning at the thickest side, slice the breast horizontally almost to the other end and open it like a book. You can proceed with this half-breast in one piece, or you may continue to cut it in half.

Spread flour in shallow baking dish. Pat chicken dry, then season with salt and pepper. Dredge chicken in flour and shake off excess.

Heat 1 tablespoon of butter in a large skillet over medium-high heat. Sauté chicken until golden brown on both sides, about 5 minutes per side. Transfer to a plate and set aside.

Add 1 tablespoon of butter. Add shallot and cook for about 1 minute or until soft. Stir in stock and wine and scrape up browned bits from bottom of pan with a flat wooden spatula. Leave brown bits in pan. Simmer wine and broth until slightly thickened, about 8 minutes.

Remove pan from heat and whisk in last 3 tablespoons of butter, dill, tarragon, mustard and accumulated chicken juices. Stir in capers and olives. Season with salt and pepper. Place chicken on plate and pour juices over chicken.

SHRIMP CREOLE

Creoles are folks of Spanish, African or French descent born in the West Indies or other parts of America populated with Spanish or French settlers. This dish probably originated in New Orleans. It can be prepared in around 30 minutes, and when served with rice constitutes a complete meal. At an attorney's hourly rate, that's pretty inexpensive.

2 tablespoons butter

2 tablespoons olive oil, divided

1 medium onion, chopped

1 celery rib, chopped

½ green bell pepper, chopped

2 cloves garlic, minced

1 (14 ounce) can diced tomatoes (do not drain)

⅓ cup cold water

½ teaspoon paprika

¼ teaspoon thyme

¼ teaspoon oregano

½ teaspoon kosher salt

½ teaspoon black pepper

¼ teaspoon (scant) red pepper flakes

½ teaspoon Worcestershire sauce

1 bay leaf

1½ pounds large shrimp, deveined with tails on

2 tablespoons water

2 teaspoons cornstarch

1-2 tablespoons freshly squeezed lemon juice

¼ cup Italian parsley, chopped

1 bunch green onions, chopped

In a large skillet over medium heat, add butter and 1 tablespoon of the olive oil. Sauté onion, celery, and bell pepper until translucent. Add garlic and cook for one more minute. Stir in undrained tomatoes, ⅓ cup water, paprika, thyme, oregano, salt, black pepper, red pepper flakes and Worcestershire sauce. Add bay leaf.

Bring to a boil, cover and simmer for 15 minutes. In the meantime, in another large skillet, sauté shrimp in 1 tablespoon olive oil just until pink. Remove bay leaf from Creole sauce.

Make a slurry by mixing 2 tablespoons water with the cornstarch. Add to the sauce. Cook and stir until thick and bubbly. Pour Creole sauce over shrimp and cook for about 2 minutes more until shrimp are done. Do not overcook shrimp. Drizzle with 1-2 tablespoons lemon juice. Sprinkle with chopped parsley and green onions. Serve over steamed rice.

SALMON & LENTILS

Lentils, a member of the legume family, are surprisingly easy to prepare. They are packed with protein, dietary fiber and Vitamin B1. Salmon, full of omega fatty acids is one of the world's leading fish for good health. Wild caught king or sockeye are the best. Lentils du Puy can be purchased in fancy stores, on the internet, or you can take a trip to France where they are plentiful. Meals like this will not only keep you away from lawyers who practice disability law, they will keep you away from doctors as well.

1 cup dry lentils (preferably lentils du Puy)
1 medium onion, chopped
2 carrots, chopped
2 celery ribs, chopped
1 tablespoon olive oil
4 garlic cloves, chopped
2 cups chicken stock
2 cups water
1 (14.5 ounce) can diced tomatoes, juice included
1 (6 ounce) can tomato paste
2 teaspoons Worcestershire sauce
½ teaspoon kosher salt
½ teaspoon freshly ground pepper
½ teaspoon dried thyme or 1 teaspoon freshly chopped thyme
¼ teaspoon each paprika, oregano, granulated garlic, sugar
Pinch red pepper flakes
1 bay leaf
¼ cup Italian parsley, chopped
4 (4 to 6 ounce) salmon filets

LENTILS: Rinse lentils and set aside. In a large, heavy skillet over medium heat, sauté onion, carrots and celery in 1 tablespoon of olive oil for about 5 minutes and until soft. Do not brown. Add garlic and stir for 1 minute until fragrant. Add lentils, chicken stock, water, diced tomatoes, tomato paste, Worcestershire sauce, salt, pepper, thyme, oregano, paprika, granulated garlic, sugar, red pepper flakes and bay leaf. Stir ingredients together and bring to a boil. Reduce heat to medium low, cover and simmer for about 20 minutes or until lentils are tender but not mushy. They should be slightly al dente. Remove bay leaf. Add parsley.

SALMON: When lentils are almost done, place a heavy 12-inch skillet over medium high heat, add 1 tablespoon olive oil and heat for 5 minutes. A highly heated pan with simmering oil is the secret to beautifully seared salmon that does not stick to the pan. Rub extra virgin olive oil over both sides of the salmon and season generously with coarse salt, dill weed and freshly ground pepper. Lightly sprinkle with light brown sugar. Do not remove the bottom skin. Place filets in the skillet and sear for 3 minutes. Do not move the filets for this period. Flip the filets, sauté for an additional 2-3 minutes or until almost cooked through.

Spoon a generous mound of lentils on the plate and place a salmon filet over the mound. Add a green veggie for beautiful color and to round out the meal.

SAUTÉED WHITE FISH FILETS WITH LEMON, BUTTER & CAPERS

This is a basic recipe to sauté virtually any white fish. For those dinners when you just want a simple piece of fish accompanied by a veggie or pasta salad, this is the gold standard. You can also use this recipe to make a fish sandwich.

4 fresh white fish filets (sole, cod, sea bass, etc.)

½ cup flour mixed with ½ teaspoon paprika & ½ teaspoon dried thyme

3 tablespoons butter

1 tablespoon olive oil

2 tablespoons capers, drained

1 lemon

2 tablespoons Italian parsley, chopped

Kosher salt and freshly ground black pepper

Pat the fish filets dry. Mix together flour, paprika and thyme in a flat dish. Dredge each filet so that entire surfaces are covered. Shake off excess flour. Sprinkle with koher salt and freshly ground black pepper. Do not dredge until just prior to cooking.

Heat a heavy 12-inch skillet , either anodized aluminum or stainless steel. Add 2 tablespoons butter and the olive oil. Make sure skillet is very hot and heat butter and oil until they begin to sizzle. That's the secret to making the filets golden brown and making sure they don't stick. Carefully lay each filet in the pan. Sauté for about 3 minutes. With a spatula, gently lift one corner to see if it is golden.

With 2 spatulas, gently flip each filet. Sauté for about 3 minutes more. With a spoon, scoop up some of the melted butter/oil and baste the top of each filet. Add capers. Squeeze juice of the lemon over fish and into the sauce. Stir gently. Add the remaining tablespoon of butter (or 2 more), to the sauce and gently mix. Sprinkle with parsley flakes.

Place filets on a platter, drizzle with sauce and capers and serve immediately.

BAKED FISH AND POTATOES

This recipe can constitute a complete meal in almost one pot.

4 Yukon Gold potatoes

½ cup flour

2-4 filets of white fish (sole, snapper, cod or rockfish)

Kosher salt and freshly ground black pepper

4 tablespoons chopped fresh thyme leaves plus 4 whole sprigs (you can use dried thyme if necessary)

2-4 tablespoons butter

4 tablespoons extra virgin olive oil

½ onion, thinly sliced

2 leeks, thinly sliced

1 red or green bell pepper, julienned (optional)

6 brown mushrooms, stems removed (optional)

5 cloves garlic, crushed

½ pound green beans (optional)

4 scallions (green onions)

1 tablespoon Italian parsley, chopped

Cut potatoes in half. Fill a large pot with water. Add potatoes and about 1 tablespoon salt. Bring to a boil and parboil for about 5 minutes. Drain potatoes, cool and cut into thin slices, about ¼-inch thick.

You can make this recipe in a metal baking pan that is both oven-proof and stove-top proof. Or, you can use a heavy 12-inch skillet. Preheat oven to 425°F.

Place the flour in a flat bottom bowl. Pat the fish filets dry. Lightly sprinkle with salt, pepper and thyme. Dredge each filet in flour. Shake off excess flour. Do not dredge until just prior to cooking. Heat a heavy 12 inch skillet or flame-proof baking pan. Add 1 tablespoon of butter and 1 tablespoon of olive oil. When oil and butter are hot, carefully place each filet in the skillet or baking pan. Sauté for about 3 minutes, then, with a spatula, carefully look under one of the filets. If it is easily lifted from the skillet and turning golden brown, carefully flip over. Cook for another 3 minutes. With a spoon, gather some of the oil in the pan and baste the tops of the filets. When the filets are fully cooked, remove skillet from heat. Cover to keep warm.

In the same cooking vessel, brush the bottom with 1 tablespoon of olive oil. Dot with butter. Cover the bottom of the dish with a layer of the potatoes, onions and leeks, plus the bell pepper slices and mushrooms, if using, and sprinkle them with salt, pepper and 1 tablespoon of the thyme leaves. Spread crushed garlic over the top. Drizzle 1 tablespoon of olive oil over the contents. Dot with butter. Bake for approximately 45 minutes or until the potatoes are crisp and golden brown and the mushrooms and bell peppers are done. Turn contents with a spatula and baste occasionally. A silicon basting brush is the best method.

If using green beans, during the last 15 minutes, add to the skillet or baking pan, mix so that they are covered with oil. Add the whole scallions and also cover with oil.

During the last 5 minutes, carefully place the fish filets over the potato mixture. Brush some of the pan juices over the filets. Sprinkle with parsley and serve immediately.

SAUTÉED HALIBUT OR COD IN TOMATO SAUCE

At home I often prepare this dish. I will use whatever white, flakey fish is fresh at the market. (And, hopefully on sale.) This is an easy recipe and very healthy. I travel to Alaska almost every year to fish for salmon. Frequently, we catch a halibut. One year, in the Bering Sea out from Dutch Harbor, I caught a 77-pound halibut. As we took photos on the dock, I was strutting around, proud as a peacock — that is, until I encountered a lady on the same dock who was displaying a 120-pound halibut. Until I learned how to cook this fish, halibut was not my favorite. Bringing home this halibut provided me with ample opportunity to experiment. The secret is to cut the filets no more than an inch thick. Cook it in a very hot skillet for no more than 2-4 minutes per side and the result will be an extremely flakey, tender tasty fish.

4 (6 ounce) halibut, sea bass or cod filets, ½" thick (2 filets, about 1 pound for two people)

¼ cup flour

½ teaspoon kosher salt

¼ teaspoon pepper

2 teaspoons extra virgin olive oil

2 large shallots or ½ onion, chopped

2 garlic cloves, minced

3 tablespoons capers, drained

2 tablespoons olives, chopped

¼ teaspoon dried basil

½ teaspoon thyme

½ teaspoon dried oregano

1 (14.5 ounce) can petite diced tomatoes

¼ cup Italian parsley, chopped

2 tablespoons butter

½ lemon, juiced

Filets should be about ½ to 1-inch thick and all about the same size. The secret to tender, juicy fish is a very hot skillet and a minimal amount of cooking.

Pat the fish filets dry. Dredge each filet in flour. Shake off excess flour. Do not dreedge until just prior to cooking or the fish could be gummy. Season fish with ¼ teaspoon salt and ¼ teaspoon pepper. Heat oil over medium-high heat in large, heavy skillet. Wait until it simmers. Filets should sizzle when placed in the pan. Depending on thickness of filets, sauté 2-4 minutes on each side or until fish flakes with a fork and is barely opaque throughout. DO NOT OVERCOOK! Transfer fish to a plate and keep warm.

Add shallot or onion to skillet, and sauté 1 to 2 minutes or until opaque and tender. Add garlic at sauté for 30 seconds. Do not brown. Add capers, olives, basil, thyme and oregano, and remaining ¼ teaspoon salt; cook 1 minute. Reduce heat to low, add tomatoes, and cook, stirring occasionally until sauce is hot. . Sprinkle with parsley. Check for seasonings. Place fish on top of sauce. Place pats of butter on top of each filet and coat with a brush. Drizzle with lemon juice. Scoop some sauce over fish. Serve over steamed rice. Can also be served with parsley boiled potatoes and/or a green veggie.

OVEN ROASTED SALMON & POTATOES

Here is a weeknight dinner that takes 30 minutes and tastes better than any restaurant could make it. And the fish and spuds can be cooked in one skillet. These potatoes are rich in color, crispy on the outside and creamy on the inside.

POTATOES
3 Yukon Gold Potatoes
6 tablespoons butter
Kosher salt, black pepper, rosemary, thyme and paprika

SALMON
1 salmon filet (about 1 pound)
2 tablespoons olive oil
Kosher salt and black pepper

POTATOES: Preheat the oven to 425°F.

Cut the potatoes in wedges, leave the skin on. Place the potato wedges in boiling water and boil for 10 minutes. Drain and wipe them dry. Over low heat, melt the butter in a heavy skillet. Place the wedges in the melted butter. Gently mix until the wedges are covered with butter. Sprinkle with salt, pepper, rosemary, thyme and paprika. Place in oven for 15 minutes. Check to see if one side of the wedges is golden brown, then turn over to brown the other side. Roast for about 10 minutes more or until they are crispy on the outside and soft in the center. Remove wedges and place in a covered dish.

SALMON: Place the skillet in which you cooked the potatoes on a burner over high heat. Pat the salmon dry. Lightly brush olive oil on both sides of the filet. Sprinkle generously with salt and pepper. Place 1 more tablespoon of olive oil in the pan and swirl around.

Place the filet, skin side up, in the skillet. If the skillet is very hot and you leave the filet alone for 5 minutes, it won't stick. Peek under the filet. If it is golden brown, flip it over with two spatulas. Cook for 3 minutes more. Tilt the pan and, with a spoon, gather the pan juices and baste the filet. This adds tremendous flavor and more color. Place the skillet in the oven and roast for about 7 minutes. Remove and drizzle with lemon juice.

FRENCH DIP TRI-TIP SANDWICHES OR TRI-TIP DINNER

Several years ago, I decided to upgrade the air conditioning and insulation in our house. I hired three highly skilled guys who were acquaintances whom I trusted. In the course of the project, our friendship grew. We ended up working side by side. We exchanged jokes and generally acted like a bunch of goofy kids.

Tri-tip gained in popularity in Santa Maria California where it was, and still is, cooked over charcoal and sliced into steaks. Until recently, it was difficult to find this cut of beef east of California — but it is becoming more plentiful. It is relatively inexpensive and extremely flavorful and satisfying. This triangular shaped roast is nestled behind the short loin, forward of the round, north of the bottom loin and south of the sirloin.

The a/c project extended over several weekends. I became the self-appointed luncheon chef. One reason, of course, was that I love to cook. But I had an ulterior motive as well. I knew that if these guys went out for lunch, they might fall in a vat of beer and never return. With my cuisine, I held them hostage.

Another reward: after the first bite, there was an outburst of wows. The comments were that they had consumed a lot of tri-tip in their lives, but never as good as mine. During the following weekends of the project, the request was for more tri-tip sandwiches. I have a suspicion that these guys stretched the project a few weekends so they could get more tri-tip. If you are cutting carbs, serve the roast with a salad and veggie.

1 tri-tip roast (3 to 4 pounds)

Kosher salt and freshly ground black pepper

1 cup dry red wine

2 cups beef stock, preferably homemade

6 crusty rolls, such as submarine or hoagie rolls

ROAST: This dish can be made in the oven or over a hot grill. I prefer making it in a large cast iron skillet by searing it over the stovetop and finishing it in the oven. Preheat the oven to 400°F. Preheat a large cast iron skillet over high heat. Rub the entire surface of the roast with a light coat of olive oil. Generously season with kosher salt and freshly ground black pepper. Place the roast in the skillet and sear on one side until crusty and brown, about 5 minutes. Flip the roast over and sear the other side. Then, with a pair of tongs, hold the roast and sear the two narrow sides so that all four sides are browned. Place the skillet with the roast in the oven and roast until medium rare, about 125°F. This will take about 30 minutes, depending on the size of the roast. Remove the roast from the skillet and place on a cutting board.

Tri-Tip & OBrien Potatoes

AU JUS: Place the skillet on a burner over a high flame. Carefully pour the wine in the skillet. With a wooden spatula, scrape the bottom of the skillet to loosen all of the brown bits — this is the fond which will enhance the flavor. Bring the wine to a boil and allow it to cook until reduced to about 3 tablespoons of liquid. Add the beef stock and bring back to a boil. Season what is now the au jus with kosher salt and pepper.

Starting at the point end of the roast, cut slices on the bias about ½-inch thick. Cut the rolls in half. Dip each slice of meat into the au jus. Dip the cut parts of the rolls into the au jus. Place about 3 slices of beef on each roll and enjoy.

You can also add thin slices of red onion and/or tomato to your sandwich.

CHERYL'S TUNA SALAD

Cheryl's tuna salad is as fabulous as her egg salad. She suggests white albacore tuna, water packed. Geisha® is her favorite brand. Keep the mayonnaise at a minimum.

---

1 (12 ounce) can water packed tuna

½ red onion, chopped

2 celery ribs, chopped

¼ cup Italian parsley, chopped

2-3 tablespoons mayonnaise

2-3 tablespoons sweet pickle relish

1 teaspoon Dijon mustard

8-10 green pimento olives, chopped

2 tablespoons capers

¼ teaspoon paprika

Remove tuna fish from the can and place in a colander. Run water over the tuna for about 3-5 minutes. With your hands and paper towels, squeeze the tuna to remove all of the water.

Mix all ingredients together. Check for flavor.

Thought for Life

Don't become a parent unless you are willing to be a parent.

CHERYL'S EGG SALAD

Cheryl makes great egg salad. She doesn't measure anything, so I had to stand at her side and write down each ingredient as she added it. Many egg salad recipes call for drowning the ingredients in mayonnaise. This recipe uses scant mayo which allows the flavor and texture of the ingredients to take center stage.

- **7 eggs, hard boiled**
- **2 celery ribs, chopped**
- **1 small red onion, chopped**
- **3 green onions, chopped**
- **12 pimento olives, halved**
- **2 tablespoons capers**
- **2 tablespoons sweet pickle relish**
- **1-2 teaspoons Dijon mustard**
- **2-3 tablespoons mayonnaise**

The best way to achieve perfectly hard boiled eggs is as follows: Place the eggs in a pot or large saucepan. Fill with cold water to about one inch above the top of the eggs. Cover and bring to a boil. As soon as the water reaches a rolling boil, turn off the heat and keep covered for 12 minutes. Remove the eggs and place under cold water for about two minutes.

This recipe works best when the eggs are still slightly warm. Crumble the eggs with your hands and place in a medium bowl. Add the chopped celery, red onion, scallions, halved olives and capers. Next, add pickle relish, mustard and mayonnaise until combined.

---— **Thought for Life** ---—

If you are fortunate enough to be gifted, don't leave the gift in the rain.

LAMB BURGERS

These taste like a lamb chop in a bun.

1 pound ground lamb shoulder
1 (4-inch) sprig rosemary, chopped or ½ teaspoon dried rosemary
4 sprigs thyme, chopped or ½ teaspoon dried thyme
½ teaspoon oregano
1 tablespoon garlic powder
Pinch kosher salt
Pinch freshly ground black pepper

Preheat grill for medium heat or place a heavy skillet on the stove. Combine all ingredients in a bowl. Mix thoroughly. Make into four patties. Do not pack them too tightly.

Grill or fry the burgers until they are slightly pink in the center, about 5 minutes per side. An instant-read thermometer inserted into the center should read 145° F. Cook a minute or so more for medium-well.

Serve on buns with lettuce and tomato or in lettuce wraps.

FABE'S SUPREME TURKEY BURGERS

These critters taste better than hamburgers — and twice as healthy.

1 pound ground turkey
1 egg, slightly beaten
¼ cup panko or breadcrumbs
1 tablespoon Dijon mustard
¼ cup celery, finely chopped
¼ cup onion, finely chopped
¼ cup green bell pepper, finely chopped
3 cloves garlic, finely chopped
3 tablespoons Italian parsley, finely chopped
½ teaspoon poultry seasoning
½ teaspoon black pepper
½ teaspoon granulated garlic
½ to ¾ teaspoon kosher salt
Pinch cayenne pepper
Pinch paprika
1 tablespoon canola oil

In a large bowl, mix all ingredients except the canola oil thoroughly. Shape a trial patty about the size of a quarter. Heat a large nonstick skillet and add 1 tablespoon canola oil. Cook the small piece and taste for flavor. Adjust seasonings if desired. Shape the remaining ingredients into four or six patties.

In the same skillet, over medium high heat, cook the patties about 5 minutes per side. Check each patty with an instant thermometer for 170° F. Do not eat rare or medium rare turkey burgers.

Serve on buns or rolled up in lettuce leaves.

FABER'S HAMBURGER & FRIES OF THE CENTURY

At times, the simplest dishes are not the easiest to prepare. How many of us have had dry and/or tasteless burgers? There is nothing like a thick burger with an abundance of flavor and juice running all over the place. To make such a burger takes just a little more effort--but it's worth it. Plus, you won't have to spend twenty bucks in one of those fancy burger joints. I strongly suggest that you grind the meat yourself. The difference in flavor and texture is remarkable--plus, you can control the quality of the meat and the percentage of fat. Who knows what goes into those supermarket packages of hamburger?

If you insist on pre-ground meat, I suggest a butcher shop where you can purchase the ground beef that is not packaged.

FOR THE GROUND MEAT

1 pound chuck roast

1 pound top sirloin steak

½ pound sweet Italian sausage

FOR THE BURGERS

1 teaspoon soy sauce

1 teaspoon Worcestershire sauce

1 egg, beaten

1 small onion, chopped

2 cloves garlic, minced

1 teaspoon Italian parsley, chopped

½ teaspoon each dried thyme, basil, oregano

½ teaspoon each granulated onion & garlic

Kosher salt & freshly ground black pepper

4 tablespoons butter, melted and cooled

Cut the chuck roast and top sirloin into 1-inch cubes. Freeze cubes for about 15 minutes before grinding. Grind meat either in an attachment to a KitchenAid mixer or in a food processor. If using a food processor, grind the meat in four batches by placing the meat in the processor and pulsing each batch about eleven times. Do not over process. If you are unable to grind the meat yourself, purchase whole steaks or roasts and ask the butcher to grind it for you.

In a large bowl, mix all of the ingredients with your hands until thoroughly incorporated. Before forming patties, tear off a small chunk and fry it in a small skillet. Taste the chunk and reseason, if necessary.

Heat your grill or skillet until it is very hot. Brush a light layer of canola oil on heating surface. My choice is to use a flat griddle atop of my gas BBQ grill.

To form patties, divide the mixture into six equal portions (or eight or four if you prefer). I prefer a 6 ounce patty. Gently form round patties. Do not press the meat too tightly together! Lay the patties on a flat surface. I like to flatten the patties by covering them with wax paper and using a rolling pin to achieve desired thickness. With your thumb, make an indentation in the center of each patty--about halfway deep into the patty. This will prevent the center from rising up while cooking.

Place the patties on the hot grill. DO NOT PRESS DOWN WITH YOUR SPATULA! Doing so will release the juice--and you want a juicy burger. Grill for about 5 minutes per side or until desired doneness. For cheeseburgers, add a slice of your favorite cheese on the burger, cover and cook for the last 1 minute or until melted.

OVEN FRIED POTATOES

What would a hamburger be without fries? But very few homes have a deep fryer. Frying in a skillet is messy. Oven fried potatoes are a great alternative. Plus (if you leave out the melted butter), my version is considerably healthier. But why leave out the melted butter? These potatoes never cease to produce vociferous "wows" from my guests.

5 large Yukon Gold or 5 medium baking potatoes

5 shallots, unpeeled, cut into quarters

5 cloves garlic, crushed

4 sprigs fresh rosemary

5 tablespoons extra virgin olive oil

3 tablespoons melted butter (optional)

1 tablespoon fresh or dried thyme

2 teaspoons paprika

Kosher salt and freshly ground black pepper

Preheat oven to 425°F. Place a large metal roasting pan or baking sheet on bottom rack in the oven.

Cut the potatoes in half, then quarters, then cut each quarter in half. Place the potatoes, shallots, garlic and rosemary in a large bowl. Sprinkle with olive oil and butter, if using. With your hands, mix well until all of the potatoes are well covered. Season with thyme, paprika, salt and pepper and mix well.

Remove the baking sheet or pan from the oven. Spread the potatoes in one even layer. Roast for about 45 minutes to 1 hour. Turn every 20 minutes. These potatoes are best if cooked until the outsides are quite brown and very crispy.

CHICKEN BURGERS

Another tasty and healthy alternative to beef burgers.

---

1 pound ground white meat chicken (or a combination of white and dark meat)

1 to 1½ cups fresh breadcrumbs, coarsely ground

¼ cup milk

¼ cup chopped onion

⅛ teaspoon cayenne pepper

¼ teaspoon granulated garlic

¼ teaspoon dried thyme

¼ teaspoon ground sage

¾ teaspoon kosher salt

Freshly ground black pepper

1 cup panko

1 teaspoon canola oil

Best to make your own ground chicken and breadcrumbs. I prefer half white and half dark meat. For breadcrumbs, use stale white bread and coarsely chop in a food processor. You can also use panko.

Place milk and breadcrumbs in a mixing bowl. Mix together to form a paste. Place chicken in a mixing bowl. Add the seasonings. Mix all ingredients with your hands. Mixture will be wet. Shape into 4-6 patties. If difficult to shape, add more breadcrumbs. Place patties in refrigerator for at least 1 hour — they will be easier to handle.

Place panko in a flat bottom bowl. Coat both sides of each patty with panko.

In a large nonstick skillet, heat oil over medium heat. Cook patties until golden brown on each side and thoroughly cooked through. For extra precaution, insert an instant thermometer in a patty — it should register 170°F. Serve on buns or wrapped in lettuce leaves.

ARMENIAN SHISH KEBAB & PILAF

KEBABS

½ cup olive oil

2 tablespoons fresh lemon juice

1 teaspoon dry white wine

¼ cup tomato paste

1 tablespoon Dijon mustard

1 tablespoon minced garlic

⅛ teaspoon salt

⅛ teaspoon black pepper

1 teaspoon oregano

1 teaspoon rosemary leaves

1 teaspoon dried sage

1 bay leaf

2 pounds boneless leg of lamb or lamb shoulder, cut into 1 ½″ cubes

1 green and 1 red bell pepper, cut into 1″ wedges each

2 large tomatoes, cut into 8 wedges

2 large onions, peeled, cut into 1″ wedges each

12 medium mushrooms, stems removed

PILAF

1 cup long grain rice

2 ounces vermicelli or orzo

3 tablespoons butter

3 cups chicken stock

1 teaspoon oregano

½ teaspoon salt

¼ teaspoon black pepper

KEBABS: Preheat grill to 425°F. Stir together olive oil, lemon juice, wine, tomato paste, mustard and garlic. Season with salt, pepper, oregano, rosemary, sage and bay leaf. Toss lamb with marinade until evenly combined, then pour into a resealable plastic bag, and marinate in refrigerator at least 8 hours, or up to 24 hours.

Remove lamb from marinade. Coat vegetables with reserved marinade. Thread lamb on skewers and alternate with peppers, tomato wedges, onions and mushrooms onto separate metal skewers. Brush vegetables with reserved marinade.

Lightly brush the grill, or griddle, with olive oil. Cook the skewers on a griddle, turning frequently. Occasionally, baste with reserved marinade. The kebabs should be fully cooked in 10-12 minutes.

PILAF: If using vermicelli, break into 1-inch pieces. Place butter in medium heavy saucepan over medium heat. When butter is melted, add pasta. Stir constantly until pasta is golden. Butter will foam. If butter is getting too brown, lower heat. Add rice and stir to coat. Add chicken stock, oregano, salt and pepper. Increase heat to high and bring stock to a boil. Cover the pan with a tightly fitting lid and reduce heat to lowest setting.

Simmer for 20 minutes without peeking. After 20 minutes, taste and reseason. Stir rice and allow to sit another 10-15 minutes until liquid is absorbed.

FABE'S BEEF KEBABS

If you love steak, you will love a steak on a stick.

MARINADE
- ¼ cup olive oil
- ¼ cup soy sauce
- 1 ½ teaspoons red wine vinegar
- 1 tablespoon Worcestershire sauce
- 2 teaspoons Dijon mustard
- 1 tablespoon brown sugar
- 1 tablespoon minced garlic
- 1 teaspoon onion powder

KEBABS
- 1 ½ pounds New York steak
- ½ red bell pepper
- ½ green bell pepper
- ½ red onion
- ½ pound brown mushrooms
- 2 Roma tomatoes

MARINADE: Combine all marinade ingredients in a resealable plastic bag. Cut steaks into ¾-inch squares. Add the squares to the marinade. Mix well to coat all pieces of steak. Place in refrigerator for 3-6 hours.

KEBABS: Use 12-inch skewers. If using wooded skewers, soak in water for 30 minutes. Cut bell peppers and red onion into 1x1-inch pieces. Remove stems from mushrooms. Cut tomatoes into quarters.

Preheat grill to 375°F. I prefer to use a cast iron griddle on the grill. It saves much of the cleanup.

Place the veggies in a small bowl. Drizzle with 2 tablespoons olive oil. Add kosher salt and pepper and mix to coat all veggies.

Remove the steak from the bag. Reserve marinade in a small bowl. Thread the meat and veggies on the skewers, beginning with a piece of steak, then add one of each veggie and so on. The amount of steak and veggies listed should fill six skewers.

Baste each kebab with reserved marinade. Place each kebab on the grill. Cook for about 4 minutes on both sides for medium rare. Place on dinner plates and brush each kebab with reserved marinade.

BBQ CHICKEN KEBABS

A delicious way to enjoy chicken and veggies in one dish.

RUB

2 teaspoons brown sugar

1 ½ teaspoons smoked paprika

1½ teaspoons kosher salt

1 teaspoon chili powder

1 teaspoon dried minced onion flakes

1 teaspoon granulated garlic

½ teaspoon dried thyme

¼ teaspoon black pepper

CHICKEN KEBABS

3 pounds boneless, skinless chicken breasts or thighs, cut into 1" chunks

8-12 slices thick bacon, cut into 3 shorter pieces

2 tablespoons olive oil

1 green bell pepper, cut into ½" pieces

1 red pepper, cut into ½" pieces

1 red onion, peeled and cut into 1" pieces

1 pint cherry tomatoes

½ fresh pineapple, cut into 1" squares (optional)

½ cup Fabe's BBQ sauce (see recipe on p. 114)

If using metal skewers, no prep is needed. If using wooden skewers, soak them in water for at least 30 minutes.

Combine spice rub ingredients in a small bowl. Set aside.

Add chicken pieces, bacon and oil in a mixing bowl and toss with about ⅔ of the rub.

To another mixing bowl, add bell peppers and onion. Add 1 tablespoon olive oil and coat all pieces. Toss with remaining rub.

Wrap bacon pieces around the chicken pieces. Thread bacon wrapped chicken, peppers, onion, tomatoes and pineapple (if using) onto kebab skewers. Make sure that the skewers pierce the bacon strips.

Lightly oil grill grates and preheat to medium high heat. Grill kebabs 8-11 minutes, turning every few minutes, until cooked through and lightly charred on all sides. Baste with BBQ sauce on both sides and cook an additional minute on each side to caramelize. Makes 8 kebabs.

SWORDFISH KEBABS

Folks are always searching for new ways to prepare fish. These kebabs present a refreshing change from beef, chicken or lamb. No worries about how to cook the fish. When the veggies are tender, the fish will be just right.

2 tablespoons chopped fresh rosemary

3 tablespoons low sodium soy sauce

1 ½ tablespoons extra virgin olive oil

1 tablespoon grated lemon zest

2 tablespoons fresh lemon juice

2 teaspoons grated orange zest

1 tablespoon fresh orange juice

1 teaspoon grated peeled fresh ginger

2 teaspoons honey

½ teaspoon salt

¼ teaspoon freshly ground black pepper

5 garlic cloves, chopped

1½ pounds swordfish steaks, cut into 1" pieces

¾ cup red onion, cut into 1" pieces

1 (8 ounce) package cherry tomatoes

1 bell pepper, cut into 1" squares

Combine first twelve ingredients in a large resealable plastic bag; add fish. Seal and marinate in refrigerator 30 minutes, turning once.

Remove fish from bag. Place marinade in a small bowl. Thread fish, red onions, tomatoes and bell pepper alternately onto four (10 inch) skewers. Place on grill rack coated with cooking spray; grill 8 minutes or until desired degree of doneness, turning once. Baste occasionally with marinade.

You can use any firm white fish, such as halibut, sea bass, or cod.

Thought for Life

Why should you brood over
whether your glass is half empty or half full?
You should rejoice!
Your glass is not empty!

ONE POT STUFFED ROAST CHICKEN & POTATOES

During the summer, fresh turkeys are hard to find. So, why not stuff a chicken and have a quasi-Thanksgiving dinner in July?

STUFFING

2 cups old white or sourdough bread, cut into ¾" squares

2 tablespoons butter, softened

1 brown onion, finely chopped

1 celery rib, finely chopped

4 cloves minced garlic

Salt, pepper, thyme, sage

½ cup chicken stock

4 tablespoons Italian parsley, chopped

CHICKEN & POTATOES

4 tablespoons butter, softened

4-5 white or fingerling potatoes, quartered

Salt, pepper, thyme, sage

1 (4 to 5 pound) whole chicken

PREPARE THE STUFFING: Preheat oven to 450°F. Place bread squares on baking sheet in one layer. Place in the oven for 5 minutes until hard, but not browned. Set aside.

Place a 12 to 14-inch ovenproof skillet or Dutch oven over medium heat. Melt 2 tablespoons of butter. Add onion and celery. Stir and cook until onion is translucent, but not brown. Add garlic and stir for 30 seconds. Add bread and mix well with vegetables. Season bread mixture with salt, pepper, thyme and sage. Add about ½ cup chicken stock and mix well until stuffing is just moist. Add parsley and mix well. Taste for seasoning and adjust. Place stuffing in a bowl and set aside. Don't allow the stuffing to become too moist. Cooking in the cavity will add more moisture.

PREPARE THE POTATOES: Next, using the same skillet or Dutch oven, add 2 tablespoons of softened butter. Then add the potatoes to the skillet. Mix until the potatoes are well coated with butter. Season with salt, pepper, thyme and sage. Cook for about 2 minutes, then remove from heat. Push the potatoes to the perimeter of the skillet and leave a space in the middle for the chicken.

ROAST THE CHICKEN: Stuff the cavity of the chicken with the prepared stuffing. **IMPORTANT:** Do not stuff until you are ready to place the chicken in the oven. Hot stuffing and cold chicken should not hang around, as it can result in possible foodborne illness. Tie the drumsticks together. Rub the entire surface of the chicken with the remaining 2 tablespoons of softened butter, then season with salt, pepper, thyme and sage.

Place the chicken in the center of the skillet or Dutch oven. Roast in preheated oven for about 1½ to 1¾ hours, depending on the size of the chicken. Rotate the pan halfway through. Using an instant thermometer, check that the thigh and breast register 170°F and the stuffing registers 165°F. **NOTE:** A stuffed chicken takes about 20 minutes longer to cook than an unstuffed chicken.

When chicken registers at the appropriate temperature, remove from oven and let it rest for 15 minutes. Remove the string and place stuffing in a serving dish. Carve and serve.

FABE'S SUCCULENT, LUSCIOUS BRAISED LAMB SHANKS WITH WHITE BEANS

Lamb shanks are fall-off-the-bone tender and extremely flavorful. Ask the butcher for the plumpest lamb shanks in the shop. Usually, one is enough for each serving. Very few restaurants serve this marvelous dish, so I love to make them at home. They are a real treat.

WHITE BEANS

1½ cups dried great northern or cannellini beans

4 strips bacon

1 medium onion, chopped

1 carrot, chopped

1 celery rib, chopped

3 cloves garlic, chopped

2 cups chicken stock

Salt and pepper

Thyme

Oregano

LAMB SHANKS

4 meaty lamb shanks (approx. 1 pound each)

Kosher salt & pepper

1 teaspoon dried oregano, plus more for sprinkling

2 tablespoons olive oil

1 medium onion, chopped

1 medium carrot, chopped

1 celery rib, chopped

8 cloves garlic, chopped

2 flat anchovies, chopped

½ bottle dry red wine

2 cups chicken stock

2 tablespoons tomato paste

1 (16 ounce) can chopped tomatoes

2 fresh thyme sprigs

1 bay leaf

4 fresh rosemary leaves

2 tablespoons lemon zest

¼ cup Italian parsley, chopped

FOR THE BEANS: Soak the beans the night before. The next day, place the beans in a stockpot and add enough water so that the level is three inches above the beans. Bring to a boil and cook until almost tender. Do not add salt.

Cook bacon in a heavy bottomed saucepan over medium high heat until just browned. Add onion, carrot, celery and garlic — stirring 4 to 5 minutes or until softened — do not brown. Add beans, bay leaf, and 1 cup stock over medium heat. Stir occasionally and add enough remaining stock to keep beans moist, rich and creamy, but not mushy, for about 30 minutes. Season with pepper, thyme & oregano. Add salt just before serving. (Adding salt to beans while cooking toughens the beans.) Keep warm.

FOR THE LAMB: Pat lamb shanks dry and season with salt, pepper & oregano. In an 8-quart heavy bottomed Dutch oven, heat olive oil over moderately high heat. In batches, brown shanks on all sides. Remove and set aside.

Place onions, carrots, celery, garlic and anchovies in the Dutch oven; season with salt and pepper and sauté until softened. Add wine and simmer until reduced to about 2 cups. Add the stock, tomato paste, tomatoes, thyme, oregano, bay leaf and shanks. Bring to a boil, reduce heat and simmer, covered, turning lamb shanks occasionally for 1½ hours. Add rosemary and simmer mixture 1 hour more, uncovered or until lamb is very tender and falling off the bone. Cook uncovered to reduce and thicken the sauce, about 10 minutes.

ASSEMBLY: When the lamb shanks are very tender, add the beans to the Dutch oven. Cook for several minutes until the flavors of the lamb and the beans meld. Mix the lemon zest and parsley together. Mix into lamb and beans. Serve immediately. **NOTE**: If you desire, the beans can be served separately and not mixed with the lamb sauce.

STU'S BEEF STEW & DUMPLINGS

From grade school on, kids would come up to me and say: "Stu, make me some stew." I was always annoyed by the joke, but teasing could have been worse.

I thought of hiring a lawyer to sue the kids for harassment, but then one day it occurred to me — I think I will make some stew and incorporate the recipe in my upcoming cookbook. That will show 'em. And if I encounter any of those kids today, I won't let them have any of my fabulous stew. That will really show 'em. So once again, great food prevails over lawyers. If you're not in the mood to make the dumplings, don't worry. This dish will be fabulous with or without them.

STEW
2 pounds chuck roast, cut up
2-4 tablespoons olive oil
1 teaspoon kosher salt, divided
1 teaspoon freshly ground black pepper, divided
1 teaspoon of thyme, divided
1 large onion, chopped
2 celery ribs, chopped
1 green bell pepper, chopped
1 bay leaf
3 strips bacon, chopped
5 cloves garlic, chopped
½ cup dry red wine
3 cups water or beef stock
1 tablespoon Worcestershire sauce
Red pepper flakes and nutmeg
2 medium potatoes, quartered
2 carrots, cut into 1″ chunks
½ pound green beans, cut into 3″ pieces
¼ pound mushrooms, sliced
½ cup frozen peas
2 tablespoons Italian parsley, chopped

DUMPLINGS
1 cup flour
½ teaspoon salt
2 teaspoons baking powder
3 tablespoons butter, softened
2 tablespoons Italian parsley, chopped
½ cup whole milk

STEW: Chop beef into 1-inch square chunks. If you have bones left, save and throw into the pot while stew is cooking. This will add flavor. In a large Dutch oven over high heat, drizzle 2 tablespoons of olive oil. Heat for 1 minute, and then add chunks of beef in 2 batches. To each batch, sprinkle ½ teaspoon each kosher salt, freshly ground black pepper and dried thyme. Brown on all sides until slightly caramelized. This will require about 10 minutes per batch. Remove beef and set aside.

Add onion, celery, bell pepper, bay leaf and bacon. Mix together about ½ teaspoon each of kosher salt, freshly ground black pepper and dried thyme. Sprinkle over vegetables. Add 1 more tablespoon of olive oil if necessary. Stir until vegetables become soft and slightly browned — beige is nice — about 5 minutes. Add garlic and stir for 30 seconds more. Add red wine and, using a wooden spatula with a flat end, scrape burned bits from bottom of Dutch oven. This is the fond which will yield great flavor.

Return meat to Dutch oven. Add water or stock and bring to a boil. Add Worcestershire sauce, a pinch of red pepper flakes and a half pinch nutmeg. Reduce heat to medium low, cover and simmer until meat is so tender that you can cut it with a spoon. This will require about 2 hours. Taste and reseason occasionally.

When it appears that the meat is just about spoon tender, add potatoes, carrots, green beans and mushrooms. Bring back to a simmer and cover. They should be tender in 15 minutes.

DUMPLINGS: While stew is cooking, gather ingredients for dumplings. Form the dumplings about ½ hour before you add the vegetables to the stew. To make the dumplings, mix flour, salt and baking powder in a medium bowl. Cut butter into chunks and add to flour mixture. With a pastry cutter or 2 forks, chop butter into flour until mixture resembles coarse crumbs. Add the chopped parsley. Finish mixing the butter-flour mixture with your hands. Add milk and mix with a spatula just until combined. Do not over-mix. Mixture will be moist and sticky.

With your hands, take a small handful of batter, enough to roll into a ball about the size of a golf ball. Form each ball but not too tightly. You should have about eight balls. Place on a plate and set aside.

FINISH THE STEW: Place 2 tablespoons of butter and 2 tablespoons of flour in a small saucepan. You are about to make a roux which will thicken and enrich the stew liquid and provide it with a silky finish. Over low heat, with a flat wooden or heatproof spatula, stir butter and flour until it comes together and forms a paste. In the south, folks are admonished never to leave the roux — it will burn without notice. Stir gently until all lumps of flour have disappeared and the roux has turned to a light tan color. Remove from heat and set aside.

Check meat and vegetables for tenderness. Remove bone and bay leaf. If meat and veggies are tender, slowly add the roux. Make sure the liquid is bubbling or the roux won't mix well. Stir and watch the liquid thicken. When it reaches the consistency of heavy cream, stop adding roux.

Place the dumplings on top of the stew. Do not immerse them in the liquid. Cover and simmer for about 15 minutes or until a toothpick inserted in the center of a dumpling comes out clean. Remove the dumplings and set aside on a plate. Add the peas and parsley to the stew, stir and cook for one minute. Adjust seasons if necessary. Serve the stew in bowls and place two dumplings over each portion.

---------- **Thought for Life** ----------

*Arrogance is a facade
exhibited by those
bereft of self-esteem
and have accomplished nothing
worthy of arrogance.*

*Those who enjoy
genuine high self-esteem,
and have soared
to great achievements,
exhibit expressions
of true humbleness,
and never regard
arrogance as worthy
...or necessary.*

SHORT RIBS BRAISED IN WINE

I used to throw monthly dinner parties "for the guys." There is nothing like a bunch of rowdy guys acting like kids. Cheryl would make plans with her friends because she claimed that when we got together, we were obnoxious. We were. Short ribs were always in demand for those dinners.

6 bone-in short ribs

Kosher salt and freshly ground black pepper

1 tablespoon oregano

4 tablespoons of olive oil

2 bay leaves

1 large brown onion, chopped

1 green bell pepper, chopped

2 celery ribs, chopped

2 carrots, chopped

3 cloves garlic

2 (6 ounce) cans tomato paste

3 cups red wine

2 cups beef stock

2 bunches fresh thyme or 1 tablespoon dried thyme

1 teaspoon sugar

1 teaspoon lemon zest

2 tablespoons of butter

¼ cup Italian parsley, chopped

Preheat oven to 375° F. Season short ribs with kosher salt, freshly ground black pepper and oregano. In a large, heavy Dutch oven, add 2 tablespoons olive oil and increase heat to high. When the oil begins to simmer, add the short ribs. Brown on all sides, about 3 minutes per side. There should be a dark brown crust on each side.

If using fresh thyme, tie bay leaves and thyme with a string into a bouquet garni.

Place onion, bell pepper, celery, carrots and garlic in a food processor. Process the veggies until they are all combined and form into a paste. Remove the browned ribs from the Dutch oven and set aside. Remove excess fat and add 2 more tablespoons olive oil.

Add the veggies to the Dutch oven. Lightly season with kosher salt, pepper and oregano. With a spatula, spread the seasoned veggies over the bottom of the pot and sear until they begin to brown, about 7 minutes. Scrape the veggies together and redistribute over the bottom of the Dutch oven and sear for an additional 3 to 4 minutes. Add tomato paste and spread over the bottom of the Dutch oven. Brown the tomato paste for about 5 minutes. Add the wine and scrape all of the brown bits from the bottom of the pot. Mix the brown bits with the other ingredients in the pot. Lower the heat to medium and reduce the mixture for 5 minutes.

Place the short ribs back into the Dutch oven in a single layer. Add the beef stock. Add the fresh thyme if using, together with the bundle. If using dried thyme, add the bay leaves and the dried thyme. Add the oregano, sugar and lemon zest. Cover the Dutch oven and place in the preheated oven. Cook until the ribs are very tender, 3 to 3½ hours. Check ribs every half hour. Add more liquid if necessary. Turn ribs over every half hour. When ribs are tender, remove cover and cook for about 20 minutes more to reduce sauce and to impart a gorgeous mahogany coat on the ribs.

Place the Dutch oven on the stovetop over a medium-low heat. Add 2 tablespoons of butter. Add parsley and mix in. Check for seasoning. Remove bouquet garni and serve. Pour sauce over ribs.

I also add a few lamb shanks for variety — plus they impart and extra level of flavor and we would get two meals for the price of one. Short ribs are great served with mashed potatoes with the sauce drizzled over the potatoes.

THE FABE'S POT ROAST OR BEEF STEW WITH BARLEY

In a way, this stew is related to beef and barley soup. Here's a secret: if you are in the mood for soup, just add some water or beef stock and you will have created a hearty soup.

½ cup flour

2 tablespoons paprika

1 tablespoon lemon zest

1 teaspoon dried thyme

1 teaspoon black pepper

1 (4 to 5 pound) chuck roast

Kosher salt

3 tablespoons olive oil

2 onions, chopped

4 carrots, chopped in 1" chunks

½ cup celery, chopped

1 green or red bell pepper, chopped

4 minced anchovy filets

4 cloves garlic, chopped

1 cup dry red wine

2 cups chicken stock

1 (28 ounce) can chopped tomatoes

1 (6 ounce) can tomato paste

1 tablespoon each mustard, ketchup

2 tablespoons Worcestershire sauce

¼ cup Italian parsley, chopped

1 bay leaf

6 Yukon Gold potatoes, quartered (optional)

1 cup barley (optional)

½ pound mushrooms, whole

1 cup frozen peas

Mix flour, paprika, zest, thyme & pepper. If you want beef stew, cut chuck roast into 1½-inch cubes. Season meat with salt, dredge in flour mixture. Shake off excess flour. In a Dutch oven, sauté meat chunks or roast in 2 tablespoons of olive oil until brown on all sides, about 8 minutes.

Transfer meat chunks or roast to platter. Add one more tablespoon of olive oil, then add the onions, celery, carrots, anchovy, bell pepper, and sauté until soft, about five minutes. Add garlic. Add wine and reduce until almost dissolved. Add stock, tomatoes, paste, mustard, ketchup, Worcestershire sauce, parsley and bay leaf. Bring to a boil.

This recipe may be cooked on the stovetop or in the oven. It seems to taste better when cooked in the oven.

OVEN METHOD: Preheat oven to 350° F. Return the meat to the pot. Cover the pot and place in oven and cook for 1½ to 3 hours or until meat is almost tender. Follow instructions below for adding barley, and/or potatoes, carrots and mushrooms.

STOVETOP METHOD: Return meat to pot, cover and reduce to a simmer. Cover the pot and. simmer about 1½ to 3 hours until meat is tender. Stew will take less time than a roast. You should be able to cut the meat with a spoon.

About 45 minutes before meat is done, add 1 cup of barley and potatoes, if desired. Add carrot chunks and mushrooms. You can use both barley and potatoes. Stir until barley and/or potatoes, mushrooms and carrots are immersed in broth. Do not overcook barley or potatoes. The barley should be al dente. For extra color and nutrition, add 1 cup of frozen peas to the stew during the final minutes. If meat is not done, remove barley with slotted spoon. Taste for seasoning.

STU'S SCRUMPTIOUS PORK CHOPS IN A WINE-MUSTARD SAUCE

I love pork chops. Too often, they are dry and tasteless. This recipe delivers some of the most juicy and flavorful pork chops you will ever consume.

COATING

4 pork loin chops (bone-in, 1-inch thick)

½ teaspoon chopped fresh rosemary

½ teaspoon dry mustard

½ teaspoon kosher salt

½ teaspoon granulated onions

½ teaspoon granulated garlic

½ teaspoon thyme

½ teaspoon freshly ground black pepper

2 tablespoons olive oil

PAN SAUCE

1 cup thinly sliced onions

½ cup dry white wine

1 tablespoon Dijon mustard

½ teaspoon fresh rosemary, chopped

½ teaspoon thyme

Kosher salt and freshly ground pepper

1 teaspoon capers

3 tablespoons flour

3 tablespoons butter

2 cups chicken stock

¼ cup heavy cream or milk

3 tablespoons Italian parsley, chopped

Thin loin chops are the best. Mix the coating and rub into the chops. In a large, heavy skillet, heat 1 tablespoon of the oil over high heat. When oil is hot, (not too hot) add the chops. They should hiss, not sputter explosively. Sear the chops on one side for 1 or 2 minutes until a beautiful brown coat appears. Adjust heat if necessary. Turn chops over and sear for 1 minute more. Reduce heat, but not to the extent that there are no more sizzling sounds.

Cover the pan and cook for an additional 3 or 4 minutes, depending on thickness of chops. The chops are done when firm but not hard when pressed with a finger. Best to test with a thermometer-they should register 145°F to 150°F. They are most juicy if removed at 145°F and allowed to rest covered until they reach 150°F.

To make the sauce, remove chops from the pan and cover with foil. Remove all but 1 tablespoon of grease from the pan, then add remaining tablespoon of olive oil. Sauté the onions for 5 minutes, then stir in the wine, Dijon mustard, herbs, salt and pepper. Scrape any brown bits from bottom of the pan and incorporate. Boil the sauce for several minutes until it turns syrupy. Add capers.

While wine mixture is cooking, place 3 tablespoons of flour and 3 tablespoons of soft butter in a heavy small saucepan. Over a low flame, mix the flour and butter until smooth. Keep mixing until a light blonde color. Do not walk away from the roux.

Add the chicken stock and bring to a boil. Add as much of the roux as you desire, stirring constantly, until the gravy reaches the desired thickness. It will not thicken unless mixture is boiling. Reduce heat to low, then add heavy cream. It will then thicken a little more. Add two more tablespoons butter.

Return the pork chops to the pan. Sprinkle with chopped parsley.

---- **Thought for Life** ----

*The Declaration of Independence
tells us
that we are endowed
with the right
to engage in the pursuit of happiness.
The challenge
is to pursue happiness
without making others unhappy.*

SKILLET SEARED RIB EYE STEAK

Years ago, I interviewed the owner of one of Chicago's leading and oldest steakhouses. We discussed what it takes to make a great steak. "The secret is in my seasoning," he said whimsically. He handed me a salt shaker. "Take a closer look," he said. I took a closer look. The salt shaker was empty.

"That's my secret seasoning," he laughed. "If you use top grade beef and cook it correctly, the steak speaks for itself. No seasoning or gooey sauces are required."

He was absolutely correct. If you are going to spend precious funds on a steak, don't waste your money with anything less that USDA Prime or a genuine Angus USDA choice. Then, sear the steak on an extremely hot grill or, my preference, a super-hot cast iron skillet. I do use some kosher salt and freshly ground black pepper — but it's just as good without them. Rib eye is my favorite. It has more marbling which means more flavor and a large bone which means more juicy. I often purchase a standing rib roast and have the butcher cut a few rib eye steaks from the roast.

1 rib eye steak, 1½ to 2 inches thick

4-6 tablespoons butter, melted

Kosher salt and freshly ground black pepper

Some chefs like to salt a steak well in advance of cooking, even up to 24 hours in advance. The main drawback of seasoning in advance is that salt applied to the outside of something tends to pull water from the center of it onto the surface. I prefer to add salt and pepper as I am cooking the steak.

To bring steak to room temperature, take the steak out of refrigerator about one hour before preparing.

Place a 12-inch cast iron skillet or griddle on the stove burners or on the grill. Light the fire under the skillet 30 minutes prior to cooking the steak. The skillet must be almost white-hot.

With paper towels or a clean kitchen towel, rub steak dry on both sides. Brush the melted butter on all sides and edges of the steak. If I cook the steak in the kitchen, I deactivate the smoke alarms. Place the steak in the skillet. Generously season the side facing up with salt and pepper. Cook for about 3 minutes. Don't move the steak around until it will move with just a light nudge. Flip steak over — the cooked side should already be charred. Cook for 3 minutes on the other side. Brush melted butter on the side just cooked, then season with salt and pepper. With a pair of tongs, pick up the steak and press the edges in the skillet to brown them. Flip the steak again and brush more butter on the top just cooked.

Continue turning, flipping and basting with butter until cooked to desired degree of doneness. (For rare, an instant thermometer should read 125°F, for medium rare, 135°F, medium, 140°F. medium well, 145°F.)

Remove steak and place on cutting board. Brush with more melted butter. Allow steak to rest for 15 minutes before serving.

STU'S GRILLED LAMB CHOPS

I love the lamb loin chops. You can also use lamb shoulder chops which have a slightly different flavor and texture.

1 tablespoon oregano

1 tablespoon fresh rosemary

1 teaspoon cumin

1 tablespoon thyme

1 tablespoon sage

1 teaspoon paprika

Pinch cayenne

4 cloves garlic

Kosher salt and freshly ground black pepper

2 tablespoons olive oil

½ cup dry red wine

1 tablespoon Worcestershire sauce

¼ cup soy sauce

4 tablespoons Dijon mustard

6 lamb loin chops, ¾" thick

Juice of 1 lime

Combine oregano, rosemary, cumin, thyme, sage, paprika, cayenne, garlic cloves, 1 teaspoon salt, 1 teaspoon pepper. Place in food processor. Add olive oil and pulse until paste forms.

Combine wine, Worcestershire sauce, soy sauce in a 13x9-inch baking pan. Coat chops well on both sides. Rub both sides of chops with half of the paste. Place in baking pan and marinate in the refrigerator for 1 hour. About 30 minutes before cooking, remove pan from refrigerator, place chops on a plate and allow chops to come to room temperature. Rub chops with mustard and remaining paste. Heat grill. If using a griddle (recommended), place griddle on grill. Lightly oil griddle with olive oil before placing on grill. I prefer a cast iron griddle.

Place chops on griddle. Sprinkle with lime juice. Reseason with salt and pepper. Depending on thickness, grill 4-6 minutes on one side, then turn over and grill about 4-6 minutes on the other side, or until medium rare, about 145°F.

ROASTED BEEF TENDERLOIN
aka CHATEAUBRIAND, aka FILET MIGNON

Perhaps the most expensive steak in the butcher shop is the filet mignon. Filet in French means "thick slice" and mignon means "dainty." Perhaps it acquired its name from the fact that it is the tenderest of beef steaks. Many steakhouse owners I've interviewed claim that a large percent of folks who order this cut are women. This cut of beef comes from the short loin, the small end of the tenderloin — thus the name beef tenderloin. If you look at a porterhouse steak, the large muscle on one side of the bone is the New York strip. The smaller, roundish muscle on the other side of the bone is the beef tenderloin, or filet mignon. A chateaubriand is the whole piece of the beef tenderloin. The average weight is seven pounds, so at twenty bucks a pound, one would set you back $140. Some butchers sell a 2 pound USDA prime roast for $300.00. One of our local butchers occasionally has USDA choice roasts for $10 per pound. If you feel overburdened with money, purchase a roast and try this recipe.

PARSLEY BUTTER

4 tablespoons butter, chopped into chunks

1 shallot, finely chopped

1 clove garlic, minced

1 tablespoon Italian parsley, chopped

¼ teaspoon each kosher salt and freshly ground black pepper

FILET

1 ½ to 2 pounds beef tenderloin

2 tablespoons soft butter

If you are cooking ½ pound steaks rather than a 2-7 pound roast, I suggest the traditional method that I use for rib-eye steaks or porterhouse steaks. I sear them and finish them in a cast iron skillet atop the stove. Alternatively, you can sear them atop the stove, then pop them in the oven at 400°F and roast until they reach your desired doneness. For a roast, I suggest the following recipe.

PARSLEY BUTTER: Make the parsley butter. Combine all ingredients in the skillet you are using to roast the steak. Melt slowly. Remove parsley butter from skillet and place in a small bowl. Cool slightly.

FILET: Bring beef to room temperature. Pat dry with paper towels. Smear all sides with butter. Season with kosher salt and black pepper. Pre-heat oven to 350°F. Place beef in a cast iron skillet and pop in oven. Roast for 30-40 minutes until it reaches a temperature (use instant thermometer) of 125°F for rare, 135°F for medium-rare. (For a 1½ pound roast, it takes about 35 minutes to reach 125°F.)

FINISH AND ASSEMBLE: Remove skillet from oven. Place beef on a plate. Wipe skillet with paper towel. Place skillet over high heat on stovetop. Smear all sides of beef with light coat of parsley butter. Return beef to skillet and sear all sides until a browned crust forms. Smear again with parsley butter. Serve immediately.

ALTERNATIVE SALTING: Salt the beef immediately after removing it from the fridge. Allowing the beef to come to room temperature, while lightly salted and covered with plastic wrap, will result in an even more juicy and tender piece of meat.

--- **Culinary Thought** ---

*Chateaubriand
is quite beyond
most any steak
you'll ever make.*

PRIME RIBS OF BEEF

Some folks love prime rib for Thanksgiving. So does my gang. I always make one. This offering delights lovers of beef. Even those folks who "don't eat beef" can't stay away from it.

1 choice or prime short end rib roast, at least 2 or 3 ribs (7 to 10 pound) Note: preferable prime grade or Angus Choice. I usually reqest the short end. It's more flavorful.

2 to 4 cloves of garlic, cut in slivers (about the thickness of toothpicks)

Kosher salt & freshly ground pepper

1 onion, sliced

1 cup dry red wine

2 cups beef stock

1 teaspoon thyme

Remove roast from refrigerator about 1 hour before cooking. Preheat oven to 475°F. With a paring knife or ice pick, drill as many holes in roast as you have garlic slivers. Insert garlic in each hole. The garlic should be spread out over the entire roast. Rub entire surface with freshly milled pepper. Just before placing roast in oven, generously rub salt over entire surface of roast.

Place onion slices over bottom of heavy roasting pan. I prefer a cast iron skillet. Make a circle with onion slices that approximate the size of the roast. After preparing roast, place it fat side up, directly atop a bed of onions. Roast for about 15 minutes. Reduce heat to 375°F. Roast for an additional 45 minutes, then check the internal temperature of the roast with an instant thermometer. For rare, remove roast from oven when thermometer registers 125°F. For medium rare, 130 to 135°F. When roast reaches desired temperature, remove from oven and pan, cover with foil.

Place the roasting pan over a stovetop burner. Increase the heat to high and with a wooden spatula, scrape the bottom of the roasting pan. Add the wine and cook until reduced to about ¼ cup. Add beef stock, mix well and season with salt, pepper and thyme for an exquisite au jus.

YORKSHIRE PUDDING

As the Yorkshire pudding magically rises in the oven, it brings down the roof as the guests stare in awe.

3 eggs
1 cup milk
1 cup flour
½ teaspoon kosher salt

The night before serving, whisk the eggs and milk. Combine flour and salt and mix with the egg-milk mixture until blended. Do not overmix. Refrigerate overnight. Stir from time to time. There will be a few lumps, but this is okay.

Preheat oven to 450°F. Pour a layer of fat drippings from whatever you have roasted, such as a prime rib, into an 11x7-inch ovenproof glass pan, just enough to coat bottom and sides. If you have no fat drippings, place 2 tablespoons of butter in the pan. Heat the pan with the fat or butter in the oven for about 2 minutes. Remove batter from refrigerator and remix. Pour into the pan. The secret to the rise is a cold batter and hot pan, so don't bring batter to room temperature. Batter should fill about one-half of the pan. Bake for about 20 minutes. Serve immediately.

You can also make these as popovers in popover pans.

STU'S BUTTERFLIED LEG OF LAMB

1 (4 pound) butterflied leg of lamb
1 cup dry red wine
¼ cup soy sauce
1 tablespoon Worcestershire sauce
2 tablespoons olive oil
1 tablespoon oregano
1 tablespoon fresh rosemary, ground
1 teaspoon cumin
1 tablespoon thyme
1 tablespoon sage, crushed
1 teaspoon paprika
4 tablespoons Dijon mustard
1 fresh lime
Kosher salt & pepper

Combine wet ingredients except mustard. Pour into a 13x9-inch baking dish. Soak lamb on both sides. Combine dry ingredients except salt and pepper — this is the rub.

After soaking lamb, rub with mustard. Then rub all over with the spice rub. Marinate for at least 4 hours. Bring lamb to room temperature one hour before cooking.

Then, add more rub and more mustard. Rub all over with lime. Season with salt and pepper. Place on high heat grill and brown on both sides. Then, put fat side down and grill for 30-40 minutes until internal temperature reaches 135°F for medium rare. Baste with remaining marinade occasionally. Before removing from grill, add more rub. Drizzle with more lime juice. Let rest for 15 minutes before serving.

This lamb may also be oven roasted. Preheat oven to 425°F. Place lamb in oven-proof baking dish. Roast for 30-40 minutes until lamb reaches 135°F. Baste with marinade occasionally.

CORNED BEEF & CABBAGE

I am not of Irish descent. Nevertheless, each year, I look forward to St. Patrick's Day. I always celebrate the event by preparing a few huge corned beef briskets and inviting over a few friends (none of whom is Irish) to celebrate St. Patty's Day. Just like O'Brien potatoes, the recipe of which is included in this book, corned beef and cabbage did not originate in Ireland. If you requested the dish on St. Patrick's Day in Ireland, they would probably throw you out of the restaurant. I'm told that the recipe was developed by Irish immigrants after they arrived in America. I don't require geographic authenticity to enjoy one of my favorite meals.

1 large corned beef brisket (Purchase either the point or flat end of the brisket. The flat end is not as fatty and has less flavor. I usually get one of each.)

1 onion

2 cloves garlic

2 bay leaves

2 tablespoons peppercorns

6 red potatoes

5 carrots

1 head cabbage, quartered & skewered

2 tablespoons butter

Italian parsley, chopped

Throw away the spices that are packed with the brisket. Place brisket in large stockpot. Cover with water. Cook in covered pot about 1 hour. Remove brisket and change water. It's a good idea to get rid of the water because the first cooking leaves blood and debris. Return brisket to clean water, add onion, garlic, bay leaves and peppercorns. Cook until tender, that is, until it will cut easily with a fork. In general, a brisket takes about 1 hour per pound.

When brisket is done, remove from the pot and set aside. Add potatoes and carrots in the same water. They will take on that beautiful corned beef flavor. Fifteen minutes before serving, add cabbage. Return brisket to pot. Cook covered until cabbage is soft and brisket is reheated. Add butter and chopped Italian parsley to potatoes, carrots and cabbage.

WIENER SCHNITZEL WITH PORK OR VEAL

During my last trip to Berlin, I tried Wiener Schnitzel in several restaurants. I alighted at the Radisson Blu hotel, a high-tech place with a giant floor-to-ceiling aquarium in the lobby. The schnitzel was the best I've ever had. I returned every night and ordered the same dish. After two nights, the waiter brought it to me without bringing a menu. It's difficult to find in the U.S., so I make it myself. Not as good as the Radisson Blu, but I keep trying.

4 boneless pork cutlets (or veal cutlets) each about 4-5 ounces and pounded to ¼" thick

¼ cup all-purpose flour

2 teaspoons coarse salt

1 teaspoon freshly ground pepper

2 large eggs

2 cups fresh breadcrumbs or panko

Canola oil or other neutral tasting oil, for frying

4 tablespoons (½ stick) unsalted butter

2 tablespoons Italian parsley, finely chopped

Lemon wedges, for serving

Purchase cutlets as thin as you can find. To prepare, place each cutlet between two sheets of plastic wrapping. With a meat mallet, or the bottom of a skillet, beat each cutlet until ¼-inch thick.

Preheat oven to 200°F. Place the flour into a shallow dish and whisk to combine with 1 teaspoon salt and the pepper. In another shallow dish, lightly beat eggs. In a third shallow dish, whisk to combine breadcrumbs and remaining teaspoon of salt.

Best method is to dredge with one hand and keep the other hand clean. Dredge one cutlet at a time in the seasoned flour, turning to coat, and shaking off excess. Next dip in the eggs, again making sure to coat completely and to allow the excess to drip back into bowl. Then coat with breadcrumbs, pressing down firmly to help them adhere to the cutlet, but being careful not to coat too thick. Place coated cutlets on piece of parchment paper or a large baking sheet.

Heat ¼-inch of oil in a large skillet over medium heat until it reaches 350°F. Working in batches to avoid crowding the pan, fry cutlets until golden brown on the bottom, 1 to 2 minutes. Flip with a flexible thin spatula and fry until the other side is golden brown and cutlets are cooked through, 1 to 2 minutes more, monitoring temperature of oil to maintain 350°F. Transfer to a baking sheet lined with a double layer of paper towels and keep warm in the oven.

Pour off and discard oil remaining in skillet, then wipe clean with paper towels. Working in batches again if necessary, melt the butter in the same skillet over medium heat until sizzling. Coat pan fried cutlets on one side with the butter, then quickly flip to coat the other side.

Arrange the cutlets on a platter, sprinkle with chopped parsley and serve with lemon wedges.

---— **Thought for Life** ———

*Breaking up is so painful.
To relieve the pain,
rather than revenge
for the perceived harm
they caused you,
offer thanks
for the joy they gave you.
Yes, the pain is excruciating.
The most powerful and effective
extra-strength pain reliever
is dignity.*

STU'S MACARONI & CHEESE

There are many iterations of mac and cheese. Some are no more than some boiled noodles with Velveeta® poured over them. I feel confident that my version will become your favorite.

1 pound elbow macaroni
½ pound bacon
½ cup grated Parmesan
2 cups sharp grated cheddar cheese
1½ cups grated Monterey Jack cheese
6 tablespoons butter
1½ cups fresh breadcrumbs
1 small onion, minced
1 cup mushrooms, chopped
½ green bell pepper, chopped small
½ red bell pepper, chopped small
1 tablespoon + 1 teaspoon flour
¾ teaspoon salt
½ teaspoon pepper
½ teaspoon parika
½ teaspoon dry mustard
3 cups milk
½ cup Italian parsley chopped
1 bunch green onions, chopped

Place macaroni in a pot of boiling water. Cook, according to package instructions, until al dente. Do not overcook. Drain and set aside. Cook bacon until crisp. Let cool, rough chop, and set aside. Wipe skillet clean and set aside. In the meantime, mix together the cheeses in a bowl and set aside. (You can use other cheeses, Mexican combo, Swiss, Gruyere Gouda, etc).

Preheat oven to 375°F. Butter a 13x9-inch casserole dish. In a small saucepan over medium heat, melt 2 tablespoons of butter. Add breadcrumbs and toss to coat. Sauté until lightly browned. Set aside.

In the 12-inch skillet, melt 4 tablespoons of butter. Add chopped onion, mushrooms, green and red bell peppers and cook just until tender. Stir in flour, salt, pepper, paprika and dry mustard until blended. Gradually stir in milk.

Cook and whisk constantly until mixture becomes smooth and thickens slightly. It should be the consistency of heavy cream. Remove from heat and, in handfuls, stir in all except 1 cup of the cheddar, until melted. Wait until each batch melts before adding the next batch of cheese.

Place ⅓ of drained macaroni in casserole. Add ⅓ melted cheese mixture and spread evenly over top of macaroni. Sprinkle ⅓ of the bacon and ⅓ of the breadcrumbs evenly over the cheese mixture. Repeat for two more layers. Top with a layer of melted cheese mixture, bacon, reserved cheese and breadcrumbs.

Bake for 20 minutes or until bubbly and the top is golden. If the top begins to brown too much, reduce temperature to 350°F and loosely cover the casserole dish with foil. Remove from oven. Sprinkle with parsley flakes and chopped green onions and serve.

Chapter 13
Old World & New World Spanish Cooking
Cuisine that is musical, colorful and delicious

STEAK PICADO & SPANISH RICE

This is a sumptuous Mexican dinner, full of flavor and texture. It's also popular in Guatemala, Panama and Cuba. Your entire house will take on the fragrance of a Mexican café.

1 ½ pounds sirloin or rib steak (rib steak is the best)

2 tablespoons vegetable oil

1 large white onion, thinly sliced

3 cloves garlic, chopped

4-5 fresh Roma tomatoes, cut into wedges [or 1 (28 ounce) can of diced tomatoes]

½ green bell pepper & ½ red bell pepper, julienned

1 jalapeño, thinly sliced

1-2 tablespoons chili powder

1 teaspoon cumin

1 teaspoon black pepper

Kosher salt to taste

Up to 2 cups water

¼ cup fresh cilantro, chopped

Cut steaks into 2-inch strips. Heat a large frying pan or cast iron skillet over medium-high heat. Add oil and brown beef on all sides. Remove and set aside.

Add the onions and cook until translucent, about two minutes. Add the garlic, tomatoes, bell peppers, and jalapeño. Mix the dry seasonings together, beginning with 1 tablespoon of chili powder, then adding more if desired.

Return beef to the pan and sprinkle in the seasonings. Add water slowly to barely cover the beef and vegetable mixture. Bring to a boil and then reduce to simmer.

Cover, reduce heat to medium and cook about 40 minutes, stirring frequently. Check that liquid hasn't evaporated. Add more liquid if necessary. Sprinkle with chipped cilantro and serve.

EXTRAORDINARY SPANISH RICE

2 tablespoons olive oil

1 onion, roughly chopped

½ green bell pepper & ½ red bell pepper, roughly chopped

3 cloves garlic, chopped

1 cup uncooked long grain rice

1 (14 ounce) can diced tomatoes with juice

2 cups water

¾ tablespoon chili powder

1 ½ teaspoons kosher salt

¼ teaspoon black pepper

Pinch cayenne pepper

2 tablespoons each green olives and capers

¼ cup fresh cilantro, chopped

In a medium pot or Dutch oven, sweat onion and bell peppers for 3 minutes. Add garlic and sweat for 1 minute. Do not burn. Add rice, move it around with a spatula to coat the grains with oil. Add tomatoes, water and spices.

Bring to a boil, then reduce heat and simmer for about 20-30 minutes until rice is tender and liquid is absorbed. Add more water if necessary. Just prior to absorption of liquid, add capers, olives and cilantro. Mix well.

ARROZ CON POLLO

This is one of those one pot meals that is satisfying and very delicious.

One whole chicken, cut into 8 pieces

2 ½ teaspoons dried oregano, divided

½ teaspoon kosher salt, plus more for sprinkling

Freshly ground black pepper

2 tablespoons olive oil

1 onion, diced

½ red bell pepper & ½ green bell pepper, diced

4 garlic cloves, chopped

½ to 1 teaspoon saffron threads

⅛ teaspoon red pepper flakes

½ cup dry red wine

1 (14 ounce) can diced tomatoes

4 cups water (or 2 cups water & 2 cups chicken stock)

2 cups Spanish bomba rice (or substitute long grain rice)

½ cup pitted green olives, sliced (preferably pimento stuffed)

¾ cup fresh or frozen green peas

½ cup Italian parsley, chopped

1 bunch green onions, chopped

Season the chicken with oregano, salt and black pepper. Rub it in well, cover and refrigerate for at least an hour or up to one day.

Preheat the oven to 350°F.

In a large, deep skillet, Dutch oven, or paella pan, heat the oil over medium-high heat. Cook the chicken pieces in a single layer, in batches if necessary, until they are well browned on all sides.

Transfer browned chicken to a plate. Add more oil to pan if necessary. Then add the onions and bell peppers to the pan, season with salt, pepper and oregano, and cook, stirring frequently, until they start to wilt. Add the garlic, saffron, red pepper flakes and ½ teaspoon of salt. Cook for one minute. Do not let these items brown.

Increase heat to high, add wine and deglaze the pan. With a spatula, scrape the brown bits from the bottom of the pan. When the wine has almost completely reduced, add the tomatoes and water to the pan. Place the chicken in the pan in a single layer, skin side up. Cover the pot tightly and bake in preheated oven for 30 minutes.

Remove the pan from the oven and add the rice. Distribute the rice in areas between the chicken pieces. Press rice down with a wooden spoon until completely covered with liquid. Cover, return to the oven and cook for 20 minutes more. Check occasionally to see if more water should be added.

After 20 minutes, remove the pan from the oven and place on stovetop, over medium heat. Add olives, peas, parsley and green onions. Cover and cook to warm the items. Add more water, if necessary. The rice should be tender and there should be a mere film of water around the rice. Adjust seasonings and serve.

---------- **Thought for Life** ----------

These are universal truths.
Everyone craves love, acceptance and respect.
Everyone craves nourishment, health and strength.
Everyone craves peace, safety and joy.
Then, why is it
that some of us erect barriers
to keep out
that which we crave?

FABE'S FISH TACOS

Folks from all over the U.S.A. travel south of the border to visit fish taco stands. They return with raves about the tacos. Here is my version. You can thank Cheryl for the guacamole recipe.

½ head green cabbage or lettuce

4 tablespoons lime juice (and more for drizzling)

½ cup mayonnaise

½ red onion, chopped

2 tablespoons fresh cilantro, chopped

Pinch kosher salt

Pinch black pepper

Pinch sugar

2 white fish filets, totaling about 1 pound (use cod, red snapper or sea bass) or 1 pound of shrimp, peeled and deveined

½ cup all-purpose flour

1 teaspoon olive oil & 1 tablespoon butter

6 corn tortillas

1 ripe tomato, chopped

Shred the cabbage or lettuce. Drizzle with lime juice. Let rest in refrigerator.

Next, prepare an aioli for the tacos by combining the mayonnaise, lime juice, onion, and cilantro. Sprinkle with salt, pepper and sugar. Let rest in refrigerator.

Season the fish filets with salt and pepper. Dredge in flour and shake off excess. In a heavy skillet, heat oil until hot. Then, add butter until just melted. Place filets in skillet. Cook on both sides, about 2 minutes per side. Cool filets for about 3 minutes, then cut into large chunks or strips. While fish is cooling, heat tortillas in the oven or heat in a dry, heavy pan over high heat until slightly browned.

Mix lettuce or cabbage with aioli sauce.

Assemble tacos with fish, lettuce or cabbage aioli mixture and tomatoes. Add shredded cheese, if desired.

These could also be made with shrimp.

CHERYL'S GUACAMOLE

3 avocados

2 limes, juiced

½ red onion, chopped

¼ cup cilantro, chopped

1 Roma tomato, chopped

½ teaspoon salt

¼ teaspoon cumin

⅛ teaspoon cayenne pepper

1 clove garlic, chopped

½ jalapeño pepper, seeded & chopped

Combine all ingredients in a bowl. Chop and smash avocado and mix all ingredients well.

Thought for Life

*When a person
acts as if they are
an authority on everything,
it's safe to conclude
the person
is an authority
on nothing.*

*Put another way:
A know-it-all
is generally
a know-nothing.*

LET THEM EAT FAJITAS

In January 2012, four East Haven, CT police officers were arrested and charged with abusing their power and allegedly discriminating against Latinos. When asked what he intended to do for the Latino community, Mayor Joseph Maturo responded, "I might have tacos when I go home."

Clearly that was an ethnically insensitive remark. But suppose the alleged police abuse and discrimination had been exerted against the French-American citizens of East Haven — and Maturo had remarked: "I might have cordon bleu when I go home." We could extend this scenario to virtually any ethnic dish: sushi, spaghetti, shrimps in lobster sauce, wiener schnitzel, vichyssoise (some claim the latter originated in the United States) or borscht — the list goes on and on. The important point for any politician to keep in mind is that if, on any day, an ethnic uprising occurs in his or her jurisdiction, he or she should forego supper that night — unless the meal is weenies and beans.

For years, debates have been raging among culinary pundits on the difference between a taco, a burrito and a fajita. Each of these delicacies involves the wrapping of beef, chicken or fish in either a flour or corn tortilla. Indifferent to the accusation that I might use this book as a marketing tool to drum up legal business, I stand intrepid and available to defend any food purveyor should he or she be sued for false advertising by attempting to sell a fajita as a taco — or vice versa.

Hereinbelow are three of my favorite fajita recipes. If you prefer to serve tacos, just call them tacos. A fajita by any name tastes as great. How wonderful it is that so many folks have emigrated to the United States bringing their art, music, language, literature, culture — and their cuisine.

For all of these recipes, heat flour or corn tortillas by wrapping them in foil and placing in a preheated 350°F oven for 10 minutes. Or, in a hot skillet, heat a tortilla on each side until it starts to brown.

FABE'S CHICKEN FAJITAS

- **2 tablespoons lemon juice**
- **2 tablespoons of vegetable oil and more for seasoning**
- **1 ½ teaspoons seasoned salt or kosher salt**
- **1 ½ teaspoons dried oregano**
- **1 ½ teaspoons ground cumin**
- **½ teaspoon chili powder**
- **½ teaspoon paprika**
- **¼ teaspoon red pepper flakes**
- **1 teaspoon granulated garlic**
- **1 ½ pounds boneless skinless chicken breasts**
- **1 each medium red and green bell pepper**
- **1 cup red onion, sliced**
- **More kosher salt & pepper**
- **4 green onions, chopped**
- **2 tablespoons fresh cilantro, chopped**
- **6 corn or flour tortillas**

Combine lemon juice and vegetable oil in a large bowl. Mix together seasonings and mix into the liquid. Cut chicken breasts into small strips. Add chicken strips and mix with the oil-lemon and seasonings until strips are well coated. Place in refrigerator for 1-3 hours. Remix occasionally.

In the meantime, slice red and green bell pepper into julienne pieces. Pour about 2 tablespoons vegetable oil into large heavy skillet. Over medium heat, sauté peppers and red onion until crisp-tender. Sprinkle with kosher salt and freshly ground black pepper. Remove from pan and keep warm.

In the same skillet, cook chicken strips and marinade for 5-6 minutes until cooked through. Do not burn. Return peppers and red onion to pan and add chopped green onions and cilantro. Mix well. Adjust seasonings.

Spoon filling down the center of tortillas. Serve with shredded cheese, chopped tomatoes and/or guacamole.

FABE'S SHRIMP FAJITAS

1 ¼ pound medium uncooked shrimp
1 fresh lime, juiced
About 2 tablespoons olive oil
½ teaspoon kosher salt
¼ teaspoon freshly ground black pepper
⅛ teaspoon chili powder

¼ teaspoon cumin
¼ teaspoon oregano
1 small red onion, sliced thin, rings separated
1 each red and green bell pepper, cut into thin strips
Kosher salt, pepper & more lime juice

¼ cup fresh cilantro, chopped
3 cloves garlic, chopped
1 bunch green onions, chopped
6 flour or corn tortillas

Peel and devein shrimp. Combine shrimp, lime juice, 1 tablespoon oil, salt, pepper, chili powder, cumin and oregano. Mix well to coat shrimp. Let sit at room temperature for 20 minutes.

Heat 1 tablespoon oil in a large non-stick skillet over medium-high heat. Sauté onions and bell peppers until soft and translucent, but still crunchy. Do not allow to brown. Sprinkle with salt and pepper and stir as they are cooking. Add half of the cilantro to the vegetables. Remove the vegetables and set aside in a bowl.

Add the shrimp and garlic to the skillet, cook and turn just until shrimp turn pink. Add a little more oil if necessary. Do not overcook. Return the vegetables to the skillet. Add the green onions and the remaining cilantro and sauté until everything is combined. Add a sprinkle of lime juice if necessary.

Lay the tortillas on a plate and spoon the shrimp and vegetables on top of the tortillas. Add shredded Mexican cheese if desired. Wrap the tortillas around the mixture and enjoy. Makes about six fajitas.

―――――――――――――――― **Thought for Life** ――――――――――――――――

A man who strikes a woman to show his strength, shows little more than his weakness.

FAJITA FABE'S STEAK FAJITAS

SALSA

2 ripe tomatoes, chopped

½ red onion, chopped

3 tablespoons cilantro, chopped

1 celery rib, chopped

½ bunch green onions, chopped

1 jalapeño pepper, chopped

2 teaspoons ground cumin

¼ teaspoon chili powder

¼ teaspoon celery salt

¼ teaspoon oregano

½ teaspoon kosher salt

¼ teaspoon black pepper

¼ teaspoon sugar

¼ cup lime juice

FAJITA FILLING

1½ pounds flank or New York strip steak

2 teaspoons kosher salt, divided

½ teaspoon black pepper, divided

½ teaspoon oregano, divided

3 tablespoons canola oil, divided

1 each red & green bell pepper, julienned

1 ½ brown onions, sliced and rings separated

4 cloves garlic, chopped

¼ cup cilantro, chopped

Lime juice

SALSA: Combine all salsa ingredients in a bowl. Taste and adjust seasoning. If you desire the salsa to consist of smaller pieces, pulse in a food processor to desired consistency. Refrigerate.

FAJITAS: Slice steak on the bias into ¼-inch strips. Just before cooking, season with salt, pepper and oregano. In a large skillet, add 2 tablespoons canola oil. Heat the oil, add the bell peppers and onion rings. Season with salt, pepper & oregano. Add garlic. Do not let the garlic burn. When peppers and onions begin to turn soft but not brown, remove ingredients from skillet and place in a bowl. Set aside.

Add 1 more tablespoon of canola oil, then place steak strips in single layer in skillet. Cook until no red meat shows, about 2 minutes per side. Return bell peppers, onions and garlic to skillet and mix well with the steak. Add cilantro and remix everything until combined. Add a few squirts of lime juice.

Place a tortilla on a plate, add the steak and vegetable mixture. Add salsa. Top with shredded lettuce, shredded Mexican cheese or other toppings of your choice.

ALMOST AUTHENTIC VALENCIA PAELLA

At first glance, this recipe may look complicated and time consuming — but it is not. The secret to this extraordinary paella is: (1) to make your own stock, if possible, (2) don't use short-cuts, (3) use top-notch ingredients, (4) plan each step and (5) have the entire array of ingredients ready at your fingertips during each segment and before the final assemblage.

I have designed this recipe to be performed in steps that will enable you to prepare some components while others are being cooked. Not only will you save time, but you will also be rewarded, with a picture that could grace the cover of any culinary magazine and a gastronomic masterpiece that will burst with a symphony of flavors and textures. Believe me, from start to finish, especially if you follow the time sequence, the entire process will take no more than two hours.

In Valencia, Spain, the birthplace of paella, I learned the art of making this dish. Once a year, I make this recipe for a group of friends. I call it the "paella festival." I've deviated slightly from the Valencia version, ergo, almost authentic.

The recipe, which calls for an 18-inch paella pan, will serve eight generously. You can reduce the ingredients by about one-third, cook them in a 15-inch pan, and serve four.

SOFRITO

2 ripe tomatoes, chopped or grated [or substitute 1 (14 ounce) can whole tomatoes]

2 tablespoons extra virgin olive oil

1 red onion, chopped

2 tablespoons Italian parsley, chopped

4 cloves garlic, minced

2 teaspoons Spanish paprika or sweet paprika

TRINITY

2 tablespoons extra virgin olive oil

1 yellow onion, medium chopped

1 each red and green bell pepper, medium chopped (see glossary for chopping terms)

1 celery rib, medium chopped

4 cloves garlic, chopped

OTHER ITEMS YOU WILL NEED

1 whole chicken, cut up (or individual pieces of your choice)

1 sausage, cut into ½" slices (chorizo, andouille or mild Italian)

2 tablespoons extra virgin olive oil (more if using paella pan)

Kosher salt, oregano, freshly ground black pepper

½ cup dry white wine

4 tablespoons of butter

1 dozen mussels & ½ dozen clams (or any combination)

4 lobster tails, cut in half

1 ½ pound raw shrimp with shells (12-15 per pound size preferred)

6-8 Dungeness crab legs

2-3 cups Bomba rice (or substitute any short grain Spanish rice, Arborio or long grain rice)

6-9 cups chicken stock

Pinch saffron

2 sprigs fresh rosemary & 1 sprig fresh thyme, tied with a string

1 handful of Italian parsley, chopped

1 bunch green onions, chopped

½ cup fresh or frozen green peas

3 ears of corn, each cut into 3 pieces and parboiled

STEP ONE: MISE EN PLACE

SOFRITO: It's a good idea to cut all of the vegetables at one time. Then, place each prepared vegetable in a separate vessel for their forthcoming usage. Read the entire recipe, then prepare and place other items for each particular step with the chopped vegetables for that step.

TRINITY: This is the foundation for many great savory dishes from braised short ribs to jambalaya. This version is more than a trinity because I have added garlic, plus one red bell pepper for color. It's also called "mirepoix."

STEP TWO: Make the sofrito and the trinity. The sofrito and the trinity are the mother's milk of authentic paella. Begin with the sofrito. If you are using canned whole tomatoes, crush and break them up with your hands. If you are using fresh tomatoes, remove skins and chop the tomatoes. Heat 2 tablespoons of extra virgin olive oil over medium heat in a separate skillet. Or, you can use the paella pan and wash it after this step. I prefer to use a separate skillet and reserve the sofrito in the skillet until ready to add to the paella pan. Sauté the red onion and parsley until they become fragrant, about 8 minutes. Add the garlic about one minute before the vegetables reach desired doneness. Add the tomatoes and their juice and 2 teaspoons of sweet paprika (preferably Spanish paprika), and cook until all of the liquid from the tomatoes has almost evaporated and the sofrito has the consistency of jam. Set aside.

To make the trinity, use the sofrito skillet. Add 2 tablespoons of extra virgin olive oil and sauté everything except the garlic until translucent, about 5 minutes. Add the garlic and sauté for 30 seconds more. Don't allow the garlic to brown. Mix the sofrito and the trinity together and set aside.

STEP THREE: Cook the chicken. You can cook the chicken in the paella pan. My preference is to use a separate skillet on the stovetop — unless I have to wash the dishes.

If using the paella pan on an outdoor grill, place it over medium high heat. If you cook the paella over a stove burner, the diameter of the burner will be less than the diameter of the paella pan and this will result in an uneven distribution of heat.

For this step, you will need the chicken parts and the sausage. First, place about 2 tablespoons of extra virgin olive oil in the pan. Heat the oil, and then add the chicken & sausage in a single layer.

Occasionally, turn the chicken and cook until all sides are golden brown. After about 5 minutes, sprinkle the chicken with kosher salt, pepper and dried oregano. It will take about 15 minutes to brown the chicken. I prefer to cook the chicken until it is ready-to-eat done, about 40 minutes more. Remove the sausage when fully cooked.

STEP FOUR: Prepare the mussels and clams. While the chicken is cooking, you can prepare the mussels and clams. In a 12-inch skillet, place enough water to come up the sides about 1 inch. Add about ½ cup dry white wine and 2 tablespoons of butter. Add the mussels and clams. You could also parboil the lobster tails, shrimp and crab legs in this pan. Cover and simmer over low heat until the clams and mussels open.

This method produces a modified court bouillon. When the clams and mussels are done, transfer them to a bowl. Also, remove lobster, shrimp and crab. Strain the juice and reserve. Discard the shrimp shells. This juice (court bouillon) will be added to the chicken stock and will yield extra flavor.

STEP FIVE: Cook the shrimp, lobster and crab. I prefer cooking the shellfish by sautéing them in a separate skillet, which produces a better flavor. Over medium heat, add 2 tablespoons butter and 1 tablespoon olive oil. Cook the shrimp, lobster and crab, turning occasionally, until the shrimp are pink. Cook crab legs and lobster for about 5 minutes. Do not overcook. Remove and set aside.

STEP SIX: Build the paella. After cooking the chicken, add another tablespoon of oil if necessary. If just starting with the paella pan, add 2 tablespoons of olive oil. Add the trinity-sofrito mixture. Add the rice and mix well until the grains are slightly coated with oil and thoroughly mixed with the sofrito-trinity. Keep stirring and cook the rice for about 1 minute. Add the chicken stock and court bouillon. The ratio of liquid to rice will be about 2 cups of stock to 1 cup of uncooked rice. The level of the liquid should be about 1-inch above the top of the rice mixture. The stock will start to bubble and reach a light boil. The rice should be completely cooked in about 15-20 minutes from this point. It is not necessary to stir the rice. You can shake the pan once or twice to distribute and level the rice. In the course of cooking the rice, it may be necessary to add more stock. I generally add it in increments of a half cup. Use water if you run out of stock.

As soon as the stock begins to bubble, crush the saffron threads to release their flavor and stir them into the stock and rice. Saffron requires boiling liquid to blossom. Add the rosemary-thyme bouquet garni. Remove after 10 minutes or it could overpower the other flavors. Add the cooked chicken and sausage and tuck into the rice. After about 5 minutes, add and stir in the chopped parsley and the chopped green onions. Add salt and pepper to taste. But be careful, as many of the ingredients will release a substantial amount of salt.

Add the cooked lobster tails and tuck them into the rice. Add the peas and stir them into the rice. The rice is done when slightly al dente and creamy. Allow the rice to toast on the bottom for a few minutes. The toasted rice is called "socarrat" and is prized in Spain. Be careful, however, not to burn the rice. During the last few seconds, add the corn, shrimp & crab just to rewarm them. Check the thick part of a breast and thigh to make certain that the chicken is cooked through. I check for 170°F with an instant thermometer.

Stir everything to fluff up the rice. Bring the pan to the table and place the chicken, sausage, clams, mussels, shrimp, corn and crab legs around the top of the rice. Move other ingredients around, mix the colors so that everything is displayed and easy to self-serve. Take a photo, then serve immediately. I guarantee that your guests will scream with delight.

NOTES: You can use many other ingredients such as artichoke hearts, green beans, olives, capers, calamari, rabbit, ham, white fish or pork ribs in this recipe. In Valencia, traditionalists use snails and duck.

ARGENTINIAN BEEF OR CHICKEN EMPANADAS

Empanadas, turnovers made with flakey pastry and filled with meat, are a Latin American treat. Other regions have similar iterations of these treats. Italian calzones consist of pasta dough folded and filled with pizza toppings. Pierogies, filled dumplings with either a sweet or savory filling, are a Polish staple. In a way, empanadas are similar to tacos or fajitas, but folded over and sealed. These are great for an informal buffet lunch or dinner.

DOUGH

2½ cups all-purpose flour

1½ teaspoons kosher salt

½ cup unsalted butter

1 large egg

¼ cup ice water

FILLING

2 teaspoons olive oil

1½ pounds ground beef or ground chicken

Kosher salt & freshly ground black pepper

½ cup yellow onion, finely diced

½ cup red or green bell pepper, finely diced

3 garlic cloves, minced

10 green olives, minced

½ teaspoon ground cumin

½ teaspoon ground paprika

½ teaspoon oregano

¼ teaspoon chili powder

¼ teaspoon red pepper flakes

4 tablespoons cilantro (divided), chopped

2 tablespoons water or beef stock

One egg plus 1 tablespoon water (for egg wash)

DOUGH: In a large bowl, mix the flour and salt together. Cut the butter into small cubes and place in a bowl. Freeze the flour mixture and the butter for 15 minutes. Place the flour mixture and the butter into a food processor. Pulse until small chunks of dough form, about the size of peas.

Place the egg in the ice water and whisk until combined. Add to flour mixture and pulse. Add more water, if necessary, one tablespoon at a time just until the dough starts to come together.

Place the dough on a floured work surface. Form into a ball. Flatten the ball and wrap in plastic wrap. Refrigerate at least one hour or overnight.

FILLING: Add the olive oil to a medium skillet and place over medium heat. After one minute, add the ground beef or ground chicken. With a wooden spoon, break up the ground beef or chicken. Sprinkle with a pinch of salt and pepper. Cook the meat until browned. Cook the chicken until no longer pink. Add the diced onion, red or green bell pepper and garlic. Cook until softened, about 5 minutes. Add the green olives, cumin, paprika, oregano, chili powder, red pepper flakes, 2 tablespoons cilantro, and a few pinches of salt. Mix well and cook about 5 minutes more, stirring occasionally. Add a few drops of water or beef stock if the mixture is too dry. Refrigerate for at least one hour.

ASSEMBLY: Roll out the disk of dough into a ⅛-inch thickness. Using a 4½-inch round cutter or the top of a bowl, cut out as many circles as you can. Reroll the scraps and cut out a few more.

Transfer the rounds to a parchment lined baking sheet. Lightly brush the edges of each with egg wash. Add a tablespoon of the meat or chicken filling to one side of the circle of dough, then fold the dough over into a half-moon shape. Do not overfill. Using the tines of a fork, seal the empanada's seam together by pressing the dough together.

Preheat the oven to 400°F. Brush the top of the empanadas with egg wash. With a knife, pierce three slits in the top to allow steam to escape. Bake for 20 to 25 minutes, until golden brown. Garnish with remaining cilantro. Eat warm or at room temperature. Serve with salsa, refried beans or Spanish rice. Makes nine 4½-inch empanadas.

NOTE: You can use the empanada filling to make fajitas. For fajitas, warm 4-6 corn tortillas. Fill with the Argentinian beef or chicken, chopped tomato, lettuce and grated cheese. Serve with *Cheryl's Guacamole* (see recipe on page 170).

FABE'S FABULOUS GAZPACHO

We all love the comfort of soup in the wintertime. As summer arrives, soup often takes a holiday. But there is nothing like a bowl of hearty, cold gazpacho on a hot summer night. Gazpacho is a favorite in Spain and Portugal. Here is my American version.

- 2 pounds Roma tomatoes
- 1 cucumber, peeled and seeded
- 1 red bell pepper
- 1 small red onion
- 1 celery rib
- 1 small jalapeño
- 2 garlic cloves
- 1 lime, juiced
- 2 tablespoons sherry vinegar
- 1 teaspoon kosher salt
- 1 teaspoon freshly ground black pepper
- 1½ teaspoons cumin
- 1 teaspoon ground coriander
- 2 teaspoons Worcestershire sauce
- ¼ cup cilantro
- Pinch sugar
- Pinch cayenne pepper
- Chopped green onions for garnish

Roughly chop the tomatoes, cucumber, bell pepper, onion, celery, jalapeño and garlic. Place these vegetables, plus the remaining items in a blender. You can also use an immersion blender or food processor. Blend or process until everything is combined into a chunky consistency. Transfer the mixture to a non-reactive container, such as a large glass bowl. Return about 2 cups of the mixture to the blender or processor and blend until puréed. Combine the puréed mixture with the chunky mixture.

Taste and adjust seasonings. Add a garnish of more chopped cilantro and chopped green onions.

NOTE: For a richer flavor, roast the bell pepper by cutting into strips, drizzling all sides with olive oil and placing on a baking sheet. Roast in a 450°F oven for 25-30 minutes or until tender.

Serve with croutons. See recipe for *Fabe's Garlic, Parmesan & Herb Croutons* on page 64. I suggest using a baguette. Cut slices about ½-inch thick and follow directions in recipe.

If you desire a soupier consistency, add an 8 ounce can of tomato sauce or tomato juice and stir to combine.

Chapter 14
My Favorite Italian Recipes

For years, I've been unable to decide if I prefer Italian or French cuisine. Both are world class. I've concluded that a decision is not required. It's like a parent can't decide (or shouldn't) which child is the favorite.

Food speaks to you.
French cuisine sings to you.
Italian cuisine is operatic.

THE FABE'S CHICKEN CACCIATORE

Cacciatore, which means "hunter's style," originated in Tuscany. The Italian-American version bears little resemblance to its progenitor, but it sure is delicious.

This is a tried and true recipe. Cook some pasta and mix it with the sauce, add a side veggie and you have a wonderful meal, complete with three food groups, for the family.

1 whole chicken, cut up

½ teaspoon salt, plus more for sprinkling

¼ teaspoon black pepper, plus more for sprinkling

1 teaspoon dried thyme

2 tablespoons olive oil

1 onion, sliced

1 celery rib, cut up

2 cloves garlic, chopped

¾ cup dry white wine

1 (28 ounce) can whole tomatoes

1 (6 ounce) can tomato paste

¼ pound mushrooms

1 green bell pepper, cut up in strips

1 teaspoon sugar

½ teaspoon dried rosemary

¼ teaspoon paprika

¼ teaspoon dried oregano

Pinch red pepper flakes

1 bay leaf

Pinch lemon juice

2 tablespoons Italian parsley, chopped

Season chicken parts with salt, pepper and ½ teaspoon dried thyme. In a Dutch oven, heat oil over medium heat. Brown the chicken in the oil on all sides until lightly browned, about 15 minutes. Remove chicken and set aside. Add onion, celery and garlic. Season with salt, pepper and ½ teaspoon dried thyme, then sweat for about 5 minutes. Drain off excess fat. Add ¼ cup of the wine and simmer until liquid just about disappears.

San Marzano whole plum tomatoes are preferred. If using whole tomatoes, break them up with your hand. Or, process until the mixture is chunky. Combine undrained tomatoes, tomato paste, remaining ½ cup wine, mushrooms, green bell pepper strips, sugar, salt, rosemary, paprika, thyme, oregano, red pepper flakes, black pepper and bay leaf. A pinch of lemon juice enlivens the flavor. If you have fresh rosemary, it is better. Substitute two sprigs.

Pour tomato mixture over chicken. If necessary, add some chicken stock or water to make sure chicken is just covered. Bring to a boil, reduce heat, cover and simmer for about 35-40 minutes or until chicken is tender. Add parsley last 5 minutes. Be sure to reseason if necessary.

To make this dish with pasta, boil one pound of a tube pasta in salted water until al dente. While pasta is boiling, remove chicken and vegetables from the pan. When pasta is done, drain and mix with sauce. Reserve about 1 cup pasta water. Return chicken and vegetables to the pot. Before serving, add some pasta water to the pot if you desire more liquid.

Legal Thought

Long before the enactment of hate crime laws, hatred of folks who were "different" flourished. This list of victims of bigotry is endless: from time to time, Italians, Irish, Poles and Asians took their place along with Africans, Hispanics and Native Americans. Just think of all of the rich culture we would be without had these folks not embraced our soil. I can't imagine life without chicken cacciatore, pizza or lasagna.

CHICKEN VESUVIO

Here is my favorite story about this recipe. We were having guests for an early dinner so that we could get to a movie on time. Generally, I work very early mornings until just mid-afternoon, so I thought I would have ample time to prepare this recipe which I had not made before. As luck would have it, on this day, I was delayed in court until very late in the afternoon. I was working as a temporary judge in traffic court and had to hear all of the cases over which I was presiding. I only had an hour or so to drive home, gather the ingredients and cook the dinner. I considered calling my friends with the suggestion that we should grab some food on the way to the movie. I detest folks who cancel a date with me, so I don't feel good about canceling plans. I arrived home around 4:45 p.m. By 6:00 p.m. this dinner was on the table and everyone loved it. The moral of the story is that it takes some practice, but if you organize properly, preparing a beautiful dish like Chicken Vesuvio is not an all-day task.

¼ cup olive oil

4 chicken thighs (bone-in & skin-on) or 4 chicken breasts (bone-in & skin-on) or a combination

Salt and freshly ground black pepper

1 ½ pounds Yukon Gold potatoes, quartered

½ tablespoon dried oregano

1 teaspoon dried thyme

¼ teaspoon red pepper flakes

6 cloves garlic, thinly sliced

1 bay leaf

2 tablespoons butter

½ cup dry white wine

½ cup chicken stock

⅔ cup peas

½ cup Italian parsley, chopped

Lemon juice

Preheat oven to 375°F. In a large Dutch oven, heat olive oil over medium-high heat.

Season chicken parts or pieces with salt and pepper. Cook for 10-12 minutes or until golden brown on all sides. Remove chicken and set aside.

Place potatoes in the same pot and season with oregano, thyme and red pepper flakes. Cook until potatoes are golden brown on all sides (about 10 minutes), stirring occasionally.

Add sliced garlic and sauté for one minute. Then add bay leaf.

Add butter, white wine and chicken stock. Scrape pot to loosen fond. Stir in peas. Simmer for 4-5 minutes.

Return the chicken in the pan and stir everything together to cover with sauce.

Bake 20-25 minutes in preheated oven. Remove from oven, stir in parsley and drizzle with lemon juice. Place chicken on platter and cover with sauce.

SHRIMP SCAMPI WITH PASTA

Popular in restaurants, scampi is easy to make at home. Purchase shrimp as large as you can find. Langostino prawns are great if you can find them. In Italy, the dish is generally made with langostinos in a butter and garlic sauce.

1 pound pasta (spaghetti, angel hair or linguine)

5 tablespoons butter

4 tablespoons extra virgin olive oil, plus 1 teaspoon (or more to taste)

2 shallots, finely diced

4 cloves garlic, minced

½ teaspoon oregano

Pinch red pepper flakes

1 pound large shrimp, peeled and deveined (For a more dramatic presentation, leave shells on.)

½ cup dry white wine

1 lemon, juiced

¼ cup Italian parsley, finely chopped

4 fresh basil leaves, torn into pieces

Pinch each kosher salt and freshly ground pepper

Green pimento olives (optional)

Bring a large pot of water boil. Add 1-2 tablespoons kosher salt; cook pasta in boiling water per package instructions until nearly al dente. Pasta will completely cook when added to sauce. Drain pasta, reserving about a cup of the pasta water. Set both aside.

In a large skillet over medium heat, melt 2 tablespoons butter with 2 tablespoons olive oil in a large skillet. Add shallots and sweat for 1-2-minutes or until translucent. Do not brown. Add garlic, oregano and red pepper flakes and stir for one minute.

Season shrimp with kosher salt and black pepper; add to the skillet and cook just until pink, about 2-3 minutes. Remove shrimp from skillet and set aside.

Pour white wine and lemon juice into skillet and bring to a boil. With a wooden spatula, scrape the bits from the bottom of the skillet — this will add flavor. Melt the remaining 3 tablespoons butter and 2 tablespoons of olive oil in the skillet and bring to a simmer. Mix pasta, shrimp, and parsley in the butter mixture until all ingredients are coated. If more liquid is needed, add some of the reserved pasta water. Add basil leaves and season with salt and black pepper. Drizzle with 1 teaspoon of olive oil and garnish with olives, if desired. Serve immediately.

FABE'S QUICK MEDITERRANEAN FISH STEW
aka CIOPPINO

As a kid, I never liked my first name. Very few guys were named Stuart. Of course, there was a famous actor named James Stewart. My first and middle name, Stuart James, was probably okay, but not to me. Kids tend to tease and make fun of other kids. Guys would come up to me and say, "Stu, make me some stew." That annoyed me — until now! I often make this dish for parties and folks rave over it. They shout with glee: "Stu, you make great stew!" Now, I love my name. I'm glad I wasn't named Cioppino or Bouillabaisse.

- 4 cloves garlic, peeled
- 4 anchovy filets
- 2 tablespoons extra virgin olive oil (plus more for drizzling), divided
- ½ teaspoon each kosher salt & freshly ground pepper (plus more to taste), divided
- 1 (15 ounce) can diced tomatoes (San Marzano preferred)
- 1 (6 ounce) can tomato paste
- ½ teaspoon ground sage
- 1 teaspoon thyme
- 2 teaspoon oregano
- 1 teaspoon sugar
- ¼ teaspoon red pepper flakes
- 4 tablespoons butter, divided
- 1 pound of a firm flaky fish (e.g., bass, cod or snapper)
- Selection of shrimp (deveined), lobster tails, scallops, clams (scrubbed), mussels (scrubbed & debearded), and crab legs
- Flour for dredging
- 4 white potatoes, quartered or 2 ears of corn
- 1 large onion, chopped
- 1 celery rib, chopped
- 1 carrot, chopped
- 1 bay leaf
- ½ cup dry white wine
- 1-2 cups water
- 1-2 tablespoons fresh lemon juice
- ½ cup Italian parsley, chopped
- 4-6 slices French bread, cut into ½" slices

Place garlic, anchovies, 1 tablespoon olive oil, pinch salt and pepper in food processor. Pulse until a paste forms. Set aside. Combine diced tomatoes, tomato paste, sage, thyme, oregano, sugar and pepper flakes in a large bowl. Mix and set aside.

Place a heavy deep skillet or Dutch oven over high heat. Add 1 tablespoon butter and 1 tablespoon oil. Pat fish filets, shrimp, lobster tails, scallops dry. Leave the shrimp and lobster tails in their shells. Gently flour the fish filets. When the fat is hot and simmering, add the fish filets, shrimp, lobster tails (meat side down) and scallops. Sauté for about 3 minutes on each side — just until they start to brown. This will create a fond and also add flavor to the fish. Remove fish and set aside. If using corn, cut two ears in half. While browning fish, add corn and brown on each side for 2 minutes per side.

Add onion, celery and carrot. Add ½ teaspoon each salt and pepper. Cook until tender, about 5 minutes. Add garlic/anchovy mixture and bay leaf and cook for 1 minute more. Add wine and cook until wine almost disappears. Scrape the bottom of the pan to incorporate fond. Add tomato mixture, about ½ cup water and potatoes. If using corn, eliminate potatoes.

Cover and simmer for about 30 minutes. Add more water to reach desired consistency — should be like a thick gravy. When potatoes are done, check seasoning. If using corn, add it in the last 5 minutes. Add lemon juice to taste. Add a few pats of butter and the parsley flakes and stir. Return the fish filets, shrimp, lobster and scallops to the pot. Then add the clams, mussels and crab legs. Cook until each is done, removing any pieces of

seafood to a bowl that are finished cooking.(Fish could disintegrate if left in pot too long.) The fish filets should be done in about 4 minutes. The shrimp will take about one minute more, followed by the scallops, crab legs and lobster tails. Wait until the clams and mussels open, but discard any that do not open. In the meantime, toast the bread.

Ladle the cioppino into bowls and serve. Toast the bread, rub with garlic cloves and olive oil, and serve alongside for dipping.

What is the difference between Mediterranean fish stew, cioppino, Yankee fish stew and bouillabaisse? I was disappointed when I discovered that cioppino did not originate in Italy. During the end of the 19th century, Italian immigrants who fished the San Francisco Bay used their excess catches of the day and made a fish soup for their families which they called cioppino. In Italy's Liguria region, they do make a fish soup that is similar. Bouillabaisse, which uses fish stock and saffron, is less tomato based. Yankee fish stew is a cream based version with potatoes. Mediterranean fish stews generally are tomato based soups with a variety of seafood and traditional Italian seasonings. This version is a iteration of Mediterranean fish stew Americanized with potatoes and corn. For a more authentic version, the potatoes and/or corn can be eliminated.

―――――――――――――――― **Legal Thought** ――――――――――――――――

America had some warlike scuffles with France around 1798. I'm not an historian, but I heard that it might have been over the Yankees stealing France's recipe for bouillabaisse. This book is not intended to give legal advice, but as an attorney, I can assure you that if you make my recipe for a party and call it bouillabaisse or cioppino, no court in the land will hold you responsible.

SPAGHETTI WITH CHERRY TOMATOES, OLIVES, CAPERS & BREADCRUMBS

This dish is also known as pasta puttanesca. As usual, I've added a few things. Please don't use store-bought breadcrumbs. Place a few slices of stale sandwich bread in the food processor, pulse until you have coarse crumbs. The difference is worth the effort. This dish tastes as close to an original in a Neopolitan restaurant as I have ever experienced.

3-4 tablespoons butter, divided (or more to taste)

2-3 tablespoons extra virgin olive oil, divided (or more to taste)

4 cloves garlic, sliced

1 ½ cups fresh coarsely chopped breadcrumbs

1 teaspoon kosher salt, divided

½ teaspoon freshly ground black pepper, divided

¼ teaspoon dried oregano, divided

2 anchovy filets, chopped

2 pints cherry or grape tomatoes, cut in half

½ cup capers, drained

1 cup olives, cut in half (combination of black pitted and green olives with pimentos)

½ teaspoon red pepper flakes

½ cup Italian parsley, chopped

½ cup freshly grated Parmesan cheese

1 pound spaghetti or angel hair pasta

In a large skillet over medium heat, melt 2 tablespoons butter and 1 tablespoons oil. Add garlic slices and sauté for 1 minute or just until they become aromatic. Do not allow them to turn brown. Remove from skillet and finely chop. Set aside. Add breadcrumbs and sauté. Sprinkle with salt, pepper and a pinch of oregano. When the crumbs turn slightly brown, remove from skillet and set aside.

In a large pasta pot, bring about 5 quarts of water to a boil. Cover and allow to boil.

Add 1 more tablespoon each of butter and oil to the skillet. Add anchovies and sauté for 30 seconds. Add tomatoes, capers and olives. Reduce heat to medium-low, cover and simmer for about 20 minutes or until the tomatoes release their juices. Return chopped garlic to skillet. Season with salt, pepper, oregano and red pepper flakes to taste. Cover and simmer for another 5 minutes. Taste and season again, if necessary. Sprinkle with parsley flakes.

Add about 2 tablespoons kosher salt to boiling water and cook pasta according to package instructions. When the pasta is about a minute shy of al dente, add pasta to the skillet. Reserve about ½ cup of pasta water before draining. Toss until the pasta is covered with the sauce. Drizzle some pasta water so sauce adheres to the pasta. Continue to drizzle the pasta water as necessary. Add 1 more tablespoon butter to enrich and emulsify. Add breadcrumbs and mix into pasta. Add more chopped parsley if desired. Serve in pasta bowls and sprinkle with cheese.

FABE'S MEAT LASAGNA

As I developed this recipe, my thought was that lasagna was, in essence, mac & cheese with Bolognese sauce. Please avoid using a jar of Ragú.® My delicious sauce is easy to make. I also stay away from pre-packaged shredded cheeses. They contain preservatives which inhibit melting. Purchase blocks or slices of cheese. You can also use ricotta cheese.

SAUCE

1 (28 ounce) can whole San Marzano tomatoes

2 (6 ounce) cans tomato paste

1 (14 ounce) can tomato sauce

1 teaspoon granulated garlic

1 tablespoon sugar

2 teaspoons kosher salt

1 teaspoon black pepper

3 teaspoons oregano

2 teaspoons basil

¼ teaspoon red pepper flakes

½ pound ground chuck

½ pound ground Italian sausage

1 tablespoon olive oil

1 onion, chopped

1 celery rib, chopped

3 garlic cloves, chopped

½ cup dry red wine

1 bay leaf

1 tablespoon lemon juice

¼ cup Italian parsley, chopped

FILLING

1 pound lasagna noodles

1 pound mozerella cheese

1 pound Romano cheese

1 pound provolone cheese

SAUCE: Place whole tomatoes, tomato paste and tomato sauce in a food processor. Add granulated garlic, sugar, salt, pepper, oregano, basil and red pepper flakes. Pulse until you reach a chunky consistency. Set aside.

In a large Dutch oven, brown the beef and sausage over medium-high heat. When browned, remove with a slotted spoon and set aside. Discard the rendered fat. Add 1 tablespoon olive oil. Add the onion and celery and cook over medium heat, just until the onion is translucent. Add the chopped garlic and braise for 30 seconds. Add red wine. Increase heat to high and cook until liquid is reduced to about 1 tablespoon. With a spatula, scrape the bottom of the Dutch oven to release the fond. Add the tomato mixture. Return the meat mixture to the Dutch oven. Add the bay leaf, reduce to a simmer, cover and cook for about 45 minutes. Stir occasionally. Add water to achieve desired consistency. Sauce should be thick like chili. During the last 5 minutes, add lemon juice and parsley. Remove bay leaf.

FILLING & ASSEMBLY: Preheat oven to 375° F. If you are not using oven-ready (no boil) noodles, cook the noodles according to package instructions. When noodles are done, drain and place in a flat dish and drizzle with sauce to keep them moist. Reserve pasta water to dilute sauce, if necessary. Grate blocks of cheese. Slices need not be shredded. You can mix grated cheeses together or use a different cheese for each layer.

Place about 1 cup of sauce in the bottom of a 13x9-inch baking pan or lasagna pan. Spread into a thin layer. Add three noodles over the sauce. You can add a half of a noodle perpendicularly if the space on the side is not filled. Add another cup of sauce over the noodles. Add about 1 ½ cups of cheese (or the slices), evenly over the sauce. Repeat two more times, ending with cheese on the top layer.

Cover the pan with foil. Bake for 45 minutes. During the last 10 minutes, remove the foil and bake until the top cheese layer is slightly browned. Cool for 20 minutes before serving. Garnish with chopped parsley.

FABE'S PASTA & MEAT SAUCE
aka UNAUTHENTIC BOLOGNESE

There are as many recipes for Bolognese sauce as there are people living in Bologna. Here is one that is full of flavor and with a smooth texture. And it takes only about 15 minutes to assemble and about 40 minutes to simmer. It usually disappears faster than it takes to cook it. This is one of the simplest, quickest and, in the opinion of many, one of the best meat sauces. This recipe can be halved.

2 tablespoons olive oil, divided

1 pound ground Italian sausage (mild or sweet)

2 pounds ground chuck

1 onion, chopped

1 small green bell pepper, diced (or combination of half red & half green bell pepper)

1 carrot, chopped small

1 celery rib, chopped small

5 garlic cloves, chopped

¼ cup dry red wine

1 (6 ounce) can tomato paste

1 (28 ounce) can plum tomatoes (San Marzano preferred)

1 (15 ounce) can tomato sauce & 1 (15 ounce) can diced tomatoes

3 teaspoons oregano

3 teaspoons basil leaves

1 bay leaf

1 ½ teaspoons brown sugar

1 teaspoon granulated garlic

1 teaspoon kosher salt

¼ teaspoon freshly ground black pepper

¼ to ½ teaspoon red pepper flakes

4 tablespoons Italian parsley, chopped

1 teaspoon fresh lemon juice

2 pounds spaghetti or tubular pasta (such as penne, rigatoni or mostaccioli)

In a large, heavy stockpot or Dutch oven, add 1 tablespoon olive oil. Mix sausage and beef and cook until brown throughout. With a potato masher, break meat into small pieces. Remove meat with slotted spoon and set aside. Remove rendered fat and discard. Add a tablespoon of olive oil, then add onions, bell pepper, carrot and celery. Cook until onions are translucent. Add garlic and stir for 30 seconds. Do not brown or burn garlic. If excessive amount of liquid gathers in the bottom of the pot, drain off or remove contents and pour liquid out. Then return contents to pot. Add red wine. Cook until wine is reduced to 2 tablespoons. Scrape bottom of pot and mix flavorful scrapings (fond) into vegetables. After wine is reduced, add half of the tomato paste. Spread it out over the bottom of the pot and cook for 2-3 minutes.

While the above ingredients are cooking, combine plum tomatoes, tomato sauce and diced tomatoes in a large bowl. With your hands, crush tomatoes and remaining tomato paste so that there are just small bits of tomato. Or, pulse in food processor just until mixture is chunky. Add oregano, basil, parsley, bay leaf, brown sugar, granulated garlic, salt, pepper and red pepper flakes, and mix well. When vegetables have softened, add tomato mixture and return meat to the pot. Mix all ingredients well.

Bring to a boil, then reduce heat to low and simmer. Cover and stir frequently. Continue to mash contents occasionally with a potato masher to obtain smaller pieces of meat. Simmer for 1 ½ hours. Adjust seasoning if necessary. Stir in chopped parsley. Remove bay leaf. Add 1 teaspoon fresh lemon juice to sauce — it brightens it up beautifully.

Meanwhile bring a large pot of water to a boil. Add 2 tablespoons kosher salt. Add 2 pounds spaghetti and stir frequently. Follow cooking instructions on the packages, which should total about 9 minutes. When the pasta is about a minute shy of al dente, add a few cups of cold water to stop the cooking process. With a pair of tongs, place pasta into sauce to finish cooking. If necessary, add a few tablespoons of the pasta water. Place helpings of pasta in bowls, add sauce and Parmesan cheese.

Culinary Thought

As I was driving to the market to purchase ingredients for the evening's dinner of pasta with Bolognese sauce, my radio was tuned to Sirius NPR. The program's host, Robert David, was playing the Trio Sonata in A Major by Arcangelo Corelli, who, along with Vivaldi and Scarlatti, was one of the giants of Italian Baroque music. I was riveted by the Baroque motif in which one instrument introduces the musical theme, another enters a few bars later, then the rest join as if each is coming out of neighboring houses and marching down the road. The technical term is a "round," similar to "row, row, row your boat gently down the stream." Next, the instruments digress from mimicking each other's melodies and engage in friendly combat with their individual contrapuntal notes. Eventually, the instruments declare a truce and meet in one harmonious chord. The moment each instrument finds its place to complete the triadic chord, the ensemble produces the resonance and depth rivaling that of an entire orchestra. I mused over the similarities between the composition of this musical journey and the preparation of my Bolognese. A sauce commences with the introduction of a sofrito, then perhaps a splash of wine followed by a crescendo of tomatoes. Just like the sonata, the depth and resonance of the sauce belies the paucity of ingredients.

This radio program is hosted by an impressive musicologist who generally offers biographical tidbits about each composer. He spoke of Corelli's acceptance into the Accademia Filarmonica di Bologna, Italy's most prestigious musical institution. Was this a coincidence? Fate? Supernatural? Here I was, contemplating the creation of Bolognese sauce at the same time Mr. David was recounting tales of Corelli's attachment to Bologna. I'm not certain if Corelli would countenance today's music, but here is what I hope he would say about my Bolognese sauce:

Bolognese

if you please.

The best since I've known 'ya

except for Bologna.

FABE'S EXTRAORDINARY MEATBALLS AND TOMATO SAUCE

There are certain food items that I could eat almost every day. Meatballs are on that list. I've had some disappointing meatball experiences in restaurants. Often they are tough, tasteless or too bready. I think you won't be disappointed with this recipe. Many chefs cook their meatballs entirely in a skillet atop the stove. In my experience, cooking them in the oven, then finishing them in the sauce produces a more evenly cooked meatball. Versatile, you can serve these as an appetizer, serve over pasta or enjoy them in a sandwich.

MEATBALLS
1 celery rib
1 onion
½ green bell pepper
1 egg
3 tablespoons milk
½ cup breadcrumbs
1 ½ pounds ground chuck
½ pound ground Italian sausage
1 teaspoon dried oregano
½ tablespoon kosher salt
½ teaspoon black pepper
½ cup Italian parsley, chopped

TOMATO SAUCE
1 (28 ounce) can whole San Marzano plum tomatoes
1 (15 ounce) can diced tomatoes
1 (6 ounce) can tomato paste
1 teaspoon each basil and oregano
1 tablespoon brown sugar
Kosher salt and freshly ground black pepper
½ teaspoon granulated garlic
Pinch red pepper flakes
2 tablespoons olive oil
1 onion, finely chopped

½ each red & green bell pepper, finely chopped
½ celery rib, finely chopped
4 cloves garlic, minced
½ cup dry red wine
1 bay leaf
1 tablespoon butter
1 tablespoon Parmesan
1-2 teaspons lemon juice
Italian parsley, chopped

MEATBALLS: Preheat oven to 425°F. Coarsely chop celery, onion and bell pepper. Place in a food processor and pulse until a fine paste forms. Italians call this pestata. Lightly beat the egg with 1 tablespoon of milk. Mix the breadcrumbs with the remaining 2 tablespoons of milk and squeeze with your hands until the crumbs are soaked. Place the meats in a large bowl and combine with your hands. Add the pestata, egg mixture, breadcrumb mixture, oregano, salt, pepper and parsley. Mix well with your hands. The mixture will be wet — that is what will make the softest meatballs you have ever eaten. Form about 15 balls, each about 3.5 ounces. Do not over-pat or squeeze. Loosely formed meatballs will come out soft and tender. Place on a baking sheet that has been lined with parchment paper. Bake for about 25 minutes or until browned on all sides. Remove from oven and place on a dish covered with a paper towel.

TOMATO SAUCE: Place the plum tomatoes, diced tomatoes, tomato paste, oregano, basil, brown sugar, salt, granulated garlic, black pepper and red pepper flakes in food processor. Pulse until coarse and chunky.

Place 2 tablespoons olive oil in a Dutch oven. Add chopped onion, bell peppers and celery. Sprinkle with kosher salt, black pepper and oregano. Cook over medium heat until soft, but not brown — stirring occasionally. Add garlic. Cook for one minute. Do not brown. Add red wine, turn heat to high and deglaze until red wine has almost disappeared.

Reduce heat to medium. Add tomato mixture to the Dutch oven. Cook for 2 minutes. Add bay leaf. Stir well. Bring to a boil, then reduce heat until sauce simmers. Cover and cook for 1 hour, stirring occasionally. Stir in 1 tablespoon butter and 1 tablespoon Parmesan. Adjust seasoning, if necessary. Spritz in 1-2 teaspoons fresh lemon juice. Add meatballs to tomato sauce, spoon some sauce over balls, cover and cook for 10 minutes. The meatballs will harden if you overcook them. Just before serving, add parsley. Stir into sauce and cook for 1 minute more, then serve.

――――――――――――――――― **Legal Thought** ―――――――――――――――――

Breaking the law is like eating bad food. Both evoke indigestion. When you break the law, deceive your neighbor or stray from your loved one, it never feels right. The indigestion attacks, not only the stomach, but your soul. Of course, for those who have no conscience, they feel no pain. But worse, they feel nothing.

BEN BENSON'S OSSO BUCO

In the 1970s and 1980s, one of the most popular steak houses in Manhattan was Ben Benson's. In those days, I traveled to New York City at least twice a year. Without exception, as soon as I arrived at my hotel, I dropped off my luggage and headed to Ben Benson's. Over the years, Ben and I became close friends. He always joined us at our table. The conversation invariably centered on cuisine. I always ordered steak. During that era, steak houses were on sabbatical, so it was a challenge to find a good steak house. One evening, Ben brought over a dish of osso buco. Stuffed with steak, baskets of bread and bowls of potatoes, I nevertheless politely sampled his offering. WOW! The best osso buco I have ever had. Ben asked me if I would convey my sentiments to the chef. He came to our table and I rhapsodized over the dish. "Any chance of getting the recipe," I asked sheepishly? Without hesitation, "Of course." Ben closed the restaurant about ten years ago. I have no doubt that he would be happy if I shared the recipe.

1 cup flour
2 tablespoons paprika
1 tablespoon lemon zest
1 teaspoon dried thyme
1 teaspoon oregano
1 teaspoon black pepper
Kosher salt
¼ cup olive oil
6 veal shanks, cut 1″ thick
2 onions, chopped
½ cup carrots, chopped
½ cup celery, chopped
4 anchovy filets, minced
4 cloves garlic, chopped
1 cup dry red wine
2 cups beef stock
2 cups chicken stock
1 (28 ounce) can whole tomatoes with their juice (San Marzano preferred)
½ cup Italian parsley, chopped
2 bay leaves

Veal shanks are frightfully expensive and hard to find. I frequently use beef shanks.

Mix flour, paprika, lemon zest, thyme, oregano and pepper. Season shanks with salt, dredge in flour mixture. In a large Dutch oven, heat olive oil over medium-high heat. Sauté shanks in batches and brown well on both sides, about 8 minutes. Transfer shanks to a platter. Add onions, carrots, celery, anchovies and sauté until onions are translucent. Add garlic. Add wine and reduce until it is almost dissolved. Deglaze the pot while the wine is reducing. Chop or process the tomatoes until the tomatoes and juices are chunky. The consistency should be like porridge. Add stocks, tomatoes, parsley and bay leaf. Bring to a boil.

Return the shanks to the pot. Cover and simmer about 1 ½ hours. When meat is tender, remove the shanks from the pot. Boil sauce uncovered until slightly reduced and thickened. For a richer flavor and thicker texture, add a roux of 3 tablespoons of butter and 3 tablespoons of flour. Return the shanks to the sauce. Reheat for 5 minutes. Sprinkle with more parsley. Serve over risotto, mashed potatoes or pasta.

Culinary Thought

How about this idea—instead of two countries declaring war against one another, why don't they declare a giant potluck dinner?

PORK CHOPS MILANESE

Veal Milanese, the predecessor of pork Milanese, originated in the Lombardian region in the city of Milan. Veal is very expensive and often hard to find. Thin pork chops or cutlets serve as a delicious substitute and my version of Amatriciana sauce is a great accompaniment.

SAUCE

- 1 tablespoon olive oil
- 3 strips bacon, chopped
- 1 onion, finely chopped
- Kosher salt & freshly ground black pepper
- 1 (28 ounce) can whole tomatoes, chopped (San Marzano preferred)
- 1 cup water
- 1 teaspoon each oregano and thyme
- 1 teaspoon sugar
- ½ teaspoon granulated garlic
- Pinch red pepper flakes

PORK CHOPS

- 4 pork chops, about ¾" thick (bone-in preferred)
- ¾ cup panko breadcrumbs
- ¼ cup Parmesan cheese
- ½ teaspoon each oregano and thyme
- ½ cup all-purpose flour
- Kosher salt (to taste)
- Freshly ground black pepper (to taste)
- 2 eggs
- 1 tablespoon water or milk
- ⅓ cup olive oil
- Garnish: parsley, lemon wedges, grated Parmesan cheese

SAUCE: Heat olive oil in a large skillet over medium heat. Add chopped bacon and sauté just until it begins to brown, about 3 minutes. Add chopped onions. Sprinkle with salt and pepper, cover and sauté just until they turn translucent, about 3 minutes.

Add the tomatoes and 1 cup of water. Stir in the oregano, thyme, sugar, granulated garlic, red pepper flakes. Season to taste with salt and pepper.

Bring to a simmer. Cover and cook until the sauce thickens. Adjust seasoning if necessary.

To serve, place some sauce on each plate, then place a chop over the sauce. Drizzle more sauce over the chop. I like this dish with a tubular pasta such as penne. Cook the penne according to package directions. Place penne on the plate and cover with sauce.

PORK CHOPS: Prepare the pork chops while making the sauce.

Place each chop between two sheets of plastic wrap. Pound with a meat mallet to achieve desired thickness, about ¼-inch thick.

In a shallow bowl, whisk together the panko, Parmesan cheese, oregano and thyme.

Place the flour in a shallow bowl and whisk in a pinch of salt and pepper. Dip each chop into the flour mixture, coating both sides completely. Shake off excess flour.

Whisk the eggs in a shallow bowl with a tablespoon of water or milk. Dip the floured chops into the beaten eggs, coating both sides completely. Let them drip over the bowl to remove excess.

Place the egg coated chops into the breadcrumb mixture and coat both sides completely with the breadcrumbs. Pat the breadcrumbs into each chop.

Heat the olive oil in a large sauté pan on medium heat. Higher heat will burn the breadcrumbs. Add two or three chops at a time, depending on the size of the pan. Don't overcrowd the pan and make sure they lay flat in the pan. Fry for 3 to 5 minutes or until golden brown.

Flip the chops and fry for a few more minutes on the second side. Fry each chop until they are golden brown on both sides and cooked through.

PORK CHOPS PIZZAIOLA

Here is a tasty way to prepare pork chops. It's another great recipe from Italy.

2 tablespoons olive oil, divided

2 thin, bone-in center cut pork loin chops (about ½" thick)

Kosher salt & freshly ground pepper

1 (15 ounce) can diced tomatoes (San Marzano preferred)

1 (6 ounce) can tomato paste

¼ teaspoon each thyme & oregano

1 bay leaf

Pinch red pepper flakes

1 small onion, chopped

3 cloves garlic, minced

1 green bell pepper, julienned

1 tablespoon Italian parsley, chopped

Heat 1 tablespoon of oil in large skillet, preferably cast iron. Allow skillet to get hot, about 10 minutes. Generously season chops with salt and pepper. Place chops in skillet and increase heat to high. Cook until browned on each side and no longer pink. Temperature measured with an instant-read meat thermometer should be about 160°F.

In the meantime, combine tomatoes, paste, thyme, oregano, bay leaf and red pepper flakes in a bowl. Remove cooked chops and place on a platter.

Reduce heat to medium. Add about 1 tablespoon more of the oil to the same skillet. Add onions and cook until slightly brown. Add garlic, stir and cook for 30 seconds. Add tomato mixture and peppers. Cover and simmer for about 15-20 minutes. Return chops to skillet, cover with some tomato mixture and cook 5 minutes more. Season with salt and pepper to taste. Spoon sauce on plates, serve the chops on top and sprinkle with parsley.

TUSCAN BEEF STEW

Cuisine from Tuscany did not become popular in the United States until the 1970s. Today, folks can't get enough of it. This version, made with lotsa wine, might be considered an Italian Beef Bourguignon. The French might not agree. I'm not sure if the Tuscans would countenance my use of barley. But it sure is good.

6 to 7 pounds boneless beef chuck roast (well-trimmed and cut into 2" chunks)

Kosher salt and coarsely ground black pepper

2 tablespoons extra-virgin olive oil

1 large yellow onion, thinly sliced

6 medium garlic cloves peeled

3 tablespoons of tomato paste

3 sprigs fresh rosemary, finely chopped (divided)

2 cups dry red wine (Chianti works well)

1-2 cups beef stock, if needed

1 teaspoon dried oregano

1 teaspoon dried thyme

Preheat the oven to 325° F. Place a rack in the lower-middle position of the oven. Place the beef in a large bowl, sprinkle with 1 tablespoon salt and 2 tablespoons pepper, then mix well.

In a large Dutch oven over medium heat, heat the oil until shimmering. Add the onion and sauté until the onions are lightly browned, 7 to 9 minutes. Add the garlic and sauté an additional 30 seconds. Add the tomato paste and rub it along the bottom of the pot, until the paste begins to brown, about 3 to 5 minutes. Mix the beef and rosemary sprigs in the onion mixture, cover and transfer to the oven. Cook for 2 hours.

Remove the pot from the oven. Stir, then return to the oven uncovered. Cook until a knife inserted into a piece of beef meets no resistance, another 1 to 1 ½ hours.

Using a slotted spoon, transfer the meat to a medium bowl. Place a strainer over a medium bowl. Pour the meat juices into the strainer and, with a large spoon, press the solids to push all of the liquid through the strainer. Discard the solids.

Pour the wine into the empty pot and bring to a boil over medium-high, scraping the bottom of the pot to incorporate the fond. Reduce to medium and simmer until the wine is syrupy and reduced to about 1 cup, about 5 to 7 minutes. If you strained the meat juices into a bowl, use a spoon to skim off and discard the fat from the surface.

Pour the defatted meat juices into the pot. If there is not much juice, add 1-2 cups of beef stock. Bring to a simmer over medium-high and cook, stirring until thickened to the consistency of heavy cream — about 5 to 7 minutes. For extra flavor and texture, make a roux with 2 tablespoons of butter and 2 tablespoons of flour. When wine mixture boils, add roux and stir to desired thickness. Return the beef to the pot, add the chopped rosemary, oregano and thyme and stir gently. Bring to a gentle simmer and cook, stirring, until the meat is heated through, 4 to 5 minutes. Stir in 2 teaspoons of pepper, then taste and season with salt.

Serve over noodles or barley. To make barley, wash 1½ cups pearl barley in a strainer.

Place barley and 2 quarts of beef stock in a pot. Add kosher salt, black pepper, 1 teaspoon each of oregano and thyme. Cook until al dente, about 30 minutes. Do not overcook.

---- **Legal Thought** ----

*Before you cosign a loan
for a friend or relative,
you should study this definition:
A cosigner
is an idiot with a pen.*

OUTSTANDING HOMEMADE PIZZA

I could eat a pizza pie every day. The war between thin and thick crust will never be resolved. Although this book should be crust-neutral, I just can't bring myself to derive any enjoyment from a thick pizza crust. Whenever I visit Chicago, I go on a pizza strike.

Although we think of Naples, Italy as the motherland of pizza, historians tell us that the delicacy originated in Greece. Turks, Croatians, Serbs and Hebrews also lay claim to the invention of pizza. We do know that, around 1889, Queen Margherita of Italy was served a pizza made with ingredients resembling the colors of the Italian flag: Tomatoes for red, mozzarella for white and basil for green. Today, the Margherita pizza is among the most popular in America and certainly, my favorite.

Several years ago, when I was visiting Rome, I decided to take a two-hour train ride to Naples. The purpose of this pilgrimage was to visit the birthplace of Italian pizza. The train chugged into the station, I disembarked and headed for the most legendary pizzeria in Naples. Within moments I was hopelessly lost.

I approached a policewoman and, in broken Italian, asked for directions. Only one word was required to communicate my objective--pizza. Her eyes lit up and she immediately understood as the word flowed from my lips. She smiled, gently took my arm and guided me to the pizzeria. Imagine--having a law officer take your arm and escort you to a place other than a jail! The instant we crossed the threshold, I felt like a kid visiting the locker room of his favorite sports team. I invited the cop to join me. She readily accepted. Within a few minutes, we were served a culinary work of art. It was like my first glimpse of the Mona Lisa. Two pizzas, each about nine inches in diameter, with a crust so thin, one could almost read a newspaper through it. Topped with a light coat of the most resplendent sauce I had ever observed, plump slices of the freshest tomatoes I've ever tasted, dripping creamy mozzarella and a scattering of fresh basil leaves. I grabbed a slice and rushed it to my lips. The first bite was like the first view of Heaven--and each bite thereafter was better than the previous one. I devoured the entire pizza in a matter of seconds--we ordered about three more.

The ride back to Rome was agonizing--I'm reminded of a scene in a movie where a man on a train gazes back at the platform as the vision of his gorgeous lover slowly disappears. As I stared, it appeared as if I received a longing, loving glance in return--not from the cop, but from the pizza joint.

CRUST — THE FOUNDATION OF GREAT PIZZA

I must concede the fact that neither I nor anyone else could ever duplicate a Neapolitan pizza. But the following crust recipe forms the base for an extremely impressive pizza. Have no fear about making a crust from scratch.

This recipe will make about two 9-inch crusts. I also like to make individual pizzas. You can get about six 5-inch crusts from this recipe. For grilling, the smaller crusts are much easier to handle.

1 tablespoon instant yeast

⅔ cup water (about 115° F)

2 cups flour [Bread flour is best or unbleached flour. If you can find 00 flour (double zero), that can also be used.]

⅓ cup cornmeal

¾ teaspoon salt

1 teaspoon ground oregano (optional)

4 teaspoons extra virgin olive oil

Combine yeast and warm water in a mixing bowl or food processor. Allow to sit for 10 minutes until the water becomes foamy on the top. In the meantime, combine 1½ cups of the flour with the cornmeal and the salt. Add the ground oregano if using. Add the olive oil to the water and yeast. Add the flour mixture, ½ cup at a time and mix or pulse until a wet dough begins to form. Add more flour mixture as needed. You may even need more flour after all of the flour-corn mixture has been added. If so, add flour 1 tablespoon at a time until a slightly sticky dough forms and pulls away from the side of the bowl. Better to have a moist, sticky dough than one that is too dry.

SAME-DAY CRUST: Place dough on a floured surface and knead until you have a smooth, shiny dough. Lightly oil a large bowl. Place the dough in the bowl and rotate the dough until it is entirely covered with a light film of oil. Cover the bowl with a towel that has been moistened with warm water. Place the bowl in a warm area and allow the dough to rise and double in size — about 2 hours.

MAKE-AHEAD CRUST: I prefer to make the crust a day ahead. After completing the above steps, place the dough in a lightly oiled bowl. Cover the bowl with plastic wrap or a clean kitchen towel. Place in fridge overnight. Remove bowl 1 hour before making pizzas.

Remove dough from the bowl and place on a cutting board. Punch dough down and let it rest for 5 minutes. Cut dough into desired number of pieces. I cut the dough into 4-ounce pieces (about the size of a plum), which produces about six disks. While shaping one portion of the dough, cover the others with the damp towel. Or, you can cut the disks in half and cut four out of each half and get eight disks.

Place the piece of dough in the center of the cutting board. Use a rolling pin to roll out the dough. Between rolling, gently pull the dough from the edges. Begin at the center and roll out away from you toward the edge. Do not roll back and forth. Turn the dough 90 degrees (from 12 o'clock to 3 o'clock) and repeat the process. Turn another 90 degrees and repeat process--then turn last 90 degrees and roll until you have a circle. Roll the dough to about ¼-inch thickness. After you have the complete circle, with the tips of your fingers, pull the dough from the center to the edges. This will make the crust even thinner. The dough may be springy and will tend to spring back to the center. Don't fight it--the dough will win every time. Let the dough rest for 2 more minutes, then begin the thinning process again. The dough is now ready for application of the toppings and baking, either in the oven or on the grill.

Working with one piece of dough at a time, pick it up with two hands and let gravity gently stretch it into an oval. For a more circular shape, move your hands around the perimeter of the dough as it stretches. Once you've achieved its desired shape, place it onto a cutting board to finish shaping.

SAUCE — THE HEART OF THE PIZZA

If the crust is the foundation then the sauce is a luxurious carpet.

1 (8 ounce) can tomato sauce

1 (6 ounce) can tomato paste

½ teaspoon sugar

1 teaspoon salt

⅛ teaspoon black pepper

¼ teaspoon garlic powder

¼ teaspoon basil

½ teaspoon oregano

¼ teaspoon marjoram

¼ teaspoon cumin

¼ teaspoon chili powder

⅛ teaspoon red pepper flakes

Place all ingredients in a heavy, medium-sized saucepan. Bring the sauce just to a boil over medium heat while stirring with a heat resistant spatula. Reduce heat to simmer and continue stirring. Scrape down the sides of the pan occasionally. Simmer for about 15 minutes. The sauce should be the consistency of thick gravy. Taste and adjust the seasoning. Cool before applying to crust.

NOTE: When placing sauce on the crust, ladle a thin layer of sauce on the dough, within 1-inch of the edges.

COOKING THE PIZZA — OVEN OR GRILL?

Before assembling your pizza, decide if you prefer the traditional oven baked version or pizza on the grill.

I will never forget the day I discovered grilled pizza. It was during the early nineties at a new Italian boutique restaurant in midtown Manhattan. The crunchiness of the crust, the majesty of the grill marks and the smokey flavor brought me to heights I had not experienced since my pilgrimage to Naples.

MAKING PIZZA ON THE GRILL: Once the dough is formed, pile the disks on top of one another with a sheet of wax paper between each. Organize all of your topping ingredients on a platter and set the platter next to the grill. Once you begin the grilling process, things will proceed with deliberate speed.

Just before the next step, stretch and shape each disk one last time. Use your fingers and stretch the dough out as much as you can. Hold up each disk and allow the dough to hang and stretch, then lay the dough on a cutting board and give one last shaping and stretch with the edges of your fingers.

Light a gas grill or prepare a wood or charcoal grill. Turn the gas grill to medium-high heat. If your gas grill has multiple burners, turn one to medium-low. Best temperature is 450°F. Use the medium-low burner after applying the toppings. If using a charcoal grill, place several layers of coal on one side and one layer of coals on the other--this creates hot and medium-low sections.

You can either place the pizza disks directly on the grill grates, or you can use a griddle placed over the grates. I prefer the griddle--less to clean up.

With a basting brush, lightly apply a coat of olive oil to one side of each disk. With a spatula, or with two hands holding and suspending the disk, gently place each disk, oiled side down, on the grill. Pull at the crust to make it thinner. Close grill cover. After about 2 minutes, gently lift each crust to see if it is becoming brown and crispy and if grill marks are forming. Watch closely for burning. The top of the crust will start to bubble--no worries. If the bottom is burning too quickly, reduce the flame or move the crust to a cooler area of the grill.

When the bottom of each crust is browned, remove the disks, either with a spatula or tongs and place each disk on a cutting board, grilled side up. Apply olive oil to the ungrilled top of each disk, then turn over, grilled side up. Lightly sprinkle with kosher salt then apply desired toppings. Place toppings within half- inch of the edge of each crust and, with a wide spatula, place each disk back on the grill, topping side up. Close cover. Using a set of tongs, rotate each disk occasionally so they will cook evenly. Within 2-5 minutes, depending on the toppings, each pizza should be ready to remove from the grill and enjoy. Remove with a wide spatula. You can assist the spatula with a pair of tongs. If each disk is no more than 6-inches in diameter, the disk should be very easy to remove from the grill.

MAKING PIZZA IN THE OVEN: Adjust oven rack to lower-middle position. If you have a baking stone, place it on the rack. Or you can place a baking sheet upside down on the rack. Preheat oven to 475°F. The easiest way to get the pizza from countertop to oven (and the safest way to keep it from falling apart), is to place the dough on a pizza peel after you shape it. First, spread a thin layer of cornmeal on the pizza peel. Then, carefully place a crust on the peel. Put your favorite topping on the crust. Then, open the oven door. Place the far edge of the peel on the far edge of the baking stone. Then slowly move the peel back and forth. The pizza should slide off the peel and onto the baking stone. Bake until the underside of the crust is golden brown, and the toppings are cooked, about 10 minutes, depending on the toppings. Gently lift a corner of the crust to make sure it is not getting too dark. When the pizza is done, gently lift the front of the pizza with your fingers and slide the peel under the pizza.

LET'S TOP THE PIZZA!

There are no limits to pizza toppings. I've seen everything from simple cheese and tomato sauce to chicken, steak and even peanut butter and sushi. There are no rules other than your own imagination and taste. One extra benefit of making pizza at home is that you can include the entire family in the process. Kids have fun stretching the dough. They can even try to throw it up in the air and catch it. Preparing the topping teaches cooking skills and cooperation. Let the kids select some toppings. If one child likes sausage and peppers and the other likes only cheese and sauce, they can construct one pizza with each of their choices on half of one pizza.

SAUSAGE AND PEPPER PIZZA

This pizza could also be made with pepperoni instead of sausage.

1 pound sweet Italian sausage, cooked

1 red or green bell pepper, roasted

1 red onion

Extra virgin olive oil

Sauce for pizza (see recipe on p. 200)

2 ripe tomatoes, thinly sliced

1 cup mozzarella cheese, grated

Before assembly, select grill or oven method for the pizza. Grill the sausage, turning frequently, until cooked through. Slice into ¼" slices. Cut onion into slices. Cut pepper into quarters. Brush onions and peppers with oil. Grill onions and peppers on each side for about 3 minutes per side. Assemble by first placing a layer of sauce on the crust, if desired. Then, place a layer of tomatoes on the crust, followed by the onions and peppers and finally, sprinkle with the cheese. Makes two 6-inch pizzas.

MEATBALL & ROASTED PEPPER PIZZA

Before assembly, select grill or oven method. See recipe for *Fabe's Extraordinary Meatballs* on page 191. Cut cooked meatballs into ¼-inch slices. Place a layer of pizza sauce on top of the pizza. Place a single layer of meatball slices on top of the sauce. Add roasted red peppers on top of the meatballs. Add cheese if desired.

ROASTED PEPPERS & ANCHOVY PIZZA

You can roast the peppers over a burner on the stovetop, but I prefer either grilling them or roasting them in the oven.

Wash and dry the peppers thoroughly. Preheat the oven to 450°F. Place the peppers on a lightly oiled baking sheet and roast for about 30-40 minutes. Turn every 10 minutes. Peppers are done when they are black charred on all sides.

Remove the peppers with tongs and place them in a brown paper bag or a large bowl covered with foil. After the peppers have cooled, the skin and charred portions should peel right off. Cut the peppers into strips and remove the seeds and white parts. Do not wash the peppers. Slightly drizzle with olive oil.

To roast on the grill, rub olive oil on grates. Place peppers over flame and roast for about 30 minutes. Turn over 10 minutes until they are charred black on all sides. Remove with tongs and cool and cut into strips as above.

Before assembly, select grill or oven method. Add a layer of pizza sauce, if desired. Place two ½-inch pepper strips and three anchovies over the sauce. Drizzle with olive oil.

SCAMPI PIZZA

This pizza should be cooked by the grill method. Use medium size shrimp, generally 21-25 to a pound. Cook shrimp first by drizzling a medium-sized pan with 1 tablespoon olive oil and 1 tablespoon butter. It's best to butterfly the shrimp. Slice each shrimp lengthwise through the middle, but not all the way through. Open the shrimp so that you have two joined halves. When oil is hot, place shrimp in pan. Sprinkle with 1 teaspoon dried oregano, 1 teaspoon dried basil, 1 teaspoon garlic powder and a pinch of kosher salt and black pepper. Cook just until pink on each side, about 2 minutes per side. Do not overcook. Stir frequently. Sprinkle a squeeze of lemon juice, then remove shrimp and set aside.

Cook pizza crusts on both sides. Remove from grill. Place a layer of pizza sauce on the cooked side of the crust. Then place a single layer of cooked shrimp on each pizza. Cover with a thin slice of tomato and red onion. Return to grill, cover and cook 3 minutes more.

TAPENADE AND TOMATO PIZZA

Cheryl does not like cheese. This is her favorite pizza.

1 cup tapenade (See recipe on p. 70)
1 Roma tomato, thinly sliced

Before assembly, select grill or oven method. Place a coat of pizza sauce over the crust. Spread a layer of tapenade over the sauce, then place slices of tomatoes on top of the tapenade. You can also add some roasted red bell peppers.

AMERICANIZED MARGHERITA PIZZA

A slightly different take on this Italian classic.

¼ **cup olive oil, for brushing and drizzling**

Pizza Sauce (see recipe on p. 200)

½ **teaspoon garlic, minced**

½ **cup loosely packed shredded mozzarella cheese**

2 tablespoons freshly grated Pecorino Romano

1 ripe tomato, thinly sliced

8 basil leaves

Before assembly, select grill or oven method. Lightly brush the crust with olive oil. Place a coat of pizza sauce over the oiled crust. Sprinkle with garlic. Spread the cheeses evenly over the sauce. Place the tomato slices on top of the cheese. Just before the pizza is done, spread a layer of basil leaves on top of the tomatoes.

ITALIAN STUFFED ARTICHOKES

The area around Watsonville in Northern California is the artichoke capital of America. During the harvest season, we occasionally journeyed to the region where we picked our artichokes. This delicacy requires some work, but it's worth the effort.

2 large artichokes

1 lemon, juiced

¾ cup breadcrumbs

½ cup Parmesan cheese, grated

4 flat anchovies, chopped

1 teaspoon capers

½ cup Italian parsley, finely chopped

4 garlic cloves, minced

¼ teaspoon kosher salt

Freshly ground black pepper

¼ teaspoon oregano

Pinch red pepper flakes

3-4 tablespoons olive oil

½ tablespoon kosher salt to add to saucepan with water

With a pair of scissors, clip the prickly tips of the leaves. Cut the stems to leave a flat surface to stand the artichokes upright in a pan. Cut approximately ½-inch off the top of each artichoke, place upside down on a work surface and press down to spread the petals. With your hands, further spread the petals to make room for the stuffing. With a grapefruit spoon, scrape out the fuzzy choke. Sprinkle the lemon juice in the interior of the artichoke to retard browning. Place some lemon juice in a bowl of water. Place the artichokes in the water and allow them to soak for 15 minutes.

To make the stuffing, place the breadcrumbs, Parmesan cheese, anchovies, capers, parsley, garlic, ¼ teaspoon salt, black pepper, oregano and red pepper flakes in a small bowl. Add enough olive oil to create a mixture that resembles a paste.

Remove the artichokes from the water. Turn upside down and drain. Once again, with one hand, spread the petals as far as possible to accommodate the stuffing. With a teaspoon, place around ⅓ cup of stuffing into each artichoke, filling as many spaces between the petals as possible. With any leftover stuffing, sprinkle it over the top of each artichoke.

Place the artichokes in a heavy saucepan with sufficient depth to accommodate the artichokes. Pour enough water around the artichokes to a level approximately 1-inch above the bottom of the artichokes. Add ½ tablespoon kosher salt to the water.

Bring the water to a boil over high heat. Cover, then reduce the heat so that the water simmers. Cook for 45-50 minutes or until the artichokes are very tender. Check occasionally to make sure that the water has remained at the same level. Add more water, if necessary. Serve immediately.

---- **Thought for Life** ----

*It takes courage
to walk the road of life.
It takes more courage
to build the road.*

FABE'S RISOTTO WITH MUSHROOMS, LEEKS & PEAS

To me, a dinner composed exclusively of risotto is extremely satisfying. Rice did not find its way to Italy until about the 16th century. Today, this short grain rice is produced in the Po Valley. The Italians cook their risotto to a creamy consistency called all'onda, or wavelike. Making it at home may seem daunting, but once you get the hang of it, you will want to make it frequently.

- About 2-3 tablespoons olive oil, divided
- About 12 tablespoons butter, divided
- 1 pound fresh mushrooms
- Kosher salt, freshly ground black pepper, fresh or dried thyme or fresh rosemary
- 6-8 cups chicken stock
- 2 leeks, white & green parts thinly sliced
- 1 shallot, chopped
- 1 cup Arborio or Carnaroli rice
- ½ cup dry white wine
- ½ cup frozen peas
- 2 tablespoons heavy cream
- ¼ cup grated Parmesan cheese
- ¼ cup Italian parsley, chopped

Melt 1 tablespoon olive oil and 2 tablespoons butter in heavy large skillet over medium-high heat. Add assorted favorite mushrooms and sprinkle with salt, pepper and thyme or rosemary, if using. Sauté mushrooms until tender and beginning to brown, about 3 to 4 minutes. Transfer mushrooms to a medium bowl. Working in three more batches, repeat with 6 tablespoons butter, remaining mushrooms, salt, pepper, and thyme.

Bring chicken stock to a simmer in medium saucepan; keep warm. Melt another 1½ tablespoons butter with olive oil in a heavy large saucepan over medium-low heat. Add leeks and shallot, sprinkle with salt, pepper and thyme and sauté until tender, about 4 to 5 minutes. Add rice and increase heat to medium. Stir until edges of rice begin to look translucent, about 3 to 4 minutes. It should make a clicking sound. Add white wine and stir until liquid is almost absorbed, about 1 minute.

Add ¾ cup warm chicken stock; stir constantly at medium speed until almost all stock is absorbed, about 1 minute.

Continue adding stock by ¾ cupful, stirring at medium speed until almost all of the stock is absorbed before adding more.

Continue adding stock ¾ cup at a time. Stir constantly until rice is mostly translucent but still opaque in the center. Rice should be al dente but not crunchy. Watch the rice carefully as it approaches doneness. Add smaller amounts of liquid to make sure it does not overcook. The final mixture should be thick enough that grains of rice are suspended in the liquid and the consistency of heavy cream. It will thicken slightly when removed from the heat. During the last 10 minutes, stir in the peas and the cooked mushrooms and continue to add stock.

Remove from heat. Stir in butter, heavy cream, Parmesan cheese, and parsley. Season with salt, pepper & thyme. Divide the mixture among serving bowls. Sprinkle with additional Parmesan cheese and parsley. Serve immediately.

Chapter 15

Cuisine of France

French chefs possess the ingenious ability to combine a few ingredients and fashion cuisine where the total is greater than the sum of its parts.

Food speaks to us. French cuisine sings to us.

MONSIEUR LE FABRE'S BEEF BOURGUIGNON

This classic French bistro dish is easy to make. Just a few spices yield an extraordinary depth of flavor. While the creation is cooking, the exquisite aromas will drift throughout the neighborhood.

1 pound assorted fresh mushrooms

6 strips bacon

5 carrots

6 ounces pearl onions

3 tablespoons extra virgin olive oil, divided

Kosher salt & freshly ground black pepper

4 pounds chuck roast, cut into 1" squares

¼ cup flour, plus more for dredging

2 teaspoons thyme, divided

2 celery ribs, chopped

1 green bell pepper, chopped

2 cloves garlic, smashed

1 (6 ounce) can tomato paste

3 cups good quality dry red wine (pinot noir or cabernet suggested)

2-3 cups beef stock, homemade preferred

3 bay leaves

2 tablespoons Worcestershire sauce

6 Yukon Gold potatoes, quartered

Italian parsley, chopped

3 tablespoons butter

1 pound frozen peas

1 pound wide egg noodles (if using)

MISE EN PLACE: Remove mushroom stems and cut mushrooms in half. Cut bacon strips into 1-inch pieces. Cut carrots into 1-inch chunks. Immerse pearl onions in a saucepan of boiling water for 2 minutes. Remove and place in a colander and run cold water over them. They will then peel very easily.

PREPARATION: In a 6-quart Dutch oven, heat 2 tablespoons of olive oil over medium, then add mushrooms. Season with salt and pepper. Allow them to brown for 1 minute without stirring them. Then, stir occasionally and sauté until browned. Transfer to a plate and set aside.

Just prior to browning the meat, dredge the meat chunks in flour and shake off excess. Add another tablespoon of olive oil to the pot and cook the meat in batches in a single layer. Season meat with 1 teaspoon of thyme, salt and pepper and brown on all sides. Remove the browned meat and transfer to a plate. Continue seasoning and browning each batch. Set aside. Preheat oven to 350°F.

Add bacon to the pot and cook over medium heat until medium brown. Add onion, celery, bell pepper and carrots. Season with salt, pepper and thyme. Cook about 6 minutes until soft and translucent. Add garlic, stir and cook for 10 seconds. Add tomato paste. Stir and cook for 1 minute. Scrape tomato paste along the bottom of the pot. Add flour, stir and cook for 1 minute until dissolved.

Add about ½ cup of the wine. With a wooden spatula, scrape the bottom of the pan to loosen all of the fond, then add the balance of the wine. This creates the intense flavor. Cook over high heat until the wine is reduced by about half. Then, add the beef stock, the bay leaves and the meat. Increase heat to high, then bring the liquid to a boil. Cover the Dutch oven with the lid and place in the oven for about 1 hour. Remove the pot from the oven and place on the stovetop. (You can also return it to the oven after adding the carrots and pearl onions, but I think you have more control on the stovetop.)

Bring liquid to a boil on stovetop over medium-high heat, then reduce heat to a simmer. Add the remaining 1 teaspoon dried thyme and about 2 tablespoons Worcestershire sauce. Add quartered potatoes. Simmer for about 1 hour more or until meat, potatoes and carrots are fork tender. Add chopped parsley. Return mushrooms to the pot and add 3 tablespoons butter. Add frozen peas.

Season to taste. Stir until butter dissolves and mushrooms and peas are warmed through. Do not overcook or mushrooms turn to mush. If desired, serve over buttered noodles.

This dish is better the second day, so it is a good idea to make it a day ahead.

Napoleon Bonaparte, born in Corsica in 1769, was a French military leader and emperor who conquered much of Europe in the early 19th century. After seizing political power in France in a 1799 coup d'état, he crowned himself emperor in 1804. Shrewd, ambitious and a skilled military strategist, Napoleon successfully waged war against various coalitions of European nations and expanded his empire. However, after a disastrous French invasion of Russia in 1812, Napoleon abdicated the throne two years later and was exiled to the island of Elba. In 1815, he briefly returned to power in his Hundred Days campaign. After a crushing defeat at the Battle of Waterloo, he abdicated once again and was exiled to the remote island of Saint Helena, where he died in 1821 at age 51. (Adapted from Napoleon Bonaparte. (2021). Retrieved from https://www.history.com/topics/france/napoleon)

At Waterloo in Belgium, Napoleon Bonaparte suffered a defeat at the hands of the Duke of Wellington, bringing an end to the Napoleonic era of European history.

A few Napoleonic quotes:

"Never interrupt your enemy when he is making a mistake."

"Envy is a declaration of inferiority."

"If you wish to be a success in the world, promise everything, deliver nothing."

A little known fact was that Napoleon could see into the future. His recently discovered quote:

"Had I fed my troops Monsieur Le Fabre's Beef Bourguignon, I could have defeated the Duke of Wellington who fed his troops Beef Wellington."

RACK OF LAMB WITH MUSTARD-THYME CRUST

When I'm asked about my most memorable meal, I usually respond with a list of about ten. Not all in the list were expensive or fancy meals. One is a two-dollar hamburger. Another was a plate of heirloom tomatoes in a vinaigrette that we had in Malta. I always include a rack of lamb we savored at the Ritz Hotel in Paris. This recipe comes very close.

¼ cup fresh breadcrumbs from stale bread or a French roll

¼ cup coarse grain Dijon mustard

1 tablespoon garlic, minced

1 tablespoon fresh thyme, chopped or 1 teaspoon dried thyme

1 tablespoon fresh rosemary or 1 teaspoon dried

1 tablespoon Italian parsley, chopped

1 teaspoon oregano

3 tablespoons olive oil

Kosher salt and freshly ground black pepper

1 rack of lamb

1 tablespoons olive oil

Additional olive oil and mustard

Place one slice of stale white bread or a French roll in the food processor. Pulse to coarse crumbs. Set aside.

Combine mustard, garlic, thyme, rosemary, parsley, oregano, and olive oil in food processor. Mix well until a thick paste is formed. In the meantime, heat a heavy skillet, preferably cast iron, over heavy heat for at least 15 minutes. Preheat oven to 450°F.

Rub all sides of the rack with an additional tablespoon of olive oil and generously season with salt and pepper. Place in the hot skillet and sear all sides until dark brown and a crust forms. Either leave lamb in ovenproof skillet or transfer to a baking sheet.

Combine the reserved breadcrumbs with the mustard mixture.

Brush lamb all over with additional mustard to make a glue. Pat crumb-mustard mixture over meaty sides of rack.

Place rack of lamb on the skillet or baking sheet, bone side up. Roast lamb until a thermometer inserted into the center registers 125°F for rare (about 20 minutes), and 130°F for medium rare (about 25 minutes). Remove lamb from oven and let rest on baking sheet or pan for 10 minutes. Carve into individual chops. Serves 2.

---- **Thought for Life** ----

One day, about five thousand years ago, a man carried the first stone to a site in Egypt. The weight of the stone was similar to the weight of an automobile. The same day, in California, a seed fell to the earth. The weight of the seed was similar to the weight of a grain of sand. Thousands more men carried thousands more stones to the Egyptian site. Not even one man planted the seed in the California soil. Today, those stones of Egypt are the 200-foot high Pyramid of Djoser. Today, that California seed is the 200-foot high tree named Methuselah. Ask yourself, "Which edifice is more miraculous?"

POMMES DE TERRE BOULANGÈRES

I love French cuisine. And there is something musical about the French language. In America, we might enjoy a bowl of spuds. A baked potato is often called a "baker." A bowl of spuds might be mashed potatoes, or "mashers." Even our French fries are called "pommes de terre frites" in France. I love spuds in almost any form. But there is nothing musical about the word, spud. Not only are Pommes de Terre Boulangères a delicious variety of potatoes, just uttering the words make them taste even better.

Pommes de terre literally means "apple (or fruit) of the earth. Boulangères literally means bread bakery. Although these potatoes are baked, I don't quite understand how the French named this delightful dish.

2 onions, thinly sliced

2 leeks, thinly chopped

2 pounds white or Yukon Gold potatoes, sliced ¼" thick

2 tablespoons butter

3 teaspoons fresh thyme or 1½ teaspoons dried thyme

Kosher salt and freshly ground black pepper

½ cup dry white wine

1½ cups chicken stock, preferably homemade

Additional butter to top potatoes

Slice onions and separate rings. Wash leeks thoroughly before chopping. Wash potatoes, but don't remove skins. Slice on a mandolin if possible. Preheat oven to 375°F.

Melt 2 tablespoons of butter over low heat in a large skillet. Add onions and leeks and cook, covered, until they are soft but not browned. Add the potatoes and coat well. Add thyme, salt and pepper and mix well.

Increase heat to medium high, add wine and deglaze by scraping the brown bits from the bottom of the skillet. This enhances the flavor. Cook over medium heat until wine is reduced to about 2 tablespoons. Add stock and cook, covered, another 15 minutes. Taste stock and adjust the seasoning if necessary.

Transfer the ingredients to a 13x9 baking dish. Dot top of potatoes with butter. Place in oven and bake for about 1 hour. Check occasionally to see if potatoes are becoming too brown — if so, cover baking dish with foil. Bake until most of the liquid has been reduced and tops of potatoes are golden brown and crusty on top. Check potatoes by inserting a knife in a potato to assure they are fully cooked. If the knife enters without resistance, the pommes de terre are fully cooked.

SCALLOPS SAUTÉED IN LEMON BUTTER

Quality scallops are a great treat. It's best to select dry scallops. Wet scallops are treated with a solution of water and a preservative, so you're paying for a large percentage of water. Dry scallops have no additives and provide a great texture and succulent flavor.

SCALLOPS
1 pound large scallops
Kosher salt & ground black pepper
1 tablespoon butter

LEMON BUTTER
2 tablespoons butter
2 cloves garlic, minced
Kosher salt & ground black pepper
2-4 teaspoons lemon juice
2 tablespoons Italian parsley, chopped

Dry scallops are the best, but hard to find. If using soaked, or wet scallops, place in a colander for half an hour before using. Before preparing this dish, place scallops on a clean dish towel and pat dry on both sides. Season with salt and pepper. Carefully remove the small muscle from the side of each scallop.

Place 1 tablespoon butter in a large nonstick skillet over medium heat. When butter is melted and sizzling, place scallops in skillet in a single layer. Cook for about 1 ½ minutes on each side until golden brown and slightly translucent in the center. With a spatula, carefully lift the edge of one scallop and peek to see if it is golden brown. The secret to tender scallops is not to overcook them. When both sides of the scallops are done, remove them from the skillet, place them in a single layer on a plate, and cover to keep warm.

In the same skillet, add 2 more tablespoons of butter. Add garlic and sauté for 30 seconds. Do not brown. Add salt, pepper and lemon juice to taste. Add parsley flakes. Gently pour over scallops and serve immediately. Serve over steamed rice with a side of veggies.

FRENCH BRAISED CHICKEN WITH WINE & MUSTARD SAUCE

There are endless ways to cook a chicken. That's a good thing, especially for those who want to restrict their intake of red meat. This is one of those one pot recipes that makes a comforting meal on a cool autumn evening. I'll eat this dish any time of the year.

2 bone-in chicken breasts, 2 bone-in thighs, 2 legs (or a whole chicken, cut up)

1 tablespoon olive oil

Kosher salt and freshly ground black pepper

2 tablespoons thyme (French thyme preferred)

4 shallots, sliced lengthwise

2 leeks, thinly sliced

1 celery rib, chopped

4 cloves garlic, thinly sliced

1 cup chicken stock

½ cup dry white wine

¼ cup whole grain mustard

4 Yukon Gold potatoes, quartered

2 carrots, sliced lengthwise

½ pound whole mushrooms

1 teaspoon tarragon

3 tablespoons butter & 3 tablespoons flour

¼ cup Italian parsley, chopped

Preheat oven to 375°F. In a large, heavy skillet or Dutch oven heat oil over medium high heat. Season chicken with salt, pepper and thyme. Working in batches, cook chicken for about 10 minutes per side or until golden brown. Transfer chicken to a plate. Add shallots, leeks, celery and garlic. Cook until soft, but not browned.

Return chicken to the pot, then add chicken stock, wine and mustard. Add potatoes, carrots and mushrooms. Immerse as many potatoes, mushrooms and carrots in the sauce as possible. Reseason with salt, pepper, thyme and tarragon.

Bake in oven for about 45 minutes or until potatoes and carrots are done and chicken registers 170°F on an instant thermometer. Meanwhile, make the roux while chicken is baking. Melt 3 tablespoons of butter in a heavy 1-quart saucepan over medium-low heat. Add 3 tablespoons of flour. NEVER LEAVE THE ROUX! It can burn in a second. Mix constantly until the roux is blonde in color. Remove from heat and set aside.

Remove the pot from the oven and place on a burner over medium-high heat. Remove all contents from the pot except the sauce. Bring the sauce to a boil, then add the roux and stir until the sauce thickens. Taste sauce and adjust seasoning with salt, pepper, thyme and tarragon. Return chicken and vegetables to the pot, spoon sauce over everything. Sprinkle with parsley. Serve immediately.

You can also eliminate the potatoes and serve over buttered noodles.

FRENCH ROAST CHICKEN WITH POTATOES

CHICKEN & POTATOES

6 tablespoons butter, softened

6 tablespoons olive oil

Kosher salt and freshly ground black pepper

½ onion, peeled

1 whole garlic, halved

4 springs each fresh thyme and rosemary (or substitute 1 tablespoon each dried)

2 pounds Yukon Gold or white potatoes, sliced ¼" thick

1 whole (3-5 pound) chicken

3 tablespoons stock or water

SAUCE

4 tablespoons butter

4 tablespoons flour

1/2 cup dry white wine

2 cups chicken stock

Kosher salt and freshly ground pepper

CHICKEN & POTATOES: Preheat oven to 450°F. Rub half of the butter on the bottom of a heavy roasting pan. Sprinkle half the olive oil over the butter. Generously season the chicken on the outside and in the cavity with salt and pepper. Insert onion, garlic, thyme and rosemary sprigs inside cavity. If using dried herbs, sprinkle half of each inside cavity and half over outside of chicken. Rub remaining half of butter and oil on outside of chicken.

Lay the potato slices on the bottom of the pan in a single layer. Place chicken, back side up, on top of potatoes. Roast for 20 minutes, then turn chicken on one of its sides and roast 20 minutes more. Then, turn chicken breast side up and continue roasting until the internal temperature registers 170°F in the breast. During the last 10 minutes, add 3 tablespoons chicken stock or water to the pan.

SAUCE: Meanwhile, make the roux while chicken is roasting. Melt 4 tablespoons of butter in a heavy 1-quart saucepan over medium-low heat. Add 4 tablespoons of flour. NEVER LEAVE THE ROUX! It can burn in a second. Mix constantly until the roux is blonde in color. Remove from heat and set aside.

Remove the chicken and potatoes from the pan and place on a carving board. Cover with foil. Drain all but 5 tablespoons of the oil from the pan. Place pan over burner at high heat. Pour about ½ cup of a dry white wine into the pan. In the meantime, scrape the brown bits off of the bottom of the pan. Boil until all but 1 tablespoon of wine remains. Add 2 cups of chicken stock and bring to a boil. Add roux and continue to boil, stirring constantly, until the roux thickens to desired consistency. Taste, then season with salt and pepper.

Carve chicken and place on dinner plates with potatoes. Drizzle with gravy and serve immediately.

FABE'S BISTRO ROAST CHICKEN WITH POTATOES & VEGGIE

This is a classic dish served in Parisian bistros. The entire house will have a Parisian fragrance.

CHICKEN

6 tablespoons butter, softened (divided)

6 tablespoons olive oil, divided

2 pounds Yukon Gold potatoes, cut into ¼" slices

1 tablespoon each of kosher salt, freshly ground black pepper & paprika

1 whole (3-5-pound) chicken

4 sprigs fresh rosemary

1 teaspoon ground thyme

½ lemon

1 head garlic, halved crosswise

2 tablespoons water

½ pound green beans

1 green or red bell pepper, cut into ½" slices (optional)

1 onion, sliced

½ cup Italian parsley, chopped

SAUCE

4 tablespoons flour

4 tablespoons butter

2 cups chicken stock

Kosher salt, freshly ground black pepper & dried thyme

3 talespoons milk (optional)

1-2 tablespoons heavy cream (otpional)

2 tablespoons butter (optional)

CHICKEN: Preheat oven to 450°F.

Butter a large, heavy roasting pan with 3 tablespoons butter and 3 tablespoons oil. Place potatoes in a single layer in roasting pan. Mix salt, pepper and paprika together and season chicken inside and out. Sprinkle seasoning over potatoes, Mix more seasonings if necessary. Rub the seasonings all over the chicken including the cavity. Place rosemary, thyme, lemon and garlic inside the cavity of the chicken. Using kitchen twine, tie the legs together to enclose. Rub entire outside of chicken with remaining 3 tablespoons each of butter and oil. Sprinkle salt, pepper, thyme and paprika over the entire surface of the chicken.

Place chicken on top of potatoes on one of its sides.

Place roasting pan in oven and roast chicken and potatoes for 20 minutes. Turn chicken onto its other side and continue roasting 20 minutes more. Turn chicken, breast side up, and add 2 tablespoons water to pan; continue roasting until juices run clear and the internal temperature reaches 170°F on an instant-read thermometer, 10 to 20 minutes more. During the last 10 minutes, add green beans to pan. Mix and cover with juices.

Note: If using peppers and onion, add to the base of the pan before layering potatoes. This will enrich the sauce. For the authentic French version, omit the onion and bell peppers.

SAUCE: Meanwhile, make the roux while chicken is roasting. Melt 4 tablespoons of butter in a heavy 1 quart saucepan over medium-low heat. Add 4 tablespoons of flour. NEVER LEAVE THE ROUX! It can burn in a second. Mix constantly until the roux is blonde in color. Remove from heat and set aside. Place 2 cups of chicken stock next to the stove.

When the chicken is done, remove the chicken, veggies and potatoes from the plan. Place on a cutting board and cover with foil. With a spoon, add about 2 tablespoons of drippings to the roux. Add another tablespoon of flour and place saucepan over low heat. Mix well until flour is fully incorporated. Remove from heat.

Add about ½ cup of the chicken stock to the pan. Place pan over high heat (a large pan will be placed over 2 burners). Using a heavy wooden spatula, vigorously scrape the bottom and sides of the pan to loosen all of the brown bits. (This is the fond.) Combine fond with stock. This is where all of the flavor is.

Add the balance of the stock. When the liquid reaches a boil, add the roux and stir vigorously with a whisk. The mixture will begin to thicken. If it becomes too thick, add more stock or water. Check for seasoning and add more salt, pepper and thyme if needed.

For extra richness, add about 3 tablespoons of milk, 1 or 2 tablespoons of heavy cream and 2 tablespoons of butter. Whisk well.

When the sauce reaches the desired consistency, carve the chicken into parts. Return the potatoes, green beans, onions and bell peppers (if using) to the bottom of the pan. Lay the chicken parts in the pan, immersing them in the sauce as much as possible. Sprinkle with chopped parsley. Place pan back in oven and reheat for 5-10 minutes.

Thought for Life

If you are too busy trying to impress others, you may be missing the opportunity to be impressed and perhaps learn and be enriched by others.

CHICKEN & POTATOES aka CHICKEN CHASSEUR

The French love one pot meals. This dish is swift and easy and makes a complete meal. This version has meat, potatoes and a green vegetable. The diced ham provides extra flavor. The word "chasseur" is French for "hunter." The Italian word for hunter is "cacciatore." Centuries ago, both Italian and French hunters hunted rabbits, fowl and other items, returned home and made a stew with their gatherings. The Italian version is more tomato based.

1 whole chicken, cut up (or 8 assorted parts)

Kosher salt, freshly ground black pepper & dried thyme (to taste)

1 cup cooked ham steak, diced

1 tablespoon each butter and extra virgin olive oil

¼ pound mushrooms, halved

1 cup pearl onions, peeled

1 medium brown onion, diced

1 shallot, diced

½ bunch scallions (green onions), chopped

1 cup dry white wine

1 cup chicken stock

3-4 Yukon Gold potatoes, sliced ¼" thick (or quartered chunks)

½ pound green beans (optional)

½ cup peas (optional)

2 tablespoons flour & 2 tablespoons butter, softened

2 tablespoons Italian parsley, chopped

Sprinkle both sides of the chicken with kosher salt, freshly ground pepper and dried thyme. In a large covered pan over medium-high heat, braise the chicken and ham in butter and olive oil. Brown the chicken for about 5 minutes per side, then remove both the chicken and ham from the pan and set aside. Add mushrooms and pearl onions to pan. Brown for about 2 minutes. Remove and set aside.

Add onion, shallot and scallion. Sprinkle with salt, pepper and thyme and braise for 3 minutes, then add garlic and cook one minute more. Do not brown. Remove excess fat.

Add wine to the pan and deglaze. With a wooden spatula, scrape the browned bits from the bottom of the pan (the fond). Simmer the sauce until wine is reduced to about 2 tablespoons.

Return chicken, ham, pearl onions and mushrooms to the pan. Add chicken stock. Add potatoes. Bring to a boil, reduce heat to simmer and cover. Cook for about 30 minutes or until chicken pieces register 170°F and potatoes are done.

During the last 10 minutes, add green beans if using. If using peas, add during the last five minutes. Make a roux while the chicken continues to cook. In a heavy 1-quart saucepan over medium-low heat, mix 2 tablespoons of butter with 2 tablespoons of flour. NEVER LEAVE THE ROUX! It can burn in a second. Mix constantly until the roux is blonde in color. Remove from heat and set aside.

Bring sauce to a boil, add roux and stir until it reaches desired thickness. Adjust seasoning. Spoon sauce over chicken and potatoes. Garnish with chopped parsley and serve.

Thought for Life

When you do the right thing, you feel so good about yourself. And that's the greatest reward in the world.

Chapter 16
The Magic of Asian Cuisine

Folks who have never cooked Asian cuisine might be intimidated to give it a try. I know that I was. Once I ventured into these exotic offerings, I saw how easy it was — and so much fun.

ASIAN SHRIMP CAKES & FRIED RICE

This is a wonderful, healthy meal. You can also wrap the cakes in lettuce or make a sandwich with a hard roll.

SHRIMP CAKES

¼ cup mayonnaise

1 pound shrimp, peeled, deveined and chopped

2 tablespoons fresh cilantro, chopped

4 green onions, chopped

2 tablespoons red onion, chopped

2 cloves garlic, chopped

2 tablespoons celery, chopped

2 tablespoons each red & green bell pepper, chopped

1 tablespoon peeled fresh ginger, chopped

1 tablespoon soy sauce

1 tablespoon oyster sauce

1 teaspoon smoked sesame oil

1 teaspoon lemon juice

½ cup panko breadcrumbs

½ teaspoon kosher salt

½ teaspoon black pepper

⅛ teaspoon cayenne pepper

More panko for coating the patties

1½ tablespoons peanut or canola oil, plus 1 teaspoon

FRIED RICE

4 cups cooked and chilled rice

3 cups water

Kosher salt and freshly ground black pepper

3 tablespoons butter, divided

2 eggs, whisked

2 carrots, diced

1 onion, diced

1 red bell pepper, chopped

½ cup frozen peas

3 cloves garlic, minced

2 teaspoons ginger, minced

3 green onions, chopped

3-4 tablespoons soy sauce

2 teaspoons oyster sauce

½ teaspoon toasted sesame oil

SHRIMP CAKES: Blend all ingredients except peanut or canola oil in a medium bowl. If the mixture is too moist, add more panko breadcrumbs. If the mixture is too dry, add more mayonnaise. Next, tear off enough of the mixture to make a small patty, about the size of a silver dollar. The patties should be slightly moist, a bit more than a hamburger patty. Form the rest of the patties after tasting the sample. Place the panko into a shallow bowl. Coat both sides of the patty in panko. In a large skillet over medium heat, add 1 teaspoon of the cooking oil. When the cooking oil shimmers, cook the patty on both sides until golden. Taste the patty and adjust seasoning of the remaining mixture if necessary. Form mixture into six patties. Place on a flat plate. Refrigerate for at least 1 hour.

Heat 1½ tablespoons cooking oil in the same skillet over medium-low heat. Coat the side of each patty in panko. Add cakes and sauté until crisp, about 5 minutes per side. Lower heat produces a golden shrimp cake without burning.

FRIED RICE: Make steamed rice the night or morning before. Place 1¾ cup of rice (Jasmine preferred), in a medium pot. Add 3 cups of water and 1 tablespoon of kosher salt. Over high heat, bring to a fast boil. Continue boiling uncovered until the water is reduced to just above the level of the rice. You will notice small holes in the top of the rice. Cover the pot and reduce the heat to low. Simmer for about 20 minutes, or until rice is soft and fluffy. Drain and refrigerate for 2 hours or overnight.

Heat ½ tablespoon butter in a wok or large sauté pan over medium heat. Heat until melted. Add whisked eggs so that it cooks flat like a small omelet. Cover and cook until firm. Remove and cut into slices. Set aside.

Add 1 more tablespoon butter to pan, heat until melted. Add carrots, onion, bell pepper and peas to pot. Season with salt and pepper and cook until all veggies are soft. Add garlic and ginger and cook 30 seconds. Add remaining butter, cooked rice, green onions, soy sauce and oyster sauce. Stir until everything is combined and evenly distributed. Cook for 3 minutes until rice is slightly fried. Add cooked eggs and stir to combine. Add sesame oil. Adjust seasoning and serve. **NOTE**: You can add and cook a protein such as chicken, shrimp or pork to the rice, or leave it vegetarian.

---------- **Legal Thought** ----------

There is a good analogy between what you eat and what you do. It has been said that you are what you eat. Each bite either enhances your health or endangers it. Each encounter we have either enhances us or is a potential lawsuit.

ASIAN SALMON BURGERS

This is a great way to get all of the health benefits from salmon. Folks love them in lettuce wraps or on a hard roll.

- 1½ pounds salmon
- 2 tablespoons Italian parsley, finely chopped
- 1 bunch scallions (green onions), finely chopped
- 4 tablespoons red & green bell pepper, finely chopped
- 1 tablespoon red onion, finely chopped
- 2 cloves garlic, finely chopped
- 2 tablespoons celery, finely chopped
- 4-5 tablespoons panko breadcrumbs
- 4 tablespoons mayonnaise
- 1 tablespoon soy sauce
- 1½ tablespoons hoisin sauce
- 1 teaspoon smoked sesame oil
- 1 teaspoon fresh ginger, chopped
- ¾ teaspoon kosher salt
- ¼ teaspoon freshly ground black pepper
- Pinch cayenne pepper
- 1-2 teaspoons lemon juice
- ½ cup panko breadcrumbs for coating

Remove skin from salmon. With a sharp chef's knife, chop salmon into ¼-inch chunks. Alternatively, chop in food processor by pulsing until the consistency of hamburger. Do not over chop. It should only take about 6-10 pulses.

Mix all ingredients (except ½ cup panko), with your hands until thoroughly combined. Tear off a piece and make a patty the size of a silver dollar. In a large skillet, heat 2 tablespoons of canola oil. When oil is hot (it will shimmer), add the patty. Cook on both sides until golden brown, about 2 minutes per side. Taste the patty and adjust the seasonings as desired.

With the remaining salmon mixture, form into 6-8 thin patties. Place ½ cup of panko breadcrumbs on a plate. Coat each side of patty with panko. Carefully place into the skillet. Cook on both sides until golden on each side, about 2 minutes per side. Remove from skillet and drain on paper towels. Serve by wrapping each patty in a lettuce leaf.

NOTE: Thin patties cook faster, they don't burn and they taste better.

CHINESE CHICKEN SALAD

This salad is so authentic, I flew to China to buy the chicken.

DRESSING
- 2 tablespoons orange juice
- 2 tablespoons hoisin sauce
- 2 tablespoons rice vinegar
- 2 cloves garlic, minced
- 1 tablespoon fresh ginger, minced
- 3 tablespoons vegetable oil
- Kosher salt & freshly ground black pepper

SALAD
- 1 cup cooked chicken breast, shredded
- 1 large navel orange
- ½ small head cabbage, shredded
- ½ small head iceberg lettuce, shredded
- 1 red bell pepper, julienned
- 1 package fresh bean sprouts
- 1 (8-ounce) can sliced water chestnuts, coarsely chopped
- 6 green onions, thinly sliced
- 1 cup crispy chow mein noodles
- ½ cup fresh cilantro leaves, coarsely chopped

DRESSING: In a small bowl, whisk the reserved orange juice, hoisin sauce, vinegar, garlic, and ginger together. Slowly add the oil and whisk until emulsified. Lightly season with salt and pepper to taste. Set aside.

SALAD: You can cook the chicken breast either by poaching or baking it. To poach, place a chicken breast in a medium saucepan. Add enough water to cover the chicken. Add kosher salt and pepper. Bring to a boil, cover and simmer for about 40 minutes or until the breast reaches 170°F. To bake the breast, preheat oven to 350°F. Place the chicken breast on a baking sheet. Lightly drizzle 1-2 tablespoons of canola oil on all surfaces and lightly sprinkle with kosher salt and pepper. Bake for about 45 minutes or until the breast reaches a temperature of 170°F.

Slice the peel from the orange. Cut orange into segments. Chop into bite-size chunks. Squeeze the chunks to obtain 2 tablespoons of orange juice. Set aside the chunks.

Place the cabbage, lettuce, bell pepper, bean sprouts, water chestnuts and green onions in a large salad bowl. Mix to combine. When ready to serve, place a helping of the veggies on each plate, then add the chicken and noodles on top. Place orange pieces around the plate. Sprinkle with cilantro. Just before serving, slowly pour the dressing over the salad.

KUNG PAO CHICKEN OR SHRIMP
aka FABE'S KUNG POW! CHICKEN OR SHRIMP

For those who love to spice up their Asian cuisine, this is the dish for you. As with any stir-fry dish, once the cooking begins, things happen quite rapidly. Have all ingredients ready and close by. Before you know it, this legendary Sichuan-Hunan masterpiece is ready to serve over steamed rice. Make this dish with chicken or shrimp.

MARINADE

1 pound large shrimp (or 1 pound boneless, skinless chicken breast)

2 tablespoons oyster sauce

1 teaspoon cornstarch

SAUCE

¼ cup white vinegar

¼ cup chicken stock

3 tablespoons dry sherry

2 tablespoons hoisin sauce

1 tablespoon soy sauce

2 teaspoons toasted sesame oil

1 teaspoon chili garlic sauce

2 teaspoons sugar

½ teaspoon each kosher salt & black pepper

VEGETABLES

3 tablespoons canola oil

4-6 small dried red chili peppers

1 celery rib, chopped

1 red bell pepper, chopped into 1" squares

4 teaspoons garlic, minced

2 teaspoons ginger, minced

2 teaspoons cornstarch dissolved in 1 tablespoon water

½ cup roasted peanuts

½ bunch green onions, chopped

If using shrimp, shell and devein shrimp. If using chicken, cut two boneless, skinless chicken breast halves into thin slices, about 1-inch long and ¼-inch wide. Combine oyster sauce and cornstarch in bowl. Mix until cornstarch dissolves. Add shrimp or chicken and coat with marinade. Let stand at room temperature for 10 minutes.

Combine sauce ingredients in a bowl. Mix well and set aside.

Place a wok over high heat. After 1 minute, add 2 tablespoons of canola oil. Add chili peppers and stir-fry until fragrant, about 5-10 seconds. Do not allow chili peppers to blacken. Add shrimp and stir-fry for 3 minutes or just until they turn pink. Remove chili peppers and shrimp and set aside. If using chicken, add chicken and stir-fry until no longer pink, about 3 minutes. Remove chicken and set aside.

Add 1 more tablespoon of oil to wok. Add celery and bell pepper. Stir-fry for 1-2 minutes. Add garlic and ginger to wok. Stir-fry for 30 seconds, then immediately return chili peppers and shrimp or chicken to wok. Stir-fry for 1 minute, then add sauce. Bring to a boil, then add cornstarch-water solution. Stir until sauce boils and thickens. Add peanuts and green onions and stir. Serve over steamed rice.

You can adjust the spiciness by adding more or less chili peppers and/or garlic chili sauce. You can make it even more spicy by cracking dried chili peppers before cooking them.

FABE'S SHRIMP FRIED RICE WITH SNOW PEAS

This is a fried rice dish that constitutes an entire meal.

1 ½ cups rice (Jasmine preferred)

3 cups water & large pinch of kosher salt

1½ tablespoons Thai fish sauce

1 tablespoon soy sauce

1 teaspoon sesame oil

1 teaspoon water

1 teaspoon sugar

2-3 tablespoons canola or peanut oil

2 eggs

2 strips bacon or 4 ounces chopped ham

1 pound large raw shrimp, peeled & deveined

1 cup pea pods

1 large shallot, chopped

4 tablespoons each red & green bell pepper, chopped

1 clove garlic, minced

1 tablespoon ginger, minced

1 bunch green onions, chopped

¼ cup fresh cilantro, minced (optional)

Place 1½ cups of rice in a medium saucepan. Add 3 cups of water and a large pinch of kosher salt. Over high heat, bring to a boil, then reduce heat, cover and lightly boil for 20 minutes or until the water level is just above the top of the rice. You will notice small craters on the top of the rice. Remove from heat and allow to sit, covered, for 15 minutes. You should have about 4 cups of very tender rice. Refrigerate for 4 hours or overnight.

Combine fish sauce, soy sauce, sesame oil, water and sugar. Set aside.

In a large, non-stick skillet or wok, heat ½ tablespoon of canola or peanut oil over medium high heat. Pour in the eggs and allow to cook for 1 minute. Then, stir and cook until just set. Transfer eggs to a plate and cut into strips. Add the bacon or ham and cook until just crisp. Remove and set aside.

Add 1 more tablespoon of canola oil to the pan. Add the shrimp. Stir-fry until just pink. Do not overcook. Remove from pan and set aside. Add pea pods and stir-fry for 1 minute, just until softened. Remove and set aside.

Add 1 more tablespoon of canola oil to the skillet. Add shallot, bell peppers and ginger and cook until softened, about 1 minute. Add garlic and cook for 30 seconds more. With your hands, mix rice to remove lumps. Add the rice and stir until heated through, about 2 minutes. Stir in the fish sauce mixture and mix well until the rice is light brown. Stir in the bacon or ham and the egg. Add the shrimp and snow peas and mix well with rice. Cook for 1 minute until heated through.

Add the green onions and chopped cilantro. Mix well. Serve immediately.

You can substitute 1 cup of chopped asparagus for the pea pods. You can also add ½ cup of thawed frozen peas and carrots.

STEAK & PEPPER STIR-FRY

A quick meal. You could add broccoli florets and enjoy all the food groups in one stir-fry.

MARINADE

2 tablespoons oyster sauce

2 teaspoons cornstarch

¼ teaspoon black pepper

1½ pounds sirloin or New York strip steak, thinly sliced against the grain

SAUCE

⅓ cup beef broth

2 tablespoons dry sherry

2 tablespoons soy sauce

1 teaspoon sugar

¼ teaspoon black pepper

STIR-FRY INGREDIENTS

2 tablespoons canola oil, divided

1 teaspoon garlic, minced

1 teaspoon ginger, minced

½ green & ½ red bell pepper, thinly julienned

1 brown onion, sliced and rings separated

Kosher salt & black pepper

2 tablespoons water

1 teaspoon cornstarch dissolved in 2 teaspoons water

1 bunch green onions, chopped

½ jalapeño, sliced (optional)

MARINADE: Combine the oyster sauce, cornstarch and black pepper. Add the meat and coat well. Set aside for 10 minutes.

SAUCE: Combine sauce ingredients and set aside.

STIR-FRY: Place a large wok over high heat. Wait 1 minute, then add 1½ tablespoons canola oil. Add beef and stir-fry until browned on all sides, about 2 minutes. Add garlic and ginger and stir-fry for 10 seconds. Remove beef, garlic and ginger and place in a bowl. Be sure to remove all of the garlic and ginger so they won't burn.

Add remaining oil to wok, then add bell peppers and onion. Lightly sprinkle with kosher salt and black pepper. Stir-fry for 1 minute, then add the 2 tablespoons of water and stir-fry until the onions and bell peppers are tender, but still crisp.

Return beef, ginger and garlic to wok. Add sauce and bring to a boil. Add cornstarch slurry and stir-fry until sauce thickens. Add chopped green onions. Cover wok and stir-fry an additional 30 seconds until everything is coated with the sauce. Serve over steamed rice or noodles. Spoon sauce over rice or noodles. Add jalapeño slices if using.

BEEF & BROCCOLI STIR-FRY

Another outstanding complete meal with meat, veggies and carbs. If you don't want the carbs, eliminate the steamed rice. Just for fun, the last time I made this, I added some bok choy.

1½ pounds flank steak, New York strip steak or top sirloin steak

½ cup soy sauce

3 tablespoons dry sherry

1 teaspoon sesame oil

2 tablespoons cornstarch

2 tablespoons brown sugar

1 small brown onion, sliced into rings

1 pound broccoli florets

3 tablespoons peanut or canola oil

1 tablespoon garlic, minced

1 tablespoon fresh ginger, minced

¼ teaspoon baking soda

1 bunch green onions, cut into ¼" pieces

¼ pound sliced mushrooms

1 bag fresh bean sprouts (optional)

Pinch red pepper flakes

Kosher salt & freshly ground black pepper

Trim fat from beef. Slice into ¼-inch slices against the grain, on a diagonal.

In a bowl, mix together the soy sauce, sherry, sesame oil, cornstarch and brown sugar. Add the beef and onion rings to the sauce and toss until well covered. Set aside.

Place broccoli florets in a pot of boiling water. Cook for 2 minutes. Remove from heat immediately and set aside.

Heat the peanut or canola oil in a heavy skillet or wok over high heat. Add the blanched broccoli florets and stir for 30-60 seconds until crisp-tender. Remove to a plate and set aside.

Add more peanut or canola oil, if necessary. With tongs, add half the meat and half the sauce to the skillet or wok. Add the garlic and ginger. Spread out the meat so as to have a single layer along the bottom of the skillet or wok. For extra tenderness and browning, sprinkle ¼ teaspoon of baking soda over the meat. Allow to cook and brown for a minute, then turn meat pieces over for 1 more minute. Cook the remaining batch of meat using the same technique.

When the second batch of meat is cooked through, add half the green onions and all of the sliced mushrooms. Next, return the first batch of cooked meat to the skillet or wok, followed by the remaining green onions and vegetables. Add bean sprouts if using. Add the remaining sauce and a pinch of red pepper. Stir everything well so that the sauce covers the meat and vegetables. Add some water, if necessary. Cover, and cook for 1-2 minutes more. Mix well so that all of the ingredients are covered with the sauce. Check for seasoning, then add a pinch of kosher salt and freshly ground black pepper, if desired. Serve immediately over steamed rice.

NOTE: You can substitute snow peas, bok choy, spinach or a combination of each.

--- **Legal Thought** ---

"A lawyer's time, experience and advice are his stock in trade."

This is a quote from Abe Lincoln. Most Americans love and respect Honest Abe. Lawyers don't sell apples. Nor do they sell spiffy automobiles, fancy clothes or journeys to exotic places. Naturally, it's more fun and less painful to pay for pretty things, food that tastes good and romantic journeys. There is nothing pretty nor romantic about a lawsuit.

FABE'S CHINESE RIBS

Tired of American BBQ ribs? These ribs offer a wonderful change of pace. Cutting the ribs and roasting the separate pieces assure a tender and flavorful rib. These ribs are great with a side dish of fried rice. I've served a platter filled with a double recipe and they disappeared in minutes.

2 slabs baby back ribs or St. Louis style ribs

½ cup hoisin sauce

⅓ cup soy sauce

3 tablespoons dry sherry

3 cloves garlic, chopped

½ teaspoon ginger, chopped

2 tablespoons sugar

¼ teaspoon red food coloring (optional)

¼ teaspoon Chinese five spice

⅛ teaspoon white pepper

The St. Louis ribs are usually more meaty. Cut the individual ribs from the slabs. Combine all of the other ingredients in a large bowl and mix well. Place ribs in the bowl and, with your hands, mix well until each rib is well coated. If you used red food coloring, your hands will look like evidence in a murder case. Cover the bowl with plastic wrap and marinate for one hour at room temperature. Remix occasionally.

Preheat oven to 350°F. Place a wire rack over a large baking sheet. (You may need two racks and two baking sheets.) Fill the sheets halfway up with water. Place ribs, bone side down, on rack and bake for 35 minutes. Do not throw sauce away. Turn ribs over and baste with reserved sauce and bake an additional 35 minutes. Flip ribs over and baste again. Bake another 35 minutes or until they begin to become glazed, tender and mahogany colored. Try one rib. The meat should be almost falling off of the bone. If not, bake a little longer. The sauce should be heated to a boil. Then poured over the ribs and served.

Note for Rib Alternatives: This recipe can be used for chicken wings. After marinating, place on the rack in the same manner as the ribs and bake at 350°F for about 1 hour 15 minutes.

This recipe also works fabulously with large (12-15 size) shrimp with shells on. Marinate shrimp for one hour and pan sauté until pink, about 5 minutes total. No need for the oven.

EXTRAORDINARY EGG ROLLS

Great as appetizers or a complete meal. Strange, most egg rolls have no eggs in them.

---

5 tablespoons canola oil, divided
¼ pound mushrooms, sautéed and finely chopped
¾ pound shrimp, sautéed and finely chopped
½ cup chicken stock
2 tablespoons soy sauce
1½ cups cabbage, shredded
2 tablespoons grated ginger
3 cloves garlic, minced
4 green onions, thinly diced
1 large carrot, sliced into matchsticks
1 small red bell pepper, sliced into matchsticks
¼ cup cilantro, chopped
1½ tablespoons sugar
2 tablespoons sesame oil
20 (6x6-inch) egg roll wrappers

Place 1 tablespoon canola oil in a skillet over medium heat. Sauté mushrooms until soft and brown. Chop finely and set aside. In the same skillet, sauté shrimp just until pink, chop finely, and set aside. In a small bowl, combine chicken stock, soy sauce and cabbage. Set aside.

In a medium skillet or wok, over medium heat, add 2 tablespoons of canola oil. Add ginger and garlic and stir-fry for 30 seconds. Do not brown. Add green onions, carrot, bell pepper and cilantro and stir-fry until softened, about 3-4 minutes. Add cabbage-broth mixture to wok. Bring to a boil and simmer until vegetables are tender, about 3-5 minutes. Add more stock or water, if necessary. With a slotted spoon, add contents of wok to a bowl. Add sugar and sesame oil. Cool for 15 minutes, then add shrimp, cilantro and mushrooms and mix until all ingredients are combined.

To assemble, take one wrapper at a time. Fill a glass of cold water. Place wrapper on a work board with one corner pointing down so that the wrapper looks like the shape of a diamond. To avoid a watery filling, use a slotted spoon to scoop the filling. Place about 1½ tablespoons of filling in the center of the wrapper. Spread the filling to within 1-inch of the center corners. Dip your finger in the water and moisten all four edges of the wrapper. Fold the two middle corners over the filling, then roll the bottom side over the filling. It will look like an open envelope. Keep rolling until you meet the top corner, then seal the edges together.

Place 2 tablespoons canola oil in a medium skillet. Over a medium-high flame, heat the oil until it simmers. Add about ⅓ of the egg rolls. You should hear a sizzle when you place them in the skillet. With tongs and a spatula, sauté and gently keep turning the egg rolls until golden brown on all sides, about 3 minutes per side. Cool for 5 minutes, then serve with dipping sauce.

For a quick and tasty dipping sauce, whisk together ¼ cup soy sauce, ¼ cup rice vinegar, 1 teaspoon sesame oil, 2 tablespoons brown sugar, 1 teaspoon each ground ginger, granulated garlic, granulated onion.

FISH WITH BABY BOK CHOY, GARLIC, GINGER & SCALLIONS

Easy to prepare. Delightful Asian flavors.

4 tablespoons oyster sauce

½ cup chicken stock

1 teaspoon cornstarch

¾ teaspoon sesame oil

¼ cup flour

1 pound halibut or other white fish, cut into 4 filets

Kosher salt & freshly ground lack pepper

2 tablespoons butter

2 tablespoons canola oil

1½ pounds baby bok choy (If using regular bok choy, cut each in half lengthwise)

2 bunches scallions (green onions), chopped

2 large cloves garlic, chopped

4 slices ginger, cut into matchsticks

Combine oyster sauce, chicken stock, cornstarch and sesame oil. Whisk to dissolve cornstarch. Set aside.

Heat a wok or nonstick skillet over medium heat for 1 minute. Place flour in a flat bowl. Dredge filets in flour. Shake off excess flour. There should be just a light film of flour on each filet. Season each filet with kosher salt and freshly ground black pepper.

Add butter and 1 tablespoon of canola oil to wok or skillet. When butter and canola oil are hot, sauté filets for 2 minutes on each side until slightly browned. Remove from wok or skillet and set aside.

Heat 1 more tablespoon of canola oil in wok or skillet, add bok choy and season with kosher salt. Toss frequently until slightly browned. Add scallions, garlic and ginger. Stir until aromatics are tender, about 2 minutes. Cook until bok choy is tender, then add sauce and mix. Stir until sauce thickens slightly. Return fish to wok or skillet. With a spoon, scoop and drizzle sauce on fish. Serve immediately.

Best served over steamed rice.

SHRIMP & BABY BOK CHOY

Until a few decades ago, many Americans, including me, had never heard of bok choy. The first time I tried it, my palate was electrified. What a marvelous taste and texture. At times, I just whip up a batch and season it with chicken stock or butter. Plus, nutritionists tell us that an average serving can provide around 60% of your daily requirements of vitamin A and is also packed with vitamin C and K. It's also a good source of fiber. A healthy food that also tastes great.

MARINADE

2 tablespoons very dry sherry

2 teaspoons cornstarch

¼ teaspoon kosher salt

¼ teaspoon freshly ground black pepper

1 pound raw shrimp (about 15-20 per pound)

SAUCE

2 tablespoons very dry sherry

2 tablespoons oyster sauce

1 teaspoon sugar

1 teaspoon seasame oil

2 teaspoons cornstarch

2 tablespoons water

VEGGIES & SPICES

3½ tablespoons canola oil, divided

1 tablespoon fresh ginger, minced

1 tablespoon garlic, minced

5 baby bok choy, quartered lengthwise

1 (8 ounce) can sliced water chestnuts

½ cup chicken stock

Mix the marinade ingredients in a flat bottomed bowl. Make sure cornstarch is dissolved. Peel and devein shrimp. Add shrimp and mix well until covered with marinade. Set aside at room temperature for 15 minutes.

Mix sauce ingredients and set aside. Mix 2 teaspoons cornstarch in 2 tablespoons water. Set aside.

Place a wok over high heat. Add 2 tablespoons canola oil. After 30 seconds, add ginger and garlic and stir-fry for 10 seconds. Do not allow garlic to brown. Add shrimp and its liquid and stir-fry for about 2 minutes. Remove shrimp and all of the ginger and garlic from wok and place in a bowl.

Add 1½ tablespoons more canola oil. Add bok choy and water chestnuts. Stir-fry for about 1-2 minutes. Add stock. Cover wok and cook until bok choy are crisp-tender, about 1 minute. Return shrimp, garlic and ginger to wok. Add sauce and cornstarch solution and stir-fry until mixture boils and thickens. Serve over steamed rice.

WOK FRIED COD WITH ASPARAGUS

This is an extremely tasty fish and veggie dish with a subtle Asian flair.

- 4 cod filets, each about ⅓ pound (or substitute red snapper, halibut or rockfish)
- 3 tablespoons oyster sauce
- 3 tablespoons chicken stock
- ½ teaspoon sesame oil
- 1 teaspoon cornstarch
- 3 green onions, chopped
- 3 cloves garlic, chopped
- 4 slices ginger, cut into strips
- 4 tablespoons canola oil, divided
- ½ cup flour
- Kosher salt and freshly ground black pepper
- 1 pound fresh asparagus
- 3-4 whole scallions (green onions), cleaned
- 3 sprigs cilantro
- ¼ cup Italian parsley, chopped

In a small bowl, combine oyster sauce, chicken stock, sesame oil and cornstarch. Stir to combine cornstarch. Set aside. Combine chopped scallions, garlic and ginger in a small bowl. Set aside.

Heat 2 tablespoons of canola oil in wok. When the oil shimmers, pat fish filets dry. Dredge in flour. Shake off excess. Season with salt and pepper and add to hot oil. Work in batches for best results. Fry on one side for 2-3 minutes. Do not move filet until after 2-3 minutes. Peek under the filet. It should be golden brown. Flip over and fry for an additional 2-3 minutes. For tender, flakey fish, do not overcook. Remove filets and place on a platter. Repeat with remaining filets.

Add remaining oil. Add asparagus and cook for 1-2 minutes. (I had some bok choy around so I threw it in.) The spears will be lightly brown underneath. Add green onions, garlic and ginger. Stir-fry for 30 seconds, then add sauce. Return fish filets to wok. Add whole scallions and cilantro sprigs. Cover and warm for 3 minutes.

Place fish and veggies on a serving platter and brush with the sauce. Serve over steamed rice. Sprinkle with chopped parsley.

CASHEW CHICKEN

A quick, complete meal for a busy night.

- 3 tablespoons soy sauce
- 1 teaspoon sesame oil
- 1 tablespoon brown sugar
- 1 pound boneless, skinless chicken breasts (about 2 breasts)
- 1 teaspoon kosher salt
- ¼ teaspoon black pepper
- ¼ teaspoon celery seeds
- 2 tablespoons canola oil, more as needed
- 1 large onion, sliced and rings separated
- 2 celery ribs, cut into ½″ pieces
- ½ pound mushrooms, sliced
- 1 large green bell pepper, cut into 1″ square
- 2 cloves garlic, minced
- 1 cup chicken stock
- 4½ teaspoons cornstarch mixed into 3 tablespoons water
- 2 cups or 1 package fresh bean sprouts
- ¼ cup cilantro, chopped
- ½ cup roasted unsalted cashews or peanuts (more if desired)

Make a marinade by combining soy sauce, sesame oil and brown sugar in a medium bowl. Cut chicken breasts into thin, 1-inch slices and place in a bowl with soy sauce mixture. Mix well to coat all pieces of chicken. Refrigerate for 20-30 minutes. Combine salt, pepper and celery seeds. Set aside.

In a wok or large nonstick skillet, add 2 tablespoons of canola oil. When heated, add onions, celery, mushrooms, bell pepper, a sprinkle of salt, pepper and celery seeds, and stir-fry onions until tender, about 3-4 minutes. Add garlic, stir-fry for 30 seconds. With a slotted spoon, remove veggies and garlic and place in a bowl. Set aside.

Remix chicken with marinade. Add chicken and marinade to wok and stir-fry until chicken is no longer pink-about 6-7 minutes. Return vegetables to skillet.

Stir chicken stock and cornstarch mixture into wok. Bring to a boil and stir until mixture thickens. Add beans sprouts, cilantro and nuts. Cover and cook until heated through. Add water if necessary. Add more salt, pepper and celery seeds to desired taste. Serve over steamed rice.

TERIYAKI CHICKEN

This is an amazingly easy dish to prepare. Serve with steamed or fried rice and a veggie of your choice. Using drumsticks and/or wings makes a great party appetizer.

Canola oil
1 teaspoon cornstarch
1 tablespoon cold water
¼ cup orange juice
¼ cup each granulated & brown sugar
½ cup soy sauce
¼ cup cider vinegar
1 clove garlic, minced
½ teaspoon ground ginger
¼ teaspoon freshly ground black pepper
2 tablespoons dry sherry
1 whole chicken, cut up (or your favorite parts)

Preheat oven to 425°F. With canola oil, lightly grease a glass 13x9 baking pan or a large nonstick skillet. Combine cornstarch and water, mixing until cornstarch is dissolved. In a small saucepan, combine cornstarch mixture, orange juice, sugars, soy sauce, vinegar, garlic, ginger, black pepper and sherry. Bring to a boil, reduce heat and simmer until sauce thickens and bubbles, about 5 minutes. Stir frequently.

Soak each piece of chicken in thickened sauce. Place chicken pieces in a single layer in baking pan. Brush some additional sauce on each piece. Bake for 30 minutes, then turn pieces over and bake an additional 30 minutes or until done. Baste every ten minutes. If using smaller pieces of chicken, such as wings only, cooking time will be less. A thick breast should register 170°F on an instant thermometer.

You can also add vegetables to the pan such as bok choy, green beans, broccoli or sliced bell peppers. Lightly coat veggies with oil, then add to the pan about 15 minutes before the chicken is completely cooked. Serve with steamed rice.

NOTE: This recipe can be doubled.

Chapter 17
Happy Holidays in the Kitchen

BUTTERFLIED TURKEY & ROAST POTATOES

A great method for preparing a turkey dinner for three or four people. It only takes about an hour and a half. Recently, I purchased a fresh turkey, the weight of which was 14 pounds. I butterflied it myself. However, most butchers will butterfly it for you. If you butterfly it yourself, there are three options. One, you can cut it all the way through the backbone and cook two halves. Two, cook one half and freeze the other for another time. Or three, you can just cut out the backbone, turn the bird over, flatten it out and roast or grill the whole bird.

I use a very sharp chef's knife and strong kitchen shears. Beginning at the neck cavity, take the knife and place it just at the edge of the spine. Cut downward toward the tail. It will require some muscle. As you proceed toward the rear cavity, you will encounter some rib bones and cartilage. Cut the rib plates and remove the small bones. It's best to use the shears for these portions of the procedure. Remove the entire backbone and tail (tail is called "pope's nose"), and use it for making stock. Turn the bird over, cavity side down. Press on the center of the breastbone until you hear a crack and the bird flattens. If you want to cut the turkey entirely in half, take the chef's knife and cut from the neck cavity down on either side of the breastbone. Keep holding the knife right up against the breastbone or you will sever and cut through the breast meat.

TO BRINE OR NOT TO BRINE: The brining controversy rages on. Brining advocates swear that the process ramps up the flavor and moisture of the bird. Detractors claim that brining renders the meat salty and stringy. Some advocates recommend the dry brining process. I tried it and the results were impressive. If you have time, I suggest the dry brining method.

Wash the turkey inside and out by running it under cold water. Pat it dry with a clean towel. Don't use the towel for anything else until after it is laundered. Or, use paper towels. For a 14 pound turkey, use 3 tablespoons of kosher salt.

Sprinkle the inside of the turkey lightly with salt. Place the turkey on its back and salt the breasts, concentrating the salt in the center, where the meat is thickest. Salt the legs, thighs and wings. Rub in the salt with your hands.

Place the turkey in a 3-gallon sealable plastic bag, press out the air and seal tightly. Place the turkey in a pan, breast-side up in the refrigerator. Refrigerate overnight or for at least 8 hours.

Remove the turkey from the bag. There should be no salt visible on the surface, and the skin should be moist but not wet. Rinse the turkey thoroughly with cold water. Pat dry inside and out with another clean towel or paper towels.

PREPARE A SEASONING RUB: In a small bowl, combine 1 teaspoon each of paprika, thyme, poultry seasoning, kosher salt and freshly ground black pepper, plus ½ teaspoon each onion powder and garlic powder.

PREPARE THE POTATOES: Cut approximately 6 medium size white or Yukon Gold potatoes into quarters. Place in a bowl and drizzle with olive oil. Sprinkle with seasoning rub. Mix with your hands so that all of the potatoes are covered with oil and seasoning.

ROASTING THE TURKEY: Preheat the oven to 450°F. Rough chop 1 onion, 1 celery rib and 1 carrot.

This is the mirepoix, the fancy French word for this vegetable combination. Spread the vegetables on the bottom of a heavy baking pan. This procedure will not only add flavor to what eventually will be the gravy, it also serves as a rack for the turkey. Drizzle about 2 tablespoons of olive oil over the entire butterflied turkey. Rub the oil all over the cavity, the breast, legs, thighs and wings. Melt 2 tablespoons of butter, cool for 10 minutes, then rub the butter over the bird as you did with the oil. Massage the seasoning rub mixture all over the outer surface of the turkey.

Place the turkey, cavity side down, on top of the mirepoix. Place the potatoes around the turkey in as much of a single layer as possible. Place in oven and roast for a total of about 1 hour, 10 minutes-1 hour 30 minutes, depending on the size of the turkey. When drippings begin to form on the bottom of the pan, baste the turkey and the potatoes with a basting brush about every 15 minutes. After about 35 minutes, rotate the pan in the oven. Move the potatoes around and turn them over from time to time. The turkey is done when an instant-read thermometer inserted into the thickest part of the breast and the thigh register 170°F. Remove the turkey from the roasting pan, place on a cutting board, wrap tightly with foil and allow to rest for at least 20 minutes. The potatoes should also be done within 1½ hours. If necessary, after you remove the turkey, cook the potatoes until they are crispy on the outside and soft in the center.

MAKING THE GRAVY: The easiest way to make a fabulous turkey gravy is the roux method. While the turkey is roasting, place 3 tablespoons of softened butter and 3 tablespoons of flour in a heavy 1-quart saucepan. Over medium-low heat, whisk the butter and flour together until combined. Continue whisking until the mixture forms into a smooth paste, about 2 minutes. NEVER LEAVE THE ROUX! It can burn in a second. Mix constantly until the roux is blonde in color. Remove from heat and set aside.

When the turkey is done and placed on the cutting board, place the roasting pan over a burner on the stove top. Over high heat, pour about 1 cup of stock into the pan and scrape the bottom of the pan to loosen the drippings which are stuck to the bottom (the fond). Pour about 2 tablespoons of the drippings into the roux pan and mix with the roux. Add about 2 more tablespoons of flour to the roux and mix well over low heat. Remove the vegetables and the remaining grease from the turkey pan. Be sure to leave the fond in the pan. Add another cup of stock to the turkey pan and simmer gently. Add the roux and whisk it into the turkey pan. The mixture will thicken. Add about ¼ cup milk or cream to the mixture. You can thicken the gravy by adding more roux. To thin the gravy, add more stock, milk or cream. Add and stir in a few tablespoons of butter for an even richer gravy. Season to taste with salt and pepper. Pour the gravy through a strainer into a gravy boat or measuring cup.

BAKED HAM WITH PINEAPPLE MUSTARD GLAZE

This ham will be gobbled up by your guests. Hopefully, enough will remain for a week of sandwiches.

1 whole or half spiral cut cooked ham

GLAZE
1 cup brown sugar
1 tablespoon cornstarch
¼ teaspoon ground ginger
¼ teaspoon salt
1 (8 ounce) can crushed pineapple
2 tablespoons lemon juice
1 tablespoon mustard
Maple syrup or honey (optional)

GLAZE: Mix brown sugar, cornstarch, ginger and salt in saucepan. Stir in pineapple, lemon juice and mustard. Stir over medium heat until mixture thickens. Boil one minute. Set aside.

Preheat oven to 275°F. Cut away skin and trim fat from ham to a thickness of about ½-inch. Place ham fat side up in shallow roasting pan. Cover entire pan and ham tightly with aluminum foil. Cook about 10 minutes per pound. A whole ham should take about 2½ to 3 hours. A half ham should take about 1½ to 2 hours. Temperature on instant-read thermometer should register 130-140°F.

Thirty minutes before ham is done, remove from oven and brush with a light coat of maple syrup or honey. Then, brush the entire ham with a light coat of the mustard glaze. When the ham is done, place on a platter and brush on another layer of glaze.

BEST PUMPKIN SPICE BREAD

This is a quick bread which means that proofing and kneading are not required.

1⅔ cups flour
¼ teaspoon baking powder
1 teaspoon baking soda
1 teaspoon cinnamon
1¾ teaspoon ground ginger
½ teaspoon nutmeg
½ teaspoon ground cloves
½ teaspoon salt
1 stick (4 ounces) butter
1¼ cups granulated sugar
2 eggs
½ cup water
1 cup canned pumpkin
½ cup pecans or walnuts, finely chopped

Preheat oven to 350°F. Butter and flour a 9x5-inch loaf pan.

Sift together flour, baking powder, baking soda, cinnamon, ginger, nutmeg, cloves and salt. Set aside.

In a stand mixer, combine butter and sugar. Beat until light and fluffy. Beat in the eggs, one at a time.

In three stages, beginning with the dry ingredients, add them alternatively with the water. Mix after each addition and scrape down the sides of the bowl. Beat in the pumpkin. Stir in the nuts if using.

Pour into the loaf pan and level top with an offset spatula. Bake for 1 hour. Cool in pan for 15 minutes. Remove bread and place on a wire rack. Cool completely.

ORANGE GINGER CRANBERRIES

I hope you don't use those canned cranberries. This recipe takes about 15 minutes to make. It can be prepared one day ahead. They are incredible.

24 ounces fresh cranberries (2 packs)

3 cups granulated sugar

1½ cups orange juice (freshly squeezed preferred)

1½ tablespoons orange zest

1½ tablespoons fresh ginger, finely minced

Combine all ingredients in a saucepan. Cook over medium heat until berries pop open, about 10 minutes. Toward the end of the cooking, skim off and discard the foam that rises to the top. Let cranberries cool. Cover and refrigerate for up to two weeks.

Serves 10.

SWEET POTATO BALLS

These little critters are always met with surprise and delight. It's a tasty and unique way to serve sweet potatoes.

5 large sweet potatoes or yams
⅔ cup brown sugar
2 tablespoons orange juice
1 teaspoon orange zest
½ teaspoon nutmeg
2 cups shredded sweetened coconut
1 teaspoon cinnamon
½ cup granulated sugar
1 bag miniature marshmallows

Bake the potatoes or yams (I prefer yams), until tender. Peel and mash. This can be done one day ahead. Stir in brown sugar, orange juice, zest and nutmeg.

In a separate bowl, mix coconut, cinnamon and granulated sugar.

Form balls about 2-inches in diameter. As you form balls, insert one marshmallow into each ball. Roll each ball generously in coconut mixture.

Place about 2-inches apart in glass baking dishes. Bake in 350°F oven for 15-20 minutes, until coconut just starts to turn light brown. Watch carefully so that marshmallows don't burst and coconut does not burn.

STU'S SECRET INGREDIENT MASHED POTATOES

Tired of the same old mashed potatoes? You will love this version.

6 medium russet potatoes, peeled and quartered
½ cup sliced green onions, sliced
2 cloves garlic, minced
Kosher salt & freshly ground black pepper
2 tablespoons butter, plus more
8 ounces sour cream
4 ounces cream cheese
4-5 tablespoons hot milk
Italian parsley, chopped

Grease a 2-quart casserole dish. Boil quartered potatoes in salted water until tender. Drain, place in a bowl and set aside. Sauté green onions and garlic in butter until tender. Mash potatoes, sour cream and cream cheese with a masher. Add green onions and garlic, plus kosher salt and pepper to taste. Add enough milk to achieve desired consistency. Transfer to the prepared casserole dish and refrigerate for up to 24 hours. Bake uncovered in 350°F oven for 45-50 minutes or until heated through. Sprinkle with parsley.

ROAST TURKEY

Contrary to popular belief, roasting a turkey is one of the easiest cooking exercises. Perhaps the size of the bird is intimidating. But I learned from flying airplanes. The bigger ones are easier to fly. Follow these few simple steps and a gorgeous bird with a sumptuous skin and moist interior will soon emerge from the oven. The debate over brining a turkey will never be resolved. I have made brined and non-brined turkeys and, to me, the difference is barely perceptible. I've been making holiday turkeys for over 60 years. I avoid nouvelle turkeys, such as Cajun or Asian. I love the old-fashion turkeys that I've enjoyed since childhood. This recipe is the easiest and the best. And I guarantee, you will love the gravy.

MIREPOIX

2 medium onions, roughly chopped

3 carrots, roughly chopped

3 celery ribs, roughly chopped

TURKEY

1 fresh turkey (14-17 pounds)

1 stick butter, softened

2 tablespoons each dried sage, rosemary, thyme

Kosher salt and freshly ground black pepper

2 tablespoons paprika

6 cups chicken or turkey stock (preferably homemade)

Remove turkey from refrigerator 1 hour before cooking. Mix the butter, herbs, ½ tablespoon each salt and pepper and paprika until well combined. Preheat oven to 425°F.

Remove all of the giblets, neck and gizzard from the cavity. Season cavity with salt and pepper. Put a handful of the mirepoix in the cavity. Sprinkle the remaining mirepoix on the bottom of the roasting pan. This will serve as the rack and will also add sumptuous flavor to the gravy.

Rub the entire surface of the turkey with a thin layer of the butter mixture. For extra flavor and moisture, place your hand between the skin and the breast and place some butter mixture between the skin and the meat.

Heat the chicken stock in a saucepan. If desired, place neck and giblets in roasting pan. Discard liver. Place the turkey on top of the mirepoix and roast for about 45 minutes. The upper surface should be getting golden brown. Reduce heat to 350°F and continue to roast for another 1 hour 15 minutes to 2 hours, depending on the size of the bird. Baste the turkey every 15 minutes with the chicken stock and the drippings.

Check the temperature with an instant-read thermometer frequently beginning at 1¼ hours. Insert the thermometer into the thickest part of the thigh without touching the bone. The thermometer should register 170°F. Any juices that run should be clear, not pink.

Remove the turkey and place on a carving board. Cut up neck meat and giblets and set aside. Cover the turkey loosely with foil and let it rest at least 30 minutes before carving. It is very simple to make a gravy to accompany the turkey. You will never purchase store-bought gravy again. Start by removing most of the grease. Then place the roasting pan on the stovetop burner(s) on high heat. Scrape the bottom of the pan with a wooden spatula to loosen all of the tasty drippings. Next, add 3 tablespoons of flour and mix with the remaining drippings until all of the flour disappears. Add 2 tablespoons of butter for richness, followed by 4 cups of chicken or turkey stock. Bring to a boil until the liquid thickens. Add ½ cup cream or milk and stir until incorporated.

———————————————————— **Legal Thought** ————————————————————

Black & white comedy movies of the 1930s often depicted scenes of pies in the face and folks getting hit over the head with frying pans. Don't do that at home. Avoid lawyers by putting your frying pans to creating gastronomic masterpieces. For example, cornbread made in a cast iron skillet is marvelous.

BASIC MAKE AHEAD CORNBREAD

It's easy to make your own cornbread. To assure firmness, make cornbread two days before using it as a stuffing. The danger is that your family will eat the cornbread before you get a chance to use it.

---

1 tablespoon plus ¼ cup vegetable oil

1 cup yellow cornmeal

1 cup all-purpose flour

2 teaspoons baking powder

1 teaspoon salt

¼ teaspoon cayenne pepper

1 cup buttermilk

1 egg

Preheat the oven to 400°F.

Pour 1 tablespoon of vegetable oil into a 9-inch baking pan or heavy cast iron skillet. Place the pan into the oven as it preheats, allowing it to heat for at least 10 minutes.

Combine the cornmeal, flour, baking powder, salt, and cayenne pepper in a large mixing bowl and stir with a wooden spoon. Add the buttermilk and egg to the mixture, and stir well to blend. Pour the cornmeal batter into the preheated pan and bake in the oven for 25 minutes or until lightly golden brown. Remove from the oven and let cool before serving or using it as stuffing.

CORNBREAD & SAUSAGE STUFFING

I think that there should be a law against those stuffings that come in a box. Every holiday, this stuffing evokes cheers from our guests. It's quick and easy to make cornbread. The problem is, while it sits in a bowl for two days, we often eat half of it before the holiday.

- **2 teaspoons unsalted butter**
- **½ pound mild Italian or andouille sausage, cut into ½" pieces**
- **1½ cups yellow onion, chopped**
- **1 cup celery, chopped**
- **1 cup green bell pepper, chopped**
- **½ pound mushrooms, sliced**
- **1 tablespoon garlic, minced**
- **Basic Cornbread recipe (see recipe on p. 248)**
- **3 slices of stale white or whole wheat bread, torn into ½" pieces**
- **Fresh corn (cut kernels from two ears)**
- **½ cup green onions, chopped**
- **1 cup pecans, coarsely chopped**
- **⅓ cup Italian parsley, chopped**
- **2 teaspoons fresh thyme, chopped**
- **1 teaspoon kosher salt**
- **½ teaspoon freshly ground black pepper**
- **⅛ teaspoon cayenne pepper**
- **1 teaspoon each dried sage and oregano**
- **2 large eggs, beaten in ¼ cup milk**
- **1 to 2 cups chicken or turkey stock, as needed**
- **Melted butter, as needed**

Preheat the oven to 350°F. Generously butter a 13x9-inch baking dish and set aside.

In a large skillet, cook the sausage until brown and the fat is rendered, about 5 minutes. Add onions, celery, bell peppers, mushrooms and garlic, and cook for 2 minutes. Remove from the heat and transfer to a large bowl to cool.

With your fingers, crumble the cornbread into the bowl. Add the bread, fresh corn, green onions, pecans, parsley, and thyme. Mix well with your hands. Add the salt, pepper, cayenne pepper, sage, oregano and egg mixture. Mix again well with your hands. Add the salt, pepper, cayenne, and eggs, and mix well with your hands. Add enough stock, ½ cup at a time, to moisten the stuffing, being careful not to make it mushy.

Transfer stuffing to the prepared baking dish and pour melted butter on top, as needed. Cover with aluminum foil and bake until heated through, about 25 minutes. Uncover and bake until golden brown, about 15 minutes. You can also fill the turkey cavity with a portion of the stuffing. **IMPORTANT:** Do not stuff the turkey until you are ready to roast it. Hot stuffing and cold turkey should not hang around, as it can result in possible foodborne illness. It's also not a good idea to make the stuffing the night before.

Yield: 8 servings. Recipe can be doubled for 16 servings. This recipe will fill one 16 pound turkey and one 13x9 baking dish.

ROAST TURKEY PARTS

If you don't want to roast an entire turkey for Thanksgiving or Christmas, you can still enjoy this traditional dinner. Most markets offer your favorite turkey parts. When summer rolls around and you have a craving for turkey, this recipe offers a solution.

TURKEY
- 1 teaspoon each paprika, sage, thyme, granulated garlic, kosher salt, black pepper, poultry seasoning
- 4-6 Yukon Gold potatoes, quartered
- 1 celery rib, chopped
- 2 carrots, chopped into 1″ pieces
- 1 onion, halved
- 2-4 tablespoons olive oil
- 4-6 turkey parts (breast, legs, thighs, wings)
- 2 tablespoons butter, softened

GRAVY
- 2 tablespoons butter, plus more for extra richness
- 2 tablespoons flour, plus more for sprinkling
- 1½ cups chicken stock
- 4 tablespoons heavy cream, optional
- Kosher salt & freshly ground black pepper

TURKEY: Preheat oven to 450°F. Mix together paprika, sage, thyme, granulated garlic, salt, pepper and poultry seasoning. Set aside. Place potatoes, celery, carrots and onion in a bowl. Drizzle with olive oil. Sprinkle with seasoning mix. Rub turkey parts with olive oil and butter. Sprinkle with seasoning mix. Place celery and onion in the middle of a large roasting pan. This should be a pan that can be placed on top of the stove later to make the gravy. Place the turkey parts over the celery and onion. Place potatoes and carrots around the turkey parts in a single layer, if possible.

Roast for 30 minutes, then reduce the heat to 400°F. After 15 minutes, baste the turkey and vegetables with accumulated juices. After 15 minutes more, turn the turkey parts and potatoes over, which should be turning to a beautiful golden brown. Baste every 15 minutes. After about 1 hour 15 minutes, check turkey parts with an instant-read thermometer. The turkey is done when the temperature reaches 170°F. If the potatoes, carrots or some turkey parts are done before others, remove them from the pan, place on a cutting board and tent with foil. Total time: about 1½ to 2 hours, depending on the size of the turkey parts.

GRAVY: Place 2 tablespoons of butter and 2 tablespoons of flour in a small saucepan. Over low heat, mix with a spatula. Stir constantly until well combined and the roux has turned blonde in color.

Remove the turkey and vegetables from the roasting pan. There should be turkey drippings and about 2 tablespoons of fat. Sprinkle with flour, then with a wooden spatula, scrape the bottom of the pan to loosen the browned drippings. Add 1½ cups chicken stock. Stir, and add the roux. Bring to a boil until the gravy thickens to desired consistency. For extra richness, add 1-2 tablespoons of butter and about 4 tablespoons heavy cream. Season to taste and stir.

CHOCOLATE GINGER CAKE

Gingerbread is very popular during the holidays. This ginger cake is not gingerbread, but it should fit right in with holiday traditions.

CAKE

6 ounces milk chocolate, chopped (or substitute milk chocolate chips)

2 ⅓ cups flour

½ cup unsweetened cocoa powder

1 teaspoon instant espresso powder (or instant coffee powder)

1 teaspoon cinnamon

¼ teaspoon ground cloves

½ teaspoon salt

1 cup canola oil

1 cup molasses

1 cup granulated sugar

1 cup water

1 ½ teaspoons baking soda

3 tablespoons fresh gingeroot, finely ground

2 eggs

2 egg yolks

FROSTING

4 ounces bittersweet chocolate, chopped

¼ teaspoon cinnamon

¼ teaspoon instant espresso powder (or instant coffee powder)

½ cup heavy cream

CAKE: Preheat oven to 350°F. Grease a 9-inch spring form pan. Place milk chocolate in a small bowl. Measure out 1 tablespoon of flour from the 2⅓ cups. Add the tablespoon of flour to coat the pieces of chocolate. In another bowl, whisk flour, cocoa, coffee powder, cinnamon, cloves and salt.

In a stand mixer with a paddle attachment, beat oil, molasses and sugar until blended. In a small saucepan, bring water to a boil. Stir in baking soda until dissolved, then stir in ginger. Add to oil-molasses mixture and beat until blended.

Add remaining flour mixture. Beat on low speed just until moistened. Do not overbeat. In a bowl, lightly beat eggs and egg yolks. Slowly mix batter until combined. Fold in milk chocolate.

Pour batter into springform pan. Level with a spatula. Bake 40-50 minutes or just until a toothpick inserted in the center comes out with just a few crumbs. Do not overbake. Cool on a wire rack for 25 minutes. Then loosen sides with a knife. Carefully remove from pan. Cool completely on wire rack before frosting.

GANACHE FROSTING: Place chocolate, cinnamon and espresso powder in a heat-proof bowl. In a small saucepan, bring cream just to a boil. Do not boil. Pour over chocolate mixture. Let stand for 1 minute. Whisk until all ingredients are combined and smooth. Cover and refrigerate for 30 minutes only. Let it get cool, but not cold. Pour over cake and frost with an offset spatula.

PUMPKIN ICE CREAM PIE

When I share this recipe with friends who rarely bake or cook, they are astounded how easy it is to make this pie from scratch. During the holidays, I make a few extra as gifts. This pie can be prepared in advance and placed in the freezer until the holiday. One friend confessed that they ate the entire pie before Thanksgiving.

CRUST

1 ½ cups graham cracker crumbs (crush or process about 12 crackers)

3 tablespoons granulated sugar

¼ teaspoon cinnamon

Pinch nutmeg

⅛ teaspoon salt

5 tablespoons butter, melted

FILLING

1 cup canned pumpkin (not pumpkin pie mix)

½ cup brown sugar

1 tablespoon orange juice

½ teaspoon cinnamon

¼ teaspoon salt

¼ teaspoon nutmeg

½ teaspoon ginger

1 quart vanilla ice cream, softened

CRUST: Preheat oven to 375°F. Combine all dry ingredients. Add melted butter and mix well. Remove and reserve ¼ cup of crumb mixture. Press remaining mixture firmly into a 9-inch pie pan. Use the bottom of a glass and pat down the crust. Pour the reserved mixture into a small baking pan and spread out the crumbs. Place pie pan and small baking pan in oven and bake for 8 minutes. Remove and cool completely.

FILLING: Combine pumpkin, brown sugar, orange juice and spices. Mix ice cream into pumpkin mixture and keep mixing until there are no longer any streaks of pumpkin. Pour into cooled crust. Freeze until ready to serve. Then, sprinkle reserved crumbs over top of filling.

HOLIDAY COOKIE MEDLEY

Every year, I make holiday cookies. One of my nicknames as a kid was "Stookie." So I put these cookies in boxes, and label them, "Stookie's Cookies — Cookies with a Law Degree." I pass them out at the gym, the courthouse and around the neighborhood.

SOFT, CHEWY PEANUT BUTTER COOKIES

½ cup butter, softened (1 stick)
1 cup packed light brown sugar
¾ cup creamy peanut butter
1 egg

½ teaspoon vanilla
1 ¼ cups flour
¼ teaspoon cinnamon
½ teaspoon baking powder

½ teaspoon baking soda
¼ teaspoon salt (scant)
Granulated sugar, to roll cookie dough

Preheat oven to 350°F. In a mixing bowl, beat butter, brown sugar, and peanut butter until well blended. Add egg and vanilla, beat well. In a separate bowl, stir together flour, cinnamon, baking powder, baking soda and salt. Gradually add to peanut butter mixture, and beat until well blended.

Shape dough into 1¼-inch balls, then roll balls in granulated sugar. Place on ungreased cookie sheet.

With the tines of a fork, flatten each ball. Flatten again in opposite direction, to form crisscross marks.

Bake 9 to 10 minutes until light brown and cookie is set. Cool slightly, then remove from cookie sheet to wire rack to cool completely. Makes about 26 cookies.

LEMON BARS

2 ¼ cups flour, divided
½ cup powdered sugar
½ pound butter (2 sticks)
4 eggs, beaten
2 cups granulated sugar
⅓ cup lemon juice
½ teaspoon baking powder
1 teaspoon lemon zest
Powdered sugar for dusting

Preheat oven to 350°F. Whisk together 2 cups of the flour with the ½ cup powdered sugar.

Cut in the butter until the mixture clings together. Press the dough into a 13x9-inch baking pan. Bake for 20-25 minutes or until crust is lightly browned.

Beat together the eggs, granulated sugar and lemon juice. Mix the remaining ¼ cup flour with the baking powder and zest. Stir into the egg mixture and pour evenly over the hot crust.

Bake for 25 minutes more. Cool, sprinkle with powdered sugar and cut into squares. These can also be made with fresh lime juice.

POWDERED SUGAR LEMONY SNOWBALLS

1 cup unsalted butter (2 sticks)
½ cup powdered sugar
1 teaspoon lemon juice
¼ teaspoon vanilla extract
½ teaspoon salt
4 teaspoons lemon zest, divided in half
2 ¼ cups flour
1 to 2 cups powdered sugar

Preheat oven to 350°F. Line two cookie sheets with parchment paper.

Beat butter, ½ cup powdered sugar, lemon juice, vanilla extract, and salt until fluffy, then stir in 2 teaspoons lemon zest.

Add the flour and mix until a stiff dough forms. If you're using a stand mixer, this will just take a minute or so. If you're using a hand mixer it will take much longer.

Scoop slightly rounded tablespoon sized cookies on cookie sheet. Leave about 1 to 2 inches between cookies. Bake for 8-12 minutes, rotating pans halfway through baking, until the cookies are no longer wet looking. Cool 10 minutes before rolling in powdered sugar.

Prepare to roll cookies by stirring 1 to 2 cups powdered sugar and lemon zest together in a flat bottom bowl. Roll cookies in powdered sugar mixture while still warm. When cookies cool completely, roll in powdered sugar mixture again.

Makes about 40 cookies.

GUMDROP COOKIES

2 ½ cups flour
1 teaspoon baking powder
½ teaspoon baking soda
¼ teaspoon salt

1 cup butter (2 sticks), room temperature
1½ cups granulated sugar, plus more for sprinkling

1 egg
1 teaspoon vanilla
1½ cups multi-colored gumdrops or jelly beans

Preheat oven to 350° F. In medium bowl, whisk together flour, baking powder, baking soda and salt. Set aside.

In a stand mixer with a paddle attachment on medium speed, cream butter and sugar until light and fluffy. Add the egg and beat until smooth. Beat in vanilla. On low speed, add flour mixture and beat until well blended. If desired, chop some of the gumdrops and stir into the batter.

Shape dough into balls, about 1-inch in diameter. Place each ball about 2-inches apart on ungreased cookie sheets. Gently flatten each ball to a circle about 1½-inches in diameter. Sprinkle some sugar on the cookies.

Bake 9 to 11 minutes or until edges are set and light brown. Cool 2 minutes, then remove from cookie sheet to cooling rack. While cookies are still warm, gently press three or four gumdrops into each cookie. Cool completely before serving.

GINGERSNAPS

¾ cup butter (1½ sticks)
1 cup plus 2 tablespoons granulated sugar, divided
1 egg

¼ cup molasses
2 cups flour
2 teaspoons baking soda
1½ teaspoons ground ginger

1 teaspoon ground cinnamon
½ teaspoon ground cloves
½ teaspoon salt

Preheat oven to 350° F. Grease two baking sheets or line with parchment paper. Cream butter and 1 cup sugar until light and fluffy. Beat in egg and molasses. In another bowl, combine flour, baking soda, ginger, cinnamon, cloves and salt. Slowly, and in three batches, add to creamed mixture and mix well.

Take level tablespoonfuls of dough and shape into balls. Dip one side into remaining sugar. Place on baking sheets, 2-inches apart, sugared side up. Bake until lightly browned and crinkly, 12-15 minutes. Do not overbake. Remove to wire racks to cool. Makes about 36 cookies.

PECAN CHOCOLATE BARS

CRUST	PECAN TOPPING	
⅓ cup pecans	¾ cup light corn syrup	2 teaspoons vanilla
2 cups flour	½ cup granulated sugar	⅛ teaspoon salt
½ cup granulated sugar	½ cup brown sugar, packed	¼ teaspoon cinnamon
½ teaspoon salt	4 eggs	1 ½ cups pecans, roughly chopped
1 ½ sticks cold butter, diced	4 tablespoons butter, melted and slightly cooled	3 ounces bittersweet chocolate chips

CRUST: Preheat oven to 350°F. Line a 13x9-inch baking pan with foil as follows: For easy removal of the bars after baking, tear off two sheets of aluminum foil long enough to line the sides and bottom of the pan. Tear off enough foil to allow a little extra to hang over the lips of the pan so that you can grab the overhang and carefully remove the cooked bars from the pan. Once pecan bars have baked and cooled, you can lift them from the pan by the foil flaps, peel them back, and cut the bars into squares. Coat the foil with baking spray or lightly brush with soft butter.

Place the pecans in a food processor and pulse until they form fine crumbs. Add the flour, sugar and salt and pulse until combined. Add the butter and continue to pulse until the dough comes together. Transfer the dough to the baking dish and, with your fingers, press the dough along the bottom and partially up the sides of the pan. Bake until the crust turns a golden brown and it is set, about 25-30 minutes.

TOPPING: While the crust is baking, in a large bowl, combine the corn syrup, sugars, eggs, melted butter, vanilla, salt and cinnamon. Whisk until combined and smooth. With a spatula, stir in the pecans.

Spread the topping evenly over the warm crust. Sprinkle the chocolate chips over the topping. Bake until the top is set and no longer jiggly, about 25-30 minutes. Lightly touch the top with your fingers.

Place the pan on a wire rack. Cool completely. Remove as described above and cut into squares. Makes about 2 dozen squares.

Thought for Life

*One who insists on always having the last word,
undoubtedly would have offered no substance
with their first word.*

Chapter 18
Sweets and Desserts

FABE'S FAVORITE BUTTER-CRISCO® DOUBLE CRUST

I'm obsessed with pie crusts. I've had some excellent crusts in restaurants, but I've also had some bad ones. Although a crust consists of four common ingredients plus water, it took me years until I was satisfied with my pie crusts. I still dabble with new techniques and ingredients all the time. This recipe is the one I use the most. The secret seems to be getting the amount of water just right. After a few tries, you will know when you have just the right amount of water. Avoid store-bought crusts. You will find that making your own crust is fun, sensual and rewarding.

3 cups unbleached flour

1-2 tablespoons granulated sugar

½ teaspoon baking powder

1 teaspoon kosher salt

½ cup butter (8 tablespoons)

6 tablespoons Crisco®

6-8 tablespoons ice water

1 teaspoon lemon juice or vodka

Egg wash (1 egg plus 1 tablespoon water, beaten)

If you want a great crust, take a few extra minutes and follow these steps: Combine flour, sugar, baking powder, salt in a bowl and place bowl in freezer for 15 minutes.

Cut butter and Crisco® into ¼ to ½-inch chunks. Place on a dish and place in freezer for 15 minutes.

I prefer to prepare this crust entirely by hand. Here is the second best method. Place flour mixture in the bowl of a stand mixer or in the bowl of a food processor. Mix in the stand mixer or pulse in the food processor to combine the ingredients. Add the chunks of butter and Crisco.® Mix at medium speed or pulse until the butter is incorporated and coated with flour. You should still have chunks of various sizes, close to the size of peas.

With the mixer running at medium speed, add 6 tablespoons ice water, spreading it over the top of the flour mixture. Add lemon juice or vodka. In food processor, pulse as you add water. Add additional water, ½ tablespoon at a time until the mixture turns a little darker and pieces of flour seem to stick together. Do not make a ball. Take a piece of dough about the size of a marble and, with your thumb and finger, pinch the dough together. If the dough sticks together, stop mixing. A dough with too much water will shrink as it bakes.

Place two sheets of wax paper or parchment paper on your work surface. Pour the dough mixture on the paper. Avoid touching the dough with your hands. The heat and oils in your hands will cause gluten to form which will make the dough tough. Form the dough into a ball by cupping your hands around the paper and bringing it together around the dough. After a ball is formed, place another sheet of paper over the ball and flatten the ball into a disk.

Now comes the fraisage. This is French for spreading the butter into streaks throughout the dough. Place a piece of wax paper between your hand and the dough. Push forward on the dough with the palm of your hand on the paper and spread the dough. Turn the disk four times and do this on all sides. With a dough cutter, cut the dough — about ⅔ for the bottom crust, ⅓ for the lattice or whole top crust.

Place each disk between two sheets of wax or parchment paper and place in refrigerator for at least 3 hours, preferably overnight.

Generously butter a 9-inch pie plate. Roll out one of the disks between the two sheets of paper. This is the easiest way to prepare the dough for transfer to the pan and without the use of more flour on the work surface. When the dough reaches a thickness of ¼-inch and a diameter of 12-inches, remove the top sheet of paper. Place the pie plate over the dough, then invert the plate with one hand under the dough. The dough should settle in the plate. Remove the last sheet of paper, press the dough into the contours of the pie dish, then fold and crimp the edges into your favorite design. Freeze the dough and pie plate for about 5 minutes. Meanwhile, make the filling.

After placing the fruit in the pie, follow these steps for a lattice crust. If you want a full crust, place the crust over the fruit and cut about six slits in the top crust.

Remove the remaining crust disk from the refrigerator. Roll out the disk until it is about ¼-inch thick and 12-inches in diameter. With a fluted pizza wheel, cut 10 strips, each about 1-inch wide. For ease of handling, place the strips on a flat plate and place in the freezer for 5-10 minutes. Place one strip in the center of the pie. Place the second strip in the center perpendicular with the first strip. Leave the strips loose so that you can go over and under every other strip. Place the next four strips each about 1-inch from the edge. Place the remaining four strips between the center strips and the strips on the edges. Gently position each strip so that each is under one perpendicular strip and over the next perpendicular strip, and so on. When you are finished laying all of the strips into a perfect lattice, crimp the edges of each strip into the edges of the bottom crust.

Fill the pie with the fruit filling. Dot the filling with chunks of butter. Lightly brush the strips with an egg wash. Then lightly brush the strips with whatever juices are remaining from the macerated fruit. The sugar in the juices will help brown the lattice. Finally, lightly sprinkle sugar over the lattice. Now, bake the pie according to pie recipe instructions.

This recipe can be halved for a single crust pie.

Culinary Thought

*A thing that raises my disgust
is a pie made with
a store-bought crust.
A crust serves
as a filling's foundation.
When flaky and tender,
it's a pallet's elation.
Filling of fresh fruit
are sublime.
They deserve a scratch crust
every time.*

FRESH PEACH PIE

One day last year, I needed some legal advice of my own and called a lawyer who was an expert in the field that related to my situation. Why would a lawyer need legal advice from another lawyer? As the saying goes, "A lawyer who represents himself has a fool for a lawyer and an idiot for a client." I took her advice, applied it to my situation and my problem disappeared. When I asked her how much I owed her, the response was, "A peach pie." I baked this pie and delivered it to her home. She sent me an email the next day and stated that her family swooned over the pie. They had never tasted anything like it. Of course, that pleased me. Plus, I had not heard the word "swoon" for years. I hope you make this pie and swoon when you devour it.

½ cup granulated sugar, plus more for sprinkling

¼ cup packed brown sugar

6 cups (4 pounds) peaches, peeled & sliced

2 tablespoons lemon juice

Zest from 1 lemon

3 tablespoons cornstarch or tapioca starch

¼ teaspoon ground nutmeg

½ teaspoon cinnamon

¼ teaspoon salt

3 tablespoon butter, softened & divided

Double pie crust (see recipe on p. 258)

Egg wash (1 egg plus 1 tablespoon water, beaten)

In a large bowl, combine sugars. Add peaches, 1 tablespoon of lemon juice, lemon zest and toss gently. Cover and let stand until about ½ to 1 cup of juice macerates, about 30 minutes to 1 hour.

Preheat oven to 400°F. Drain peaches over a sieve and reserve juice. Combine cornstarch or tapioca, nutmeg, cinnamon and salt. Pour reserved juice into a saucepan and add cornstarch-cinnamon mixture. Over medium heat, whisk until the dry ingredients have dissolved. Bring to a boil and reduce heat just until mixture thickens, about 1 minute. Immediately remove saucepan from heat, add 1 tablespoon butter and remaining tablespoon of lemon juice and place mixture in a clean bowl or the mixture will thicken too much. Add peaches and gently mix until all of the peaches are coated with the mixture. Taste and adjust seasoning, if necessary.

Place the bottom crust in the buttered 9-inch deep pie plate. Flute the edges. Add peach mixture. Take 2 more tablespoons of butter and dot the top of the peaches with chunks of butter. Apply top crust and crimp to the edges of the bottom crust. Brush top crust with egg wash, sprinkle with sugar. Place pie on a baking sheet and bake for 1 hour or until the crust is golden brown and the filling is bubbly. Halfway through baking, rotate baking sheet. Cool on a wire rack for 3 hours before serving.

WORLD CLASS SKILLET APPLE PIE

When I first encountered this recipe, I thought there was a mistake in the directions. I was fearful that the placement of the bottom crust over a warm butter-brown sugar mixture would melt the crust. After some exhaustive research, I learned that this method was a traditional southern practice. What did I have to lose? I could always eat the top crust and the apples. I prepared the pie, brought several slices to the gym and handed them out to my friends. The gym erupted in pandemonium. When asked which pies are my all-time favorites, skillet apple pie is at the top of the list. During future trips to the gym with slices of this pie, I am thinking of bringing along a bodyguard—although he or she might grab the pie from me.

---

2 pounds Granny Smith apples

2 pounds Golden Delicious apples

Juice from 1 lemon

1 teaspoon ground cinnamon

¼ teaspoon nutmeg

1 tablespoon flour

¼ teaspoon salt

¾ cup granulated sugar, plus 2 tablespoons for sprinkling

½ cup butter (1 stick)

1 cup firmly packed light brown sugar

Double pie crust (see recipe on p. 258)

Preheat oven to 350°F.

Peel all the apples, and cut them into ½-inch thick wedges. Squeeze the lemon juice over the apples. Toss apples with cinnamon, nutmeg, flour, salt and ¾ cup of granulated sugar.

Melt butter in a 10-inch cast iron skillet over medium heat. Add brown sugar and cook, stirring constantly, 1 to 2 minutes or until sugar is dissolved. Remove from heat. Reserve ¼ cup of butter mixture to brush on top crust.

Cool butter mixture slightly, and place one pie crust in skillet over brown sugar mixture. Spoon apple mixture over pie crust, and top with remaining pie crust.

Brush top of pie crust with reserved brown sugar mixture, then sprinkle with 2 tablespoons of granulated sugar. If necessary, reheat reserved brown sugar mixture over low heat. Add a tablepoon of milk to thin it out if needed. Cut four or five slits on the top crust to allow for steam to escape.

Place a baking sheet in the oven. Place the skillet on the baking sheet. Bake for 1 hour to 1 hour and 10 minutes or until top crust is golden brown and the mixture is bubbly. To avoid excessive browning, cover the pie with aluminum foil during the last 10 minutes. Cool on a wire rack 30 minutes before serving. Serve with ice cream.

FABE'S STRAWBERRY CHIFFON PIE

This pie looks complicated. With a little patience, it's quite easy to make. Not only does it make a spectacular presentation, it tastes luscious and refreshing. I've rarely met a person who does not love strawberries.

CRUST
- 1½ cups graham cracker crumbs
- ¼ cup granulated sugar
- ¼ teaspoon cinnamon
- 5 tablespoons butter, melted

FILLING
- 1 package unflavored gelatin
- ¼ cup cold water
- 1½ cups strawberry purée (made from about 2½ cups fresh sliced strawberries)
- 1½ to 2 tablespoons fresh lemon juice + 1 tablespoon orange juice
- 2 egg whites
- ¼ cream of tartar
- ¼ cup granulated sugar
- ½ cup heavy cream

TOPPING/GARNISH
- 1 cup heavy cream

GARNISH
- Assorted strawberries, halved
- About ¼ cup red currant jelly or orange marmalade, melted

CRUST: Preheat oven to 375°F. In a medium bowl, combine the cracker crumbs, sugar and cinnamon. Add the melted butter and mix well. Reserve ¼ cup of the mixture. Place the remaining mixture in a 9-inch regular pie pan and distribute along the bottom and up the sides. Use the bottom of a glass to pat the crumb mixture and build a nice even mound along the sides. Sprinkle the ¼ cup of reserved crumbs on a cookie sheet. Place pie pan and cookie sheet in the oven side by side. Bake for 8 minutes until the crust sets. Watch the reserved crumbs closely, as they will start to burn before the 8 minutes are up. When the reserved crumbs start to burn on the edges, remove immediately. Let the pie crust cool completely. Pour the reserved crumbs in a small bowl to use for the topping.

FILLING: Sprinkle the gelatin over the water and let soak for 5 minutes. It will become the texture of wet sand. Place the mixture in a small saucepan over low heat and stir until dissolved. Remove from heat and cool.

While the gelatin is cooling, place the sliced strawberries in a blender. Add the lemon and orange juices so that the mixture blends easily. Blend until there are no lumps of strawberries. The mixture should resemble the consistency of a thick milkshake.

When the gelatin reaches room temperature, stir the gelatin into the strawberries.

Place the egg whites and ¼ teaspoon of cream of tartar in a stand mixture. Beat the egg whites slowly, then increase speed and beat until frothy. Gradually beat in the sugar one tablespoon at a time. Continue to beat until soft peaks form. Stir about one quarter of the egg whites into the strawberry gelatin mixture. Begin folding in the remaining egg whites but do not fold them in completely.

Beat the cream until stiff peaks form. Fold it into the strawberry mixture until everything is smooth and incorporated. You should see no patches of white. Try a taste. Add small amounts of sugar if necessary. It should be sweet and tart (chances are you won't need more sugar). Pour the mixture into the baked crust and spread evenly. Refrigerate until set, at least 4 hours.

TOPPING/GARNISH: Best to apply the topping one hour before serving. Beat the heavy cream until stiff peaks form. Spread the whipped cream over the top of the pie, or make a circle around the edge. Sprinkle the reserved crumbs over the top of the entire pie. Place strawberry halves in a design of your choice over the top of pie. Melt the jelly or marmalade in a small saucepan over low heat and brush each strawberry. Refrigerate until ready to serve.

--- **Legal Thought** ---

The law provides predictability in our daily transactions. If you agree to sell me goods or provide a service for a specific sum of money, the law insists that you deliver the goods or perform the service and also insists that I keep my promise and pay you for the goods or service. If either of us breaks our promise, the law provides remedies.

MAPLE-PECAN ICE BOX PIE

Pecan pie is one of America's favorites. Chock full of pecans with a touch of maple syrup, this recipe elevates pecan pie to a new flavorful dimension. If you've never made a pie from scratch before, try this one. You will never purchase a store-bought pie again!

CRUST

1⅓ cups graham cracker crumbs

1 tablespoon granulated sugar

⅛ teaspoon salt

¼ teaspoon cinnamon

5 tablespoons butter, melted

FILLING

¾ cup butter (1½ sticks)

¾ cup firmly packed brown sugar

¼ cup light corn syrup

¼ cup pure maple syrup

3 tablespoons heavy cream

3 cups pecan halves (12 ounces)

⅛ teaspoon cinnamon

¼ teaspoon vanilla

CRUST: To make the graham cracker crumbs, place about 12-15 graham crackers in a food processor and pulse until they reach the consistency of sand. **NOTE:** One sheet contains four graham crackers, so 12 graham crackers equals three sheets. Preheat the oven to 350°F. In a large bowl, combine the crumbs, sugar, salt and cinnamon. Pour the melted butter over the dry ingredients and mix until all of the dry ingredients are coated with the melted butter. Pour the mixture into a 9-inch pie pan. Pat the mixture in an even layer on the bottom of the pan and up the sides. Use a rounded glass or measuring cup to pat down the crust. Place the pie pan in the oven and bake for 8 minutes or until the mixture browns slightly. Watch carefully as the crust can burn in an instant. Remove from the oven and place on a wire rack. Cool completely.

FILLING: Meanwhile, make the filling. Place the butter, brown sugar, corn syrup and maple syrup in a heavy saucepan. Bring to a boil. Stir frequently. Add the heavy cream, pecans and the cinnamon. Return to a boil, then reduce the heat and simmer for 12 minutes. Turn off the heat and stir in vanilla. Pour the pecan mixture into the crust. Pat down mixture and move halves of pecan around to fill up any empty spaces. Cool to room temperature, then cover with plastic wrap and refrigerate until filling sets, from 3 hours up to 1 day.

LEMON PIE WITH MERINGUE CRUST

What I love about this pie is that you kill two birds with one stone. Most lemon meringue pies have a bottom pastry crust and meringue topping. Why not eliminate the pastry crust and make a meringue crust and fill it with luscious lemon cream? Plus, no worries about what to do with leftover egg yolks or whites.

CRUST
- 4 egg whites
- ¼ teaspoon cream of tartar
- 1 cup sugar

FILLING
- 4 egg yolks
- ¼ teaspoon salt
- ½ cup granulated sugar
- ⅓ to ½ cup fresh lemon juice (do not use bottled)
- 1 cup heavy cream (additional 1 cup for optional topping)
- 1 tablespoon lemon zest

CRUST: Separate eggs while they are cold and reserve the yolks. Bring egg whites to room temperature for best results. Preheat oven to 275°F. Generously butter a 9 inch pie plate. Beat egg whites and cream of tartar until foamy. Beat in sugar, 1 tablespoon at a time until formation of stiff and glossy peaks, about 10 minutes. Place meringue in pie pan and press with back of a tablespoon on bottom and up sides until a crust is formed. Bake 1 hour until firm and creamy white. Turn off oven and leave meringue in oven with door closed for 1 hour. The crust should be hard to the touch and faintly browned.

FILLING: Beat the egg yolks until light yellow in color. Stir in the salt, sugar and lemon juice. In a saucepan over medium heat, stir constantly until mixture thickens, about 5 minutes. Cool completely. Using a mixer, whip the heavy cream until stiff peaks form.

Fold the filling mixture and lemon zest into the whipped cream. It is best to fold ⅓ of the lemon mixture into the cream in three batches. Fold gently until there are no streaks of white or yellow. Do not overfold.

Pour filling into the pie crust and refrigerate for at least 4 hours.

As an optional topping, using a mixer with the whisk attachment, whip an additional cup of heavy cream to stiff peaks. Spread or pipe over lemon custard.

MIXED BERRY ICE BOX PIE

Ice box pies are easy to make and very often taste better than fully baked pies. They are called ice box pies because the filling does its "baking" in the fridge. The oven is required only to make the simple graham cracker crust. Mixed berry pies are also known as bumble berry pies. If you can't make up your mind and you have a hankering for strawberry, blueberry or raspberry pie, why not include all three in one pie?

CRUST
- 1 ⅓ cups graham cracker crumbs
- 1 tablespoon granulated sugar
- ½ teaspoon cinnamon
- ⅛ teaspoon salt
- 5 tablespoons butter, melted

FILLING
- 2 cups fresh raspberries
- 2 cups fresh blueberries
- 2 cups fresh strawberries, halved
- 1 cup seedless raspberry jam
- 2 teaspoons fresh lemon juice

CRUST: Preheat oven to 350°F. To make the graham cracker crumbs, place about 12 graham crackers in a food processor and pulse until they reach the consistency of sand. **NOTE**: One sheet contains four graham crackers, so 12 graham crackers equals three sheets. Combine graham cracker crumbs, sugar, cinnamon and salt in a medium bowl. Add melted butter and mix well until combined. Press the crumb mixture into a 9-inch pie plate. Use a rounded cup or glass to pat down the crust on the bottom and up the sides of the pan. Bake for 8 minutes. Cool completely.

FILLING: Use only fresh fruit. Pat the fruit dry, then place in a large bowl. Place the jam in a medium saucepan. Over medium heat, warm the jam just until it begins to simmer. Remove the pan from the heat and stir in lemon juice. Pour the hot jam over the berries. Toss them gently to coat all of the berries.

Place the berry mixture into the crust. Cover with plastic wrap and place in the fridge, until the filling is completely set for at least three hours and up to six hours. This pie is best the day it is made.

MILK CHOCOLATE PUDDING PIE

This is a no-bake pie with flavor and texture similar to the best French silk chocolate pies. Generally, I'm opposed to crusts made from store-bought cookies. But I've made an exception. How does pudding differ from custard? Both use eggs, but pudding employs a cornstarch thickener. Make this pie for a dinner party dessert and you will receive a standing ovation.

CRUST
24 chocolate sandwich cookies
¼ cup butter, melted

FILLING
5 milk chocolate bars (1.55 ounces each) or 7.75 ounces milk chocolate chips
⅔ cup granulated sugar
6 tablespoons cornstarch
2 tablespoons cocoa
½ teaspoon salt
4 egg yolks
3 cups milk
2 tablespoons butter, softened
1 tablespoon vanilla extract
1 cup heavy cream

CRUST: In a food processor, pulse chocolate sandwich cookies until they form coarse crumbs. Add butter and blend until completely combined. Press crumb mixture into bottom and evenly up sides of a deep dish 9-inch pie dish. (Try to make crust about ⅛-inch thick evenly all around.) Refrigerate at least 1 hour before adding filling.

FILLING: If using chocolate bars, break into pieces and set aside. Stir together sugar, cornstarch, cocoa and salt in 2-quart saucepan. Combine egg yolks and milk in a measuring cup. Gradually blend milk mixture into sugar mixture.

Cook over medium heat, stirring constantly, until mixture comes to a boil. Boil and stir 1 minute. It will rapidly begin to thicken. Immediately remove from heat.

Stir in butter and vanilla. Add chocolate bar pieces or chocolate chips. Stir until melted and mixture is well blended. Pour through a strainer into crumb crust.

Let cool before covering with plastic wrap. Refrigerate for several hours or until chilled and firm. Remove plastic wrap and prepare whipped topping. Pour 1 cup heavy cream in the bowl of a mixer. Using the whisk attachment, whip until soft peaks form. Garnish with whipped cream and pieces of a chocolate bar or chocolate shavings.

FABE'S QUICK LUSCIOUS LEMON PIE

This pie should convince anyone that a homemade pie is easy and fun to make. The graham cracker crust is very flavorful. If you make this pie and serve it at a party or present it as a gift, I guarantee that folks will think you spent hours making it. You can substitute limes, key limes, or combine lime and lemon juice.

CRUST

- 1½ cups graham cracker crumbs
- 1 tablespoon granulated sugar
- ⅛ teaspoon salt
- ¼ teaspoon cinnamon
- 5 tablespoons butter, melted

FILLING

- 1 (14 ounce) can sweetened condensed milk
- ½ cup fresh lemon juice
- 1 cup heavy cream

CRUST: To make the graham cracker crumbs, place about 12-15 graham crackers in a food processor and pulse until they reach the consistency of sand. **NOTE**: One sheet contains four graham crackers, so 12 graham crackers equals three sheets. Preheat the oven to 350°F. In a large bowl, combine the crumbs, sugar, salt and cinnamon. Pour the melted butter over the dry ingredients and mix until all of the dry ingredients are coated with the melted butter. Remove about ¼ cup of the butter-graham cracker mixture and spread it evenly on a small cookie sheet or in a small skillet. Pour the remainder of the mixture into a 9-inch pie pan. Pat the mixture in an even layer on the bottom of the pan and up the sides. Use a rounded glass or measuring cup to pat down the crust. Place the pie pan and the cookie sheet or skillet in the oven and bake for 8 minutes or until the mixtures brown slightly. Watch carefully as the crust/crumbs can burn in an instant. Remove from the oven and place on a wire rack. Cool completely.

FILLING: Place the sweetened condensed milk and lemon juice in a large bowl. Whisk until combined. Using a mixer, whip the heavy cream until stiff peaks form. Fold the whipped cream into the lemon mixture. Pour into the cooled crust. Refrigerate overnight or for at least 3 hours until set. Just before serving, sprinkle the reserved graham cracker mixture evenly over the top of the filling. You can also whip ½ cup of heavy cream and spread it over the top of the pie, then sprinkle reserved crumbs over the whipped cream topping.

WORLD CLASS RHUBARB PIE

Although I file my rhubarb pie recipe under fruit pie, rhubarb is actually a vegetable. However, I'm told that a New York court declared it to be a fruit, and I always obey the law. Around late spring, rhubarb appears in many parts of the country, including my home state of Wisconsin. We used to pick it and eat it raw. Some folks add strawberries to their rhubarb pie. In my opinion, there should be a law against that practice. I even obey the proposed law--no strawberries! If asked, "What is your favorite pie?" Rhubarb is always my answer.

FILLING

1½ cups granulated sugar

⅓ cup + 1 tablespoon flour

¼ teaspoon cinnamon

¼ teaspoon nutmeg

5-6 cups rhubarb (approximately 2 pounds)

Juice & zest from 1 lemon

1 tablespoon orange zest (scant)

½ teaspoon vanilla

½ teaspoon brown sugar dissolved in ½ teaspoon water

CRUST

Double crust (see recipe on p. 258)

2 tablespoons butter (to dot filling)

1 egg + ½ teaspoon milk (for egg wash)

Granulated sugar for sprinkling

FILLING: Preheat oven to 400° F. Mix sugar, flour and spices. Cut rhubarb into ½ x ½ -inch thick pieces. Mix dry ingredients with rhubarb. Add remaining filling ingredients. Allow mixture to stand for about 15-20 minutes so that it macerates. Rhubarb will not macerate as much as berries. When liquid is released from rhubarb, taste and adjust seasonings. Mix occasionally. Make sure all dry ingredients are incorporated and not visible.

CRUST: Roll out one disk to about 12-inches in diameter. Butter the bottom of a 9-inch deep dish pie plate. Place the disk in the pie plate and form into a crust. Add rhubarb mixture including liquid. Dot the top of the mixture with small chunks of butter. Add full crust or lattice top. Mix one whole egg with ½ teaspoon of milk and brush top crust with a light coat of egg wash. Sprinkle with sugar. Place pie on a baking sheet. Cover rim of crust with foil. Bake for approximately 25 minutes, then reduce temperature to 375° F and bake an additional 40-60 minutes, or until crust is brown and the filling is bubbling. It may take over 60 minutes before you get a good bubble. Otherwise, it may be slightly runny. Cool completely.

PEANUT BUTTER CHOCOLATE GANACHE CHIFFON PIE

This is a superb pie for folks who love chocolate and peanut butter. It's virtually a no-bake pie.

CRUST
1⅓ cups graham cracker crumbs
1 tablespoon granulated sugar
¼ teaspoon salt
5 tablespoons butter, melted

FILLING
1 cup creamy peanut butter
2 cups heavy cream
¾ cup + 2 tablespoons powdered sugar
2 teaspoons vanilla

GANACHE
4 ounces bittersweet or semi-sweet baking chocolate bar
½ cup heavy cream

CRUST: To make the graham cracker crumbs, place about 12 graham crackers in a food processor and pulse until they reach the consistency of sand. **NOTE:** One sheet contains four graham crackers, so 12 graham crackers equals three sheets. Preheat oven to 350°F. In a large, heat resistant bowl, mix graham cracker crumbs, sugar and salt until combined.

Add melted butter to graham cracker mixture. Mix well until all of the ingredients are coated with melted butter. Place mixture in a 9-inch pie plate. With your hands, press crust on the bottom and up the sides of the pie pan. With a rounded measuring cup, pat the bottom and sides of the crust to flatten. Bake for 8 minutes until set. Cool completely.

FILLING: Place the peanut butter in a large bowl. Place the 2 cups of heavy cream in a mixing bowl fitted with a whisk attachment. Whisk until soft peaks form. Add the powdered sugar and vanilla. Continue whisking until stiff peaks form.

Gently fold about 1 cup of the whipped cream into the peanut butter. Then, add the lightened peanut butter mixture back to the remainder of the whipped cream. Gently fold until there are no steaks of cream or peanut butter. Gently pour the filling into the cooled pie crust. Smooth with a rubber spatula. Cover with plastic wrap and refrigerate for at least 3 hours.

GANACHE: Finely chop the chocolate. Place in a heat-resistant bowl and set aside. In a small saucepan, over medium-low heat, bring the ½ cup of heavy cream just to a simmer. Do not boil.

Pour the heated cream into the bowl of chopped chocolate. Allow to sit for 1 minute. With a rubber spatula, mix the cream and chocolate until smooth and resembles hot fudge. Cool for 10 minutes, then spread over the pie to about ½-inch from the edge of the peanut butter filling. Refrigerate for at least 3 hours, then serve. Keep remaining pie, if any, in fridge. **NOTE:** You can make a chocolate cookie crust instead. Process enough chocolate wafers to yield 1½ cups of finely ground crumbs. Combine crumbs in a heat-resistant bowl and mix in ⅛ teaspoon salt and ½ teaspoon vanilla. Add 5 tablespoons of melted butter and combine. Follow remaining instructions for crust assembly, oven temperature and baking time above.

---------- **Culinary Thought** ----------

*I love to watch food fights in the movies. I must confess that, in real life,
I've participated in a few. I have a great idea for an adult food fight—or it can be a version
where you can involve and teach your kids some culinary skills.
Organize a group of friends, or your friend's kids.
Have each contestant prepare a special culinary offering.
Then, invite everyone over for a pot-luck contest
with prizes for the winners.
Better yet, make arrangements to take the offerings to a food bank.*

FABE'S APPLE CIDER DONUT CAKE

I'm not a cake person. I am a donut person. This cake is an enormous donut disguised as a cake. It is light, airy and moist.

APPLE CIDER MIXTURE

- 1 large (or 2 small) Granny Smith apples
- 1½ cups apple cider
- ½ cup milk

CAKE BATTER

- 2½ cups flour
- 1½ teaspoons baking powder
- ½ teaspoon baking soda
- 1 teaspoon salt
- ½ teaspoon nutmeg (freshly grated is best)
- ¼ teaspoon cinnamon
- 8 tablespoons (1 stick) butter, softened
- ¾ cup granulated sugar
- ½ cup brown sugar
- 3 eggs, room temperature
- ¼ cup vegetable oil
- 1 teaspoon vanilla

CINNAMON SUGAR TOPPING

- ¼ cup granulated sugar
- 1 teaspoon cinnamon
- ⅛ teaspoon nutmeg
- ⅛ teaspoon salt
- 2 tablespoons butter, melted

APPLE CIDER MIXTURE: Peel, core, and chop the apples. Combine with apple cider in a saucepan. Bring to a boil, then simmer over medium heat for 10-12 minutes, until apples are tender. The mixture will foam up when it boils. Cool for 5 minutes, then purée, using an immersion blender or food processor.

Combine 1 cup of apple mixture with milk. Mix and set aside.

CAKE BATTER: Preheat oven to 350°F. Very generously butter and flour (or use baking spray) a 10-cup Bundt cake pan. Set aside.

Combine flour, baking powder, baking soda, salt, nutmeg and cinnamon in a mixing bowl. Set aside.

Place butter and sugars in the bowl of a stand mixer with the paddle attachment. Cream butter and sugars on medium speed for 3 minutes, until light and fluffy. Add eggs, one by one. Add oil and vanilla, and mix for another minute, until well incorporated.

Alternate adding the flour and apple mixtures in batches, beginning and ending with the flour mixture. Scrape the bottom of the mixer bowl to mix well.

Pour batter into Bundt cake pan and bake for 35-50 minutes. After 35 minutes, insert a toothpick into center of cake. It should come out with just a few crumbs on it. Do not overbake.

Cool cake in the pan for 10 minutes, then carefully invert onto a cake platter.

CINNAMON SUGAR TOPPING: Combine granulated sugar, cinnamon, nutmeg, and salt. While cake is still warm, lightly brush with melted butter. Coat cake with cinnamon sugar. Allow cake to cool for 1½ hours before serving.

WORLD CLASS BANANA COCONUT CREAM PIE

Most folks love everything I cook for them. But some dishes stand above others. I can always tell by expression on their faces and a roaring "wow" with the first bite. This pie produces a "wow" every time. Plus, it's a snap to make. The problem: I want to eat it before the guests arrive.

CRUST

1⅓ cups graham cracker crumbs

¼ cup butter, melted

⅓ cup sweetened coconut flakes

⅛ teaspoon salt

FILLING

3 tablespoons cold water

1 envelope unflavored gelatin

1 (14 ounce) can unsweetened coconut milk

1 (15 ounce) can cream of coconut

¾ cup heavy cream

2 bananas, sliced

TOPPING

½ cup heavy cream

¾ cup sweetened coconut flakes

CRUST: To make the graham cracker crumbs, place about 12 graham crackers in a food processor and pulse until they reach the consistency of sand. **NOTE:** One sheet contains four graham crackers, so 12 graham crackers equals three sheets. Set aside. Preheat oven to 350°F. Combine butter, coconut and salt. Add graham cracker crumbs to coconut mixture and stir until crumbs are moistened. Then press crust mixture over bottom and sides of a 9-inch deep dish pie plate. Bake until the crust is slightly brown, about 6-8 minutes. Cool completely.

While the crust is cooling, toast the ¾ cup of coconut and set aside for the topping. To toast the coconut flakes, spread them on a cookie sheet and bake at 350°F for about 5 minutes or until light brown. Watch the flakes closely as they will burn in a split second.

FILLING: Place cold water in a bowl and sprinkle with gelatin. Let stand to dissolve.

Combine coconut milk and cream of coconut in a saucepan. Bring just to a boil and stir occasionally. Remove from heat and stir in gelatin mixture. Transfer contents to a stainless steel bowl and place the bowl in an ice bath. Whisk occasionally until the mixture has started to thicken, about 20-40 minutes. Cool completely.

Using a stand mixer with the whisk attachment, whip the ¾ cup of heavy cream to soft peaks. Gently fold whipped cream into the coconut mixture.

Line the bottom of the cooled pie shell with a single layer of bananas. Scoop half of the filling over the bananas. Lay another layer of bananas over the coconut cream. Fill with remaining filling. Cover with plastic wrap and chill for at least 6 hours, preferably overnight.

TOPPING: Just before serving, whip the ½ cup of heavy cream using a stand mixer with the whisk attachment, until stiff peaks form. With an offset spatula, gently spread the whipped cream over the top of the pie, then sprinkle the reserved toasted coconut flakes over the topping.

GERMAN CHOCOLATE PIE

This pie is a thing of beauty and tastes even better than it looks.

CRUST

1 (16 ounce) package chocolate sandwich cookies

8 tablespoons (1 stick) butter, melted

FILLING

6 ounces semi-sweet baking chocolate bar

8 tablespoons (1 stick) butter, softened

½ teaspoon espresso powder

½ teaspoon cinnamon

2 ¼ cups heavy cream

½ teaspoon vanilla

TOPPING

2 ounces (½ stick) butter

2 egg yolks

½ cup brown sugar

½ cup half-and-half

7 ounces sweetened coconut flakes

1 teaspoon vanilla

½ cup pecans, chopped

CRUST: In a food processor, pulse chocolate sandwich cookies into large crumbs. In a large bowl, combine cookie crumbs and melted butter until well combined. Press mixture into a deep 9-inch pie pan. Pat down crust on bottom and up the sides of the pan. Freeze for 30 minutes or up to 2 hours.

FILLING: Chop chocolate into fine pieces. Cut butter into small chunks. Set aside. Add espresso powder and cinnamon to the chocolate pieces. In a medium saucepan, bring heavy cream just to a simmer. Do not boil. Remove from heat. Add chocolate mixture to hot cream and allow to stand for 30 seconds. With a whisk, mix well until the mixture looks like hot fudge. Add chunks of butter and whisk until the butter is melted and combined. Stir in vanilla and mix well.

Pour the chocolate mixture into the chilled pie crust. Cover with plastic wrap and refrigerate for at least 2 hours. Filling should be set completely.

TOPPING: Chop butter into small chunks. Place egg yolks in a medium bowl and whisk slightly. Set aside. In a medium saucepan, combine brown sugar, half-and-half and butter. Over medium heat, bring just to a boil. Whisk constantly until sugar is dissolved and butter is fully melted and combined.

Add about ⅓ of the hot cream mixture to the egg yolks to temper them. Whisk cream mixture and eggs together. Add another ⅓ of the cream mixture to the egg yolks and repeat. Return the egg-cream mixture to the pan and cook for 2-3 minutes over medium heat until the mixture thickens to consistency of sour cream. Do not boil. If there are any lumps of egg in the mixture, strain into a bowl through a strainer.

Remove from heat and stir in coconut and vanilla. Gently spoon the topping over the pie. With an offset spatula, gently spread the mixture over the top of the pie. The mixture should be up to ½-inch from the edges of the topping so that some of the topping on the edges is visible. Sprinkle the pecan pieces over the topping. Refrigerate for at least 1 hour more before serving.

AUNT BEDE'S CHEESECAKE

When I was growing up in Wisconsin in the 1930s and 1940s, my parents hung out with about six other couples. They were all very close. They got together several times a week, were loyal customers to each other's businesses and professions and were always there if one needed the other. If we were playing with the kids of one of these couples, when lunchtime came around, we just stayed at their house for the meal. They were more like family than friends. In those days, the kids did not address the adults by their first names. It would have been awkward to address them as Mr. or Mrs. So the kids addressed them by "Aunt" or "Uncle." For example, Aunt Ruth, Uncle Ben and so on. Uncle Joe often took me fishing. His wife, Aunt Bede was not a good cook. But somehow, she got her hands on this cheesecake recipe. It took off like wildfire. I've made hundreds of cheesecakes and this one is in most demand. No cookbook is complete without at least one cheesecake recipe. I want to share this one in Aunt Bede's memory.

CRUST

1½ cups graham crackers, finely ground (NOTE: 12-15 graham creackers equals 3-4 sheets)

¼ cup granulated sugar

¼ teaspoon cinnamon

Pinch of nutmeg

5 tablespoons butter, melted

FILLING

2 eggs, separated

½ cup granulated sugar (scant)

9 ounces cream cheese (room temperature)

8 ounces sour cream (room temperature)

1 teaspoon vanilla (scant)

1 teaspoon lemon zest

CRUST: Mix the dry ingredients together. Add melted butter slowly and mix. Do not oversaturate.

Reserve ¼ cup of crust mixture for sprinkling top of cheesecake. Pat the rest down into a deep 9-inch pie pan. Place reserved crust mixture in an ovenproof pan. Brown crust for 7 minutes at 375°F. Cool completely. Brown reserved crumbs for 5 minutes. Cool and set reserved crumbs aside.

FILLING: Mix egg yolks and sugar. Add cream cheese, sour cream, vanilla and lemon zest. Beat egg whites to soft peak stage. Fold in beaten egg whites.

Place filling in the 9-inch pie plate lined with the graham cracker crust. Bake at 350°F for 30 minutes or until set. Leave in open oven for 40 minutes.

Remove from oven. Cool at room temperature for two hours. Refrigerate at least six hours or overnight. Sprinkle top of cheesecake with reserved graham cracker mixture just before serving. Serve cold or at room temperature.

MY ALL-TIME FAVORITE CHOCOLATE CAKE

There are hundreds of recipes for traditional chocolate cakes. I've tried many of them. During a trip to the south, I discovered a recipe on a package of Martha White® cake flour. I purchased a bag of the flour, came home, and tried the recipe. It was excellent, but something was missing. So, I modified the recipe, made this cake, and never looked back. I added a few touches: instant coffee or espresso powder and cinnamon, which significantly enhanced the flavor. This is truly a world-class cake. It's moist, light and brings expressions of joy to everyone who eats it. Martha White® flour products are still on the market, but alas, they no longer make cake flour. Other brands are available online or in the supermarket. Be sure to use cake flour and sift it before measuring. For a crowd, I suggest the 13x9 version which produces more portions that are easier to cut and serve.

CAKE

½ cup (1 stick) butter

4 ounces unsweetened baking chocolate

2 eggs

2 cups buttermilk

2 teaspoons vanilla

2½ cups sifted cake flour

2 cups granulated sugar

2 teaspoons baking soda

1 teaspoon salt

FROSTING

2 cups granulated sugar

1 teaspoon espresso powder

½ cup (1 stick) butter

3 ounces unsweetened baking chocolate

⅔ cup milk

½ teaspoon salt

2 teaspoons vanilla

CAKE: Preheat oven to 350°F. Grease and flour two 8-inch square or two 9-inch round cake pans. Or, grease and flour one 13x9-inch pan. In a heavy saucepan, melt butter and chocolate together over low heat. Let cool.

Beat eggs until frothy, about 2 minutes. Add buttermilk and vanilla and mix until combined. In a separate bowl, combine dry ingredients and stir into buttermilk mixture. Add melted butter & chocolate mixture and blend until there are no streaks.

Pour into pans and bake 30 minutes or until cake pulls away from sides of pans. If using a 13x9 pan, it takes about 35 minutes. Don't overbake! Let cake cool completely before frosting.

FROSTING: Mix all ingredients except vanilla in 3-quart saucepan. Heat to a rolling boil, stirring occasionally. Boil 1 minute without stirring. Place saucepan in an ice bath. Beat until smooth & spreadable. Stir in vanilla. Spread evenly over the cake.

---— **Thought for Life** ———

*Inferior ingredients in a cake
Will not make a s superior cake.
Inferior thoughts and deeds
Will not make a superior person.*

APPLE PIE BARS

When I'm in the mood for apple pie, but too lazy to make one, these apple pie bars will satisfy my craving in half the time. These bars are always received with standing ovations.

CRUST

1 stick butter, room temperature

½ cup granulated sugar

⅛ cup packed brown sugar

1 ¼ cups all-purpose flour

¼ teaspoon kosher salt

FILLING

¼ cup packed brown sugar

½ teaspoon ground cinnamon

¼ teaspoon nutmeg

¼ teaspoon kosher salt

2 medium Granny Smith apples

2 medium Golden Delicious apples

Juice of ½ lemon

½ teaspoon vanilla

TOPPING

4 tablespoons butter, slightly softened

½ cup flour

¼ cup brown sugar

¼ cup granulated sugar

¼ teaspoon cinnamon

⅛ teaspoon nutmeg

¼ teaspoon salt

CRUST: Preheat oven to 350° F. Butter the bottom of an 8-inch baking pan. In a food processor, beat butter and sugars together until light and fluffy. Add flour and salt and pulse until just combined and crumbly. With your fingers, press the mixture on the bottom and ½ -inch up the sides of the pan. As you press the dough, it will come together as a crust. Set aside the food processor for the topping. Bake for 20 minutes or until lightly golden.

FILLING: Combine brown sugar, cinnamon, nutmeg and salt in a bowl. Set aside. Peel, core and slice apples to about ¼-inch thickness. You should have about 4 cups of apples. In a large bowl, combine apples with lemon juice, vanilla and brown sugar mixture. Mix well with your hands so that every apple slice is coated. Spread apples evenly over warm crust. There will be some juice in the bottom of the bowl. Drizzle over apples.

TOPPING: Cut butter into chunks. Place all items in a food processor. Pulse just until crumbly. Don't overprocess. Remove from food processor and sprinkle evenly over the apples. Try to cover all of the apples. Bake for one hour or until the top is golden. With a paring knife, carefully pierce an apple slice to make sure apples are soft. Cool on wire rack for 30 minutes, then cut into squares.

This recipe can be doubled and baked in a 13x9-inch baking pan.

STUIE'S GOOEY BROWNIES

These are so gooey, they almost fall apart. But sooo good.

BROWNIES

¾ cup flour

¼ cup unsweetened cocoa powder

1 teaspoon salt

8 ounces semi-sweet chocolate chips

12 tablespoons butter

1 teaspoon cinnamon

1 teaspoon instant espresso powder

2 eggs

1¼ cups granulated sugar

2 teaspoons vanilla

FROSTING

¼ cup whole milk

2 tablespoons butter, softened

4 ounces bittersweet chocolate, chopped

BROWNIES: Preheat oven to 350°F. Line an 8x8-inch baking pan with parchment paper. Lightly butter the parchment paper. Whisk together the flour, cocoa powder and salt.

Reserve half of the chocolate chips in a small bowl. In a small heavy saucepan over low heat, melt the other half of the chocolate along with the butter. Watch carefully. When the chocolate and butter are melted, stir in the cinnamon and espresso powder and mix until dissolved. Remove from heat immediately. Place melted chocolate in a bowl and cool slightly.

In a stand mixer fitted with a paddle attachment, mix the eggs and sugar until light and fluffy. Beat in the vanilla.

Whisk in the melted chocolate mixture. Make sure it is cool or the eggs will curdle. I suggest mixing in a small amount of the flour mixture with the melted chocolate mixture to cool it down.

On low speed, carefully mix in the remaining flour mixture. Do not overmix or the brownies will not be gooey. With a rubber spatula, fold in the reserved chocolate chips. Transfer the batter to the baking pan. Level the top with the spatula.

Bake for 20-25 minutes. After 20 minutes, the brownies will be gooey and slightly runny. Allow the brownies to cool completely. They will firm up after two hours.

FROSTING: Meanwhile, prepare frosting while brownies are cooling. Place milk and butter in a medium saucepan over medium heat. Cook until butter melts and small bubbles appear around the edges of the pan. Do not boil. Add finely chopped chocolate and let stand for five minutes. Stir to combine. Let thicken for one hour. Spread frosting evenly over cooled brownies.

Legal Thought

Lend money to a friend?
You will lose the money,
And lose the friend.

LEMON CUPCAKES WITH LEMON ICING

When given a lemon, make lemon cupcakes.

CUPCAKES

½ cup (1 stick) butter, softened to room temperature

1 cup granulated sugar

2 large eggs, at room temperature

1½ teaspoons vanilla

1½ cups all-purpose flour

2 teaspoons baking powder

½ teaspoon salt

½ cup whole milk

⅓ cup fresh lemon juice

1½ tablespoons lemon zest

ICING

1 ¾ cups powdered sugar

¼ cup lemon juice

Zest of one lemon

1 teaspoon butter, very soft

Pinch salt

CUPCAKES: Preheat the oven to 350°F. Line a 12-cup muffin pan with cupcake liners.

Beat the butter and sugar together on medium-high speed in a large bowl until creamed, about 2 minutes. Add eggs and vanilla extract, then beat on medium-high speed until combined, about 1 minute. Set aside.

In a medium bowl, whisk the flour, baking powder, and salt. Pour the dry ingredients into the wet ingredients. Mix on low speed, then slowly add the milk, lemon juice, and lemon zest. Mix just until combined. Do not overmix this batter.

Spoon batter into 12 cupcake liners to about ⅔ full. Bake for about 18-22 minutes, or until a toothpick inserted into the middle of one cupcake comes out clean. Cool completely before frosting.

ICING: Place all ingredients into a medium bowl. Mix well until smooth. Pour over cupcakes.

BANANA CAKE

Of all the cakes that I have baked, this banana cake is one for which I get the most requests. Martha White® cake flour is no longer on the market. I use SwansDown® or Softasilk® cake flour. I prefer to make this cake in a 13x9-inch pan. It's easier to assemble and easier to serve.

CAKE

3 cups sifted cake flour

1 teaspoon baking soda

1 teaspoon salt

¼ cup buttermilk

1 cup (2 sticks butter, softened)

2 cups sugar

2 eggs

2 cups mashed ripe bananas

1 teaspoon vanilla

1 cup pecans, chopped

FROSTING

¼ cup (half stick) butter, softened

½ cup mashed ripe bananas

1-2 teaspoons fresh lemon juice

1 pound confectioners sugar (about 4 cups)

CAKE: Preheat oven to 350°F. Grease and flour two 8-inch square or two 9-inch round cake pans. Or, grease and flour one 13x9-inch cake pan (my preference).

Be sure to sift flour before measuring. I suggest sifting the flour until you obtain 3 cups. Then add the baking soda and salt and sift again. I use a large mesh strainer for sifting.

If you don't have buttermilk, add 1 teaspoon white vinegar to ¼ cup of whole milk. Stir and let rest for 5 minutes.

Place butter and sugar in the bowl of a stand mixer. Cream until light and fluffy. Add eggs, one at a time, beating well after each addition.

Add mashed bananas and vanilla. Mix well. Add ⅓ of the flour mixture followed by ⅓ of the buttermilk. Repeat the process two more times. Stir in the pecans. Do not overmix.

Pour into prepared pans. Level tops with a spatula. Bake 40-45 minutes or until a toothpick inserted in the center come out with just a few crumbs on it. Do not overbake. For a 13x9 pan, bake 50-60 minutes.

Cool on a wire rack for 15 minutes, then carefully remove from pan(s) and cool completely.

FROSTING: In a stand mixer, cream butter until fluffy. Stir in mashed bananas and lemon juice. Blend well. Gradually beat in confectioners sugar until frosting is of spreading consistency.

Epilogue

And so, I travel down the road.
today, the courthouse.
Where my love of law transports me
to bring succor to a frightened soul,
perhaps brought here
by his own disregard.

And so, I travel down the road.
Today, a fragrant dough
of nascent bread
placed in a warm bowl.
It begins to rise.
A miracle,
not by machine,
but by nature's placid touch.
Just as a child grows
within its mother,
awaiting birth
with the hope
it will bring much joy,
as will the bread.

And so, I travel down the road.
I walk past folks
in all colors.
All speaking different sounds.
Imagine the nihility
of a symphony
with but one note.
Or a painting
with but one color.
I strive to be surrounded,
and nourished
by many colors
and many sounds.

And so, I travel down the road.
Where years ago,
each time I passed,
a great blue heron greeted me.
Perhaps today,
he will recognize me once again.
And greet me one more time.

And so, I travel down the road.
This time way above
the highway which I see below.
Leading to where my wheels
will gently meet the runway.
My beloved aircraft's engine
drones with steadfast loyalty
to take me home.
Soon appears the water tower,
the city's name
emblazoned on its wall.
Assuring me
that I am home.
In moments I hear
the airport's invitation.
"Clear to land."

How many more times
will the courtroom beckon me,
will the bread bestow its bouquet,
will life's sounds and colors
bring me sustenance,
felicity and joy?

How many more times
will the tower guide me home,
will the heron lift its wings
to say hello?

A Few Additional Thoughts

―――――――――――――――― **Legal Thought** ――――――――――――――――

Would you rather hear: "I'll see you in court!" or, "I'll see you in my kitchen"?

―――――――――――――――― **Culinary Thought** ――――――――――――――――

Hunger is nature's way of reminding us that we must nourish ourselves. A cook can be thought of as one of nature's workers.

―――――――――――――――― **Legal Thought** ――――――――――――――――

A lawsuit could arise from anything you do each day. So, do each day smart!

―――――――――――――――― **Thought for Life** ――――――――――――――――

I often wonder.
Who changes the light bulbs
on the sun?

---------- **Thought for Life** ----------

The Magic of Reality

Fantasy can soothe, comfort, stimulate and excite the mind. But not as much as the magic of reality. The existence of natural things is so awesome and mysterious that it thrusts us into deep thought and contemplation. Philosophers have attempted to uncover the mystery of reality for centuries. Our presence on and departure from the earth are realities. Yet, no one can explain it.

Fantasies, such as movies, magic tricks and games are explainable. But let's examine just one reality. Imagine a seed the size of a grain of sand. A thousand years ago, it finds its way into the soils somewhere in the Sierra Nevada Mountain range. At the same time, thousands of men construct the great pyramids of Egypt. Today, a tree stands majestically in the forest. The pyramid, as high as the tree, also claims its presence. Not one man, not one stone was required to build the tree. The tree grew because it was a tree. The pyramid grew to honor a fantasy of eternal life of a pharaoh. Which structure is the greater magic?

---------- **Thought for Life** ----------

Hypotheticals
are hyper farcical.
Why respond to facts
that don't exist?
Folly enough to enter a baited trap.
Extreme folly to enter a trap
that has no bait.
Here's an example.
If challenged with a hypothetical
would you respond?

Thought for Life

We all love to build memories.
Today's holidays, birthdays,
school days, vacations,
and get-togethers with friends
are tomorrow's memories.

Memories are constructed
for the moment
and to fill emptiness
in later years.

Building memories
is a worthy pursuit
for the moment
and for later.

A worthier pursuit
should be considered.

Instead of emptiness
in later years,
build new memories
for yourself
in that moment
and for others
later.

Legal Thought and Thought for Life

The Tinman wanted a heart.
The Scarecrow wanted a brain.
The Cowardly Lion wanted courage.

Those who drift and stumble
off the road of decency and the law
should ask the Wizard
for a conscience and common sense.

But learn this.
The only Wizard
who can give you a conscience
and common sense is You.
Your own conscience and common sense
can teach you more about decency and the law
than can any lawyer
or a roomful of law books.

GLOSSARY OF COOKING TERMS

This list will assist both the novice and experienced cooks with terms used throughout this and many other cookbooks. The list is not intended to be exhaustive.

The majority of culinary terms and techniques originated in France and Italy. I love to use these foreign expressions when I'm talking about cooking. It just seems more fun to tell a cooking companion to "please make a bouquet garni with these bay leaves, thyme and parsley sprigs," rather than saying, "tie up this stuff with some string." It's even more fun if I say it with a goofy French accent.

I often repeat this corny joke: "What's the difference between chocolate pudding and chocolate mousse?"

Answer: "About five dollars."

ACIDITY	The amount of acid in a product, such as lemon juice, vinegar or wine, used to enhance the flavor of a recipe. Acidity is also important as a means of tenderizing meats. It's amazing how a quick squeeze of lemon juice just as a sauce is ready to serve lightens up the flavor.
AL DENTE	An Italian term, meaning "to the tooth" that refers to a slight resistance when the pasta is bitten. This is the preferred level of doneness for pasta.
AROMATICS	Certain vegetales, spices and herbs used to impart flavor and fragrance to foods. See *mirepoix*.
BAIN-MARIE	A term for a water bath where ramekins or a cheesecake in a spring form pan is placed in another larger vessel that is partially filled with water. The water bath enables the product to cook more evenly and smoothly. The term also includes a substitute for a double boiler which includes two pots, the bottom pot filled with simmering water and the top pot filled with an ingredient that you desire to melt, such as chocolate. Absent a double boiler, a heatproof bowl can be placed over a pot of simmering water and the chocolate placed in the heatproof bowl.
BAKE	To cook food in the oven surrounded by dry heat. The term is somewhat confusing and interchangeable with roasting. Baking is usually associated with cooking pastry items and small cuts of meat while roasting generally involves cooking large cuts of meat.
BASTE	To add liquid to the surface of meat by spooning or brushing the liquid from the pan. Sometimes I prepare a special basting liquid.
BEURRE MANIÉ	French term for butter mixed by hand with flour. A means of making a thickener, primarily used to thicken sauces. I prefer a roux.
BLANCH	The process of plunging food into boiling water to partially cook the item. Potatoes are often blanched, then dried and placed in a roasting pan. Peaches are blanched to loosen the skin so that the fruit is easily peeled. Blanching is usually followed by an ice bath to stop the cooking process.

BOUQUET GARNI	A bunch of fresh herbs, such as parsley and thyme leaves, tied together with string. One end of the string is tied to the pot handle, The bouquet is then immersed in a sauce or soup to enhance the flavor. It is easily removed by just grabbing the string.
BRAISE	A cooking method by which food, such as meat or vegetables, is first browned, then slowly cooked in a tightly covered vessel with a small amount of liquid over low heat. Braising differs from frying in that frying is cooking in oil, often at high heat. To sauté means to cook, usually uncovered, over a higher heat for a shorter period of time.
BRINE	A method of making meat more tender and juicy by placing meat in a solution of water and salt and sometimes sugar.
BROIL	A method of cooking meat placed directly under a high heat source in the oven.
BROWN	A method of putting a sear or crust on meat to retain the juices prior to roasting or using in a stew. Browning is done in a heavy skillet over high heat.
BRUISE	A method of partially crushing an ingredient to release its flavor. Often done with garlic cloves.
BUTTER	A common dairy product used in cooking and baking. Unsalted butter is recommended, especially in baking, so the cook can control the amount of salt used.
BUTTERFLY	To split a food product down the center to make two thinner pieces. Usually the meat (such as a whole chicken, leg of lamb or shrimp) is cut through the midline, almost to the end, then opened like a book or butterfly.
CARAMELIZE	The process of releasing the natural sugars in foods, such as onions. As the foods are cooked and the sugars released, the food takes on a brown color similar to caramel. To caramelize is also the process of cooking sugar and water to form a syrup that eventually becomes caramel.
CHIFFON	An airy, fluffy mixture, usually in a pie or cake. Accomplished by folding in whipped cream or egg whites.
CHIFFONADE	In French, it means "little ribbons." Chiffonade is a method of quickly chopping vegetables, such as lettuce, by tightly rolling up the leaves and then shredding them. It's similar to julienne, which applies to firmer vegetables.
CHOP	Chopping refers to cutting food, often vegetables. It usually means to cut the vegetable into large squares. A rough or coarse chop means to create larger chunks of about ¾-inch, while a fine chop is smaller at ¼-inch.
CLARIFIED BUTTER	This is unsalted butter which has been heated to separate the milk solids from the fats. The purpose is to enable the use of the butter at higher temperatures.
COAT	A means of covering food with an outer coating, say of a sauce or a flour. For example, in making some rice dishes, the raw rice is swirled around the cooking oil to coat the grains prior to adding liquid.

CONFIT	An ancient French method of preserving meat. Today, it's a technique of slowly cooking a meat (frequently duck), in its own fat for several hours. The result is an intensely flavored meat.
COOL	To allow food to rest at room temperature for a specific period of time.
CREAM	A method of mixing butter or other fat with another substance to create a smooth and fluffy texture. The term is frequently used in baking where butter and sugar are mixed at high speed until the ingredients are light and fluffy.
CRISP	To reconstitute freshness, usually referring to fresh vegetables. Soaking celery or carrots in ice water will often bring back their crispiness.
CRISP-TENDER	When food, usually vegetables, are cooked and still retain some raw crispness.
CUBE	To cut food into even squares, usually about a ½-inch in diameter.
CUTTING IN	A method of mixing cold butter with dry ingredients such as flour. This is done by placing the butter in a bowl with the flour, and chopping the mixture with two knives, a pastry cutter or forks until you have small chunks of butter evenly distributed within and coated with the flour. Cutting in can also be accomplished with a food processor.
DASH	A dash is the introduction of a small amount of liquid to a mixture. It amounts to a few drops. The term is frequently used by bartenders, such as a dash of bitters. Cooks also use the term, such as a dash of hot sauce.
DEGLAZE	The process of adding a liquid to a pan after meat and/or vegetables have been browned, or caramelized. Adding the liquid, usually wine or water, and scraping the bottom of the pan with a flat spatula releases the fond and enhances the flavor of the sauce.
DEMI-GLACE	A rich meat sauce beginning with the roasting of bones, then reducing the liquid repeatedly until you end up with a small amount of gorgeous sauce.
DICE	Dicing is more uniform than chopping and is somewhat smaller. It is about the diameter of a pea.
DISSOLVE	The process of stirring a dry ingredient into a liquid until the dry ingredient disappears.
DOT	To scatter small amounts of an ingredient over a food mixture. For example, after placing the fruit filling into a pie pan, small chunks of butter are usually scattered over the filling.
DOUBLE BOILER	See *bain-marie*.
DREDGE	To lightly coat food to be fried, usually with flour or bread crumbs.
DRIZZLE	The process of slowly spreading a liquid over food, such as melted chocolate over the tops of cookies.
DUST	Sprinkle lightly with a dry ingredient such as flour or powdered sugar.

EGG WASH	Egg yolks, or the whole egg, whisked with a small amount of milk or water. The egg wash is then lightly brushed over a pastry to create a gloss.
EMULSION	A mixture of one liquid with another. Usually involves liquids that do not blend easily, such as oil and vinegar. If you make a vinaigrette by mixing oil and vinegar and place them in a covered container and shake the container, the heavier liquid will temporarily suspend in the lighter liquid. This is called an emulsion.
FERMENTATION	A process by which food is altered by bacterial enzymes, microorganisms or yeast. For example, adding yeast and to bread flour ferments the dough and gives it the flavor. Beer is created by fermentation. Fermentation is any metabolic process in which microorganisms' activity creates a desirable change in food and beverages, whether it's increasing flavor, preserving foodstuffs or providing health benefits. Although the word is creepy, fermentation generally is a good thing.
FLUTE	To bring edges of pastry dough together to make an attractive edge, such as a pie crust.
FOLD	A method of creating a light, airy final food product. It's accomplished by gently adding a lighter mixture, such as whipped egg whites or whipped cream, into a heavier mixture, such as a chocolate cake batter. A spatula or whisk are gently rotated through the mixtures just until they are combined.
FOND	Fond consists of those small brown bits that stick to the bottom of the pan or Dutch oven after browning the meat and vegetables. It's essential to incorporate these brown treasures into the sauce. Fond significantly enhances the flavor. Fond is released by deglazing the pan with a liquid, usually wine or water. See deglaze above. The term "fond" is derived from the Latin "fundus" which means bottom.
FRY	The process of cooking food over medium or high heat with the use of oil or fat. This is different from panfrying, which is to place food in a cold skillet using little or no fat. Frying is also different from braising, which uses liquid instead of oil, and sautéing, which uses a smaller amount of fat.
GANACHE	A glaze, icing, frosting, sauce, or filling for pastries made from chocolate and heavy cream.
GLAZE	To brush or apply something to create a gloss, such as brushing heated fruit jelly on fruit.
GREASE	Used as a verb in cooking, greasing is the process of placing a coat of fat such as butter into a pan. It prevents the batter or other product from sticking to the pan. The term is used along with the verb "flour" which means to lightly coat the pan with flour after it has been greased. At times, bakers refer to "buttering" the pan when butter is specified.
ICE BATH	An ice bath is merely ice water. It is used to quickly stop the cooking process, especially when blanching or parboiling ingredients. It is also used to cool items such as a frosting. The frosting is placed in a bowl which is placed in another bowl of ice water.

INFUSION	The process of extracting a flavor from a solid product, such as tea leaves in water or chopped garlic in olive oil.
JULIENNE	The process of cutting foods, often vegetables, into thin strips.
KNEAD	Kneading means to work bread dough, either by machine or by hand, for the purpose of developing the glutens in the flour, which is what gives baked goods their structure, flavor and texture.
LEAVEN	To leaven is to add an agent which will cause a dough to rise and lighten. Baking powder, baking soda, yeast and beaten eggs are common leaveners.
MACERATE	The process of soaking fruit in liquid and sugar to soften it and release its juices is called maceration. For example, when apple slices are prepared for a pie, they are coated in sugar and lemon juice and will give off liquid.
MARINADE	A liquid that contains seasonings in which foods, such as meats and vegetables, are soaked (marinated) to impart flavors.
MINCE	Mincing is a very fine chop. When mincing garlic, it should be almost like a paste.
MIREPOIX	A flavor base made by cooking chopped onion, carrot and celery, in this case called *aromatics*, usually with butter or oil, or other fat. The purpose is to impart the flavors from the vegetables to the sauce, soup, meat or stew. Mirepoix also can serve as a base upon which to place a piece before roasting. Another term for mirepoix is the *Holy Trinity*, consisting of onions, celery and bell pepper.
MISE EN PLACE	A French culinary term which means "putting everything in place." Simply put, it's the process of getting all of your tools and ingredients together ahead of time before you cook.
PARBOIL	To parboil is to partially boil food, usually vegetables, for just a few minutes.
PINCH	A small quantity of a seasoning, such as salt. The amount you can pinch between your fingertips, usually about ⅛ of a teaspoon.
POACH	Cook something in simmering liquid just below boiling point.
PROOF	The bubbly reaction when yeast is added to water. Proofing is also the act of allowing bread dough to rest. During this rest period, yeast ferments the dough and produces gasses, thereby leavening the dough.
PURÉE	A cooked food, usually vegetables or fruits, that has been ground, blended or sieved to a smooth consistency of a creamy paste or liquid.
RENDER	To melt animal fat from meat, such as bacon.
RIBBON	A term describing the appearance, usually of an egg and sugar mixture that is cooking. As the mixture is whisked, it thickens. When the whisk is lifted from the mixture, the batter falls back into the mixture in a ribbon-like pattern.
ROAST	See *bake*.

ROLLING BOIL	A rolling boil occurs when a liquid is boiled rapidly with lots of bubbling.
ROUX	A combination of equal parts of flour and fat cooked together and used to thicken sauces. The flour is added to the melted fat, butter or oil on the stovetop, blended until smooth, and cooked to the desired level of brownness. Roux ranges in color from light blonde to dark brown.
SAUTÉ	A French term used to describe the cooking of foods in a shallow pan using high heat. The food is cooked in the pan uncovered, in a small quantity of butter or oil. Unlike frying where the food is cooked over higher heat with more fat, sautéed food obtains its flavor and doneness from the pan's heat. Braise also differs from sauté, where food is first browned, then slowly cooked in a tightly covered vessel with a small amount of liquid over low heat.
SEAR	Searing and sautéing both involve cooking food in a shallow pan on the stovetop. Searing is used to produce only a flavorful brown crust on thick cuts of meat. Sautéing is used to cook smaller pieces of food or thinner cuts of meat all the way through.
SET	When a batter sets, such as in a cookie being baked, the surface begins to harden. The edges of the cookie will be slightly firm and dry to the touch and the top of the cookie will no longer look wet.
SHIMMER	As you heat a liquid or a fat, the surface will appear to jiggle like gelatin, which is referred to as shimmer.
SHRED	To cut into long, thin pieces.
SIFT	The process of passing a dry ingredient, such as flour or powdered sugar, through a mesh bottom sieve or sifter. This allows the ingredient to aerate by making it lighter and more uniform in texture. To sift together dry ingredients, such as flour and baking powder is to combine them through a sifting device so that there is even distribution of the ingredients.
SIMMER	Heated liquids, usually water, will form small bubbles around the edges of the pan. At this point, the water is below boiling temperature and is simmering.
SLURRY	A mixture of water or stock and a thickening agent, such as cornstarch or flour. The agent is mixed until it dissolves in the liquid, at which point it is called a slurry. It is then added to the soup or sauce which, when boiled, will thicken.
SPATCHCOCK	See *butterfly*.
STOCK	Stock, also called broth, is a savory cooking liquid that forms the basis of many dishes, particularly soups, stews and sauces. Making stock involves simmering animal bones or meat, seafood, or vegetables in water or wine, often for an extended period of time until the flavors are infused in the liquid.
SUGAR	There are around a dozen types of sugar. For this book, we use granulated sugar, confectioners sugar and brown sugar. Sugars are made from sugar cane or sugar beets. I prefer pure cane sugar. Granulated, or white sugar, is the most common. Powdered, or confectioners sugar, is white sugar that has been

ground into a fine powder with some cornstarch added for stability. Brown sugar, which is granulated sugar with molasses added, is sold as light brown and dark brown. I use the light variety whenever brown sugar is called for.

SWEAT To sweat means to cook an item, such as chopped onions, garlic or celery, over low heat in a small amount of fat, usually in a covered pan or pot. Sweating will soften the vegetables and release their moisture. The vegetables will become translucent, not brown.

TEMPER The process by which the temperature of an ingredient is altered. For example, if eggs are introduced to a heated cream, some of the cream is added to the eggs to equalize their temperature so that the eggs will not curdle when added to the hot cream.

TRANSLUCENT The point that a vegetable, usually onions, is no longer opaque but not quite transparent.

WATER BATH A pan of hot water placed in the oven to add moisture to the oven. Used in baking cheesecakes to prevent them from cracking. See *bain-marie*.

WHISK As a noun, a whisk is a cooking utensil with a handle attached to wire loops that can be used to blend ingredients smoothly and to incorporate air into a mixture. As a verb, to whisk is to blend ingredients together, which can be accomplished with a whisk or other mixing tool.

ZEST In cooking, zest is used as both a noun and a verb. As a noun, the zest is the scraped colored skin from citrus fruit, such as an orange or a lemon. As a verb, to zest a lemon or orange means to gently remove the colored skin with a grater to add flavor to foods.

INDEX

A

Apple
Cider Donut Cake 272
Pancake 56
Pie Bars 278
Skillet Pie 261

Artichokes, Stuffed 206

Asparagus Parmesan 112

B

Banana
Cake 281
Chocolate Chip Bread 93
Coconut Cream Pie 273

BBQ
Butterflied Chicken 121
Chicken Kebabs 144
Ribs 114
Rub 114
Sauce 114

Beans
Baked Beans — Quick Version 99
Boston-California Baked Beans 98
Braised Lamb Shanks with White Beans 147
Fagioli (beans) with Pasta 82
in Vegetable and Breadcrumb Medley 97

Beef
Bourguignon 210
and Broccoli Stir-Fry 230
Corned Beef & Cabbage 161
Empanadas 178
Hamburgers 139
Kebabs 143
Meatballs in Tomato Sauce 191
Pot Roast or Beef Stew with Barley 151
Prime Rib 158
Rib Eye Steak 154
Roasted Beef Tenderloin (aka Chateaubriand/Filet Mignon) 156
Short Ribs Braised in Wine 150
Steak Fajitas 174
Steak & Pepper Stir-Fry 229
Steak Picado 166
Stew & Dumplings 148
Tri-Tip 134
Tuscan Stew 196

Beets
with Orange Juice & Brown Sugar 112

Bok Choy
with Fish, Garlic, Ginger & Scallions 234
with Garlic, Ginger & Spinach 101
with Shrimp 235

Bread
Banana Chocolate Chip 93
French Baguettes 90
French Bread & Rolls 88
Pumpkin Spice 243
Rolls, Crunchy Hard 92
White Sandwich Bread 87
Whole Wheat Sandwich Bread 94

Broccoli
Sautéed with Cauliflower & Carrots 110
Sir-Fry with Beef 230
in Vegetable and Breadcrumb Medley 97

Brussels Sprouts
Braised 96
with Gremolata 96
in Vegetable and Breadcrumb Medley 97

Burgers
Asian Salmon 224
Asian Shrimp Cakes 222
Beef/Pork 139
Chicken 141
Lamb 138
Turkey 138

C

Cabbage and Corned Beef 161

Cakes
Apple Cider Donut 272
Banana 281
Cheesecake 275
Chocolate 276
Chocolate Ginger 251
Coffee 57

Carrots
Glazed 110
Sautéed with Broccoli & Cauliflower 110

Cauliflower
with Broccoli & Carrots 110

Chicken
Arroz con Pollo 168
BBQ Kebabs 144
Bistro Roast Chicken with Potatoes & Veggie 218
Braised with Wine & Mustard Sauce 216
Burgers 141
Butterflied with BBQ Sauce 121
Cacciatore 182
Cashew 237
Chinese Chicken Salad 225
and Dumplings 77
Empanadas 178
Fajitas 172
Honey Soy Wings 74
Kung Pao (or Shrimp) 226
Noodle Soup 84
and Potatoes (Chicken Chasseur) 220
Roasted 124

Roasted with Potatoes 217
Sautéed Breasts 127
Stock 86
Stuffed, Roasted with Potatoes 146
Teriyaki 238
Tortilla Soup 80
Vesuvio 183
Chili 116
Chinese Ribs 232
Chocolate
   Brownies 279
   Cake 276
   Chocolate Chip Banana Bread 93
   Chocolate Ginger Cake 251
   German Chocolate Pie 274
   Milk Chocolate Pudding Pie 267
   Peanut Butter Chocolate Ganache Chiffon Pie 270
   Pecan Chocolate Bars 256
Cookies
   Gingersnaps 255
   Gumdrop 255
   Peanut Butter 253
   Powdered Sugar Lemony Snowballs 254
Cornbread
   Basic Make Ahead 248
   and Sausage Stuffing 249
Cranberries, Orange Ginger 244
Croutons
   with Garlic, Parmesan & Herb 64
Crust
   Double Pie 258

D

Desserts
   Bars
      Apple Pie 278
      Brownies 279
      Lemon 254
      Pecan Chocolate 256
      Butter-Crisco® Double Crust 258
   Cakes
      Apple Cider Donut 272
      Banana 281

      Cheesecake 275
      Chocolate 276
      Chocolate Ginger 251
      Coffee 57
   Cookies
      Gingersnaps 255
      Gumdrop 255
      Peanut Butter 253
      Powdered Sugar Lemony Snowballs 254
   Lemon Cupcakes with Lemon Icing 280
   Pies
      Banana Coconut Cream 273
      German Chocolate 274
      Lemon 268
      Lemon with Meringue Crust 265
      Maple-Pecan Ice Box 264
      Milk Chocolate Pudding 267
      Mixed Berry Ice Box 266
      Peach 260
      Peanut Butter Chocolate Ganache Chiffon 270
      Pumpkin Ice Cream 252
      Rhubarb 269
      Skillet Apple 261
      Strawberry Chiffon 262
Dressings
   Caesar 63
   Thousand Island 68
Duck
   Roasted with Orange/Raspberry Sauce 122

E

Egg Rolls 233
Empanadas (Beef or Chicken) 178

F

Fajitas
   Chicken 172
   Shrimp 173
   Steak 174
Fish
   with Baby Bok Choy, Garlic, Ginger & Scallions 234

   Baked with Potatoes 131
   Cod With Asparagus 236
   Halibut Or Cod In Tomato Sauce 132
   Salmon & Potatoes 133
   Stew (Cioppino) 185
   Swordfish Kebabs 145
   Tacos 170
   White Fish Filets with Lemon, Butter & Capers 130
French Toast 58

G

Granola 60
Green Beans
   and Bacon 100
   with Meat Loaf & Potatoes 118
   and Tomato Casserole 105
   in Vegetable And Breadcrumb Medley 97
Gremolata
   with Brussels Sprouts 96
Guacamole 170

H

Ham
   Ham with Pineapple Mustard Glaze 242
   Lentil & Ham Hock Soup 83

K

Kebabs
   Armenian Shish Kebab with Pilaf 142
   BBQ Chicken 144
   Beef 143
   Swordfish 145

L

Lamb
   Armenian Shish Kebab 142
   Braised Shanks with White Beans 147
   Burgers 138
   Butterflied Leg 160

Crown Roast with Mustard Crust
    & Wine Pan Sauce 117
Grilled Chops 155
Rack with Mustard-Thyme Crust
    212

Lasagna with Meat 188

Lemon
Bars 254
Cupcakes with Lemon Icing 280
Pie 268
Pie with Meringue Crust 265
Powdered Sugar Lemony
    Snowballs 254
Scallops Sautéed in Lemon Butter
    215
White Fish Filets with Lemon,
    Butter & Capers 130

M

Macaroni & Cheese 164
Meatballs in Tomato Sauce 191
Meat Loaf
with Potatoes & Green Beans
    118

Mushrooms
and Beef Barley Soup 78
Risotto with Leeks & Peas 208
Stuffed with Breadcrumbs and
    Parmesan 71
in Wild Rice with Pecans &
    Shallots 109

O

Olives
Roasted 70
in Spaghetti with Cherry
    Tomatoes, Capers &
    Breadcrumbs 187
Tapenade 70

Omelet, Spanish
59

Osso Buco 193

P

Paella 175
Pasta
and Fagioli (Beans) Soup 82
Meat Lasagna 188
and Meat Sauce (Unauthentic
    Bolognese) 189
with Shrimp Scampi 184
Spaghetti With Cherry Tomatoes,
    Olives, Capers &
    Breadcrumbs 187

Peppers
and Steak Stir-Fry 229
Stuffed Baby Bell 72
Stuffed Bell 120
in Vegetable And Breadcrumb
    Medley 97

Pies
Banana Coconut Cream 273
German Chocolate 274
Lemon 268
Lemon with Meringue Crust 265
Maple-Pecan Ice Box 264
Milk Chocolate Pudding 267
Mixed Berry Ice Box 266
Peach 260
Peanut Butter Chocolate Ganache
    Chiffon 270
Pumpkin Ice Cream 252
Rhubarb 269
Skillet Apple 261
Strawberry Chiffon 262

Pizza
Americanized Margherita 205
Crust 199
Meatball & Roasted Pepper 202
Oven or Grill 200–201
Roasted Peppers & Anchovy 203
Sauce 200
Sausage and Pepper 202
Scampi 203
Tapenade and Tomato 204

Pork
BBQ Ribs 114
Chinese Ribs 232
Chops Milanese 194
Chops Pizzaiola 195
Chops in a Wine-Mustard Sauce
    152
Wiener Schnitzel 162

Potatoes
and Baked Fish 131
Bistro Roast Chicken with Veggie
    218
and Chicken (Chicken Chasseur)
    220
Crispy, Roasted 104
with Roast Chicken 217
Mashed 245
Mashed Casserole 107
with Meat Loaf & Green Beans
    118
O'Brien 106
Oven Fried 140
with Oven Roasted Salmon 133
Pan Fried 108
Pommes De Terre Boulangères
    214
Roasted with Butterflied Turkey
    240
Salad
    Anti-Mao 102
    French 103
Stuffed Roast Chicken and 146
Sweet Potato Balls 245

Pumpkin
Ice Cream Pie 252
Spice Bread 243

R

Rice
Arroz con Pollo 168
Fried with Asian Shrimp Cakes
    222
Fried with Shrimp and Snow Peas
    228
Risotto with Mushrooms, Leeks
    & Peas 208
Spanish 166
Wild Rice with Pecans,
    Mushrooms and Shallots
    109

S

Salads
Barley, with Fresh Veggies 62
Chinese Chicken 225
Corn and Tomato 65
Egg 137
Niçoise 66
Potato
    Anti-Mao 102

French 103
Tomato Onion 69
Tuna 136
Salmon
Asian Burgers 224
and Lentils 129
Oven Roasted with Potatoes 133
Sauces
BBQ 114
Cherry Tomatoes, Olives, Capers & Breadcrumbs 187
Meat Sauce (Unauthentic Bolognese) 189
Pizza 200
Scallops in Lemon Butter 215
Shrimp
Asian Cakes & Fried Rice 222
and Baby Bok Choy 235
Creole 128
Fajitas 173
Fried Rice With Snow Peas 228
Kung Pao 226
Scampi with Pasta 184
Wonton Soup 76
Soups
Beef & Mushroom Barley 78
Butternut Squash 81
Chicken & Dumplings 77
Chicken Noodle 84
Chicken Tortilla 80
Gazpacho 180
Lentil & Ham Hock 83
Pasta e Fagioli 82
Shrimp Wonton 76
Split Pea 75
Stock, Chicken or Turkey
see also Stock 86
Stews
Beef with Barley 151
Beef with Dumplings 148
Fish (Cioppino) 185
Tuscan Beef 196
Stir-Fry
Beef & Broccoli 230
Cashew Chicken 237
Kung Pao Chicken or Shrimp 226
Shrimp & Baby Bok Choy 235
Shrimp Fried Rice with Snow Peas 228
Steak & Pepper 229
Stock, Chicken or Turkey 86
Stuffing
Basic Make Ahead 248
Cornbread & Sausage 249

T

Tacos, Fish 170
Tomatoes
Corn and Tomato Salad 65
Halibut or Cod in Tomato Sauce 132
and Onion Salad 69
Pizza Sauce 200
Spaghetti with Cherry Tomatoes, Olives, Capers & Breadcrumbs 187
Tuna Salad 136
Turkey
Burgers 138
Butterflied with Roast Potatoes 240
Roast 246
Roast Turkey Parts 250
Stock 86

V

Vegetables or Veggies
Artichokes, Stuffed 206
Asparagus with Cod 236
Asparagus Parmesan 112
Barley Salad 62
Beets With Orange Juice & Brown Sugar 112
Bok Choy with Fish, Garlic, Ginger & Scallions 234
Bok Choy with Garlic, Ginger & Spinach 101
Bok Choy with Shrimp 235
Breadcrumb Medley 97
Broccoli with Cauliflower & Carrots 110
Brussels Sprouts, Braised 96
Brussels Sprouts with Gremolata 96
Glazed Carrots 110
Green Beans & Bacon 100
Green Beans and Tomato Casserole 105

W

Wiener Schnitzel 162

Y

Yorkshire Pudding 159

www.ingramcontent.com/pod-product-compliance
Lightning Source LLC
Chambersburg PA
CBHW061118010526
44112CB00024B/2901